SONGS IN THE NIGHT

by

G. Herbert Schmidt

This book contains the unabridged story of Gustav (or Gustave) Herbert Schmidt (1891–1958) from English editions of his books, *Songs in the Night* and *The Journey Home*. Chapters 1 to 37 are from *Songs in the Night* (1947 ed.). Chapters 38 to 61 are from *The Journey Home* (1948).

All Scripture quotations are from the King James Version.

ISBN-13: 978-1-952139-98-7

Table of Contents

Part III: Into the Haven of Safety

Part IV: The Journey Home

A Biographical Introduction

THIS BOOK is not a autobiography of G. Herbert Schmidt, but an account of God's remarkable dealings with him during World War II and the aftermath. It may be helpful to some readers to better understand his complex early life.

While his father was born in Lwówek, Poland, Herbert Schmidt was born in 1891 under the Russian Empire, in a province known as Volhynia (probably in western Ukraine). He was thus acquainted with several Slavic languages, and could read and write not only Polish, but German, Russian, and English. His family had moved east in search of opportunity, but found poverty and hardship in rural Volhynia. In 1896, his mother died and was buried in Hannopil, Ukraine, when he was only four years old.

Herbert Schmidt surrendered to Christ at a meeting in Bydgoszcz, Poland, in 1909. A year later, he immigrated to the United States. He received ministerial training at the Rochester Bible Institute from 1915 to 1918. In 1918, he was ordained with the Assemblies of God and was commissioned as their first missionary to eastern Europe. He also became field superintendent of the Russian and Eastern European Mission, which was in cooperation with the Assemblies of God from 1927 to 1940.

In 1919, he came to Sweden where he met and married his first wife Carrie, who had come from Norway. They adopted a daughter, Gerda, whom they tragically lost in 1924. Herbert was struck by sorrow yet again when his wife Carrie died, on Christmas Day, 1929. In the 1930s, he married Margaret Neumann. In his books, Schmidt does not mention that Margaret was a German citizen, and when their daughters, Ruth and Karin, were born, she passed on this citizenship to them. This explains why the threat of concentration camp fell on him especially.

On March 2, 1930, Schmidt became the founding dean of the Bible Institute in Danzig (Gdański Instytut Biblijny), the first Pentecostal theological college in Central and Eastern Europe. Giving instruction in Russian and German, the school offered grounding in biblical theology and Pentecostal doctrine to hundreds of students from Poland, Russia, Ukraine, Bulgaria, Yugoslavia, Estonia, Latvia, Lithuania, Czechia, Slovakia, Hungaria, Romania, and Germany. Several prominent British Pentecostals, including Donald Gee, visited Poland regularly and taught in Danzig. Under pressure from Nazi authorities, the school was closed in June 1938. Despite the tension in Europe, the Schmidts returned to Poland after a furlough, arriving in June 1939, where this book begins. There were around 500 Pentecostal churches in eastern Europe, with 20,000 members.

The work did not cease, of course, after the events in this book, as the afterword tells. After Schmidt's 1946 return to the United States, he quickly found opportunities to minister. On his way to California, where he settled, he preached at Central Assembly of God in Springfield, Missouri. He found other opportunities at conferences and missions conventions. Nevertheless, he wrote in his diary in 1947 that he felt "at times out of place—a decoration."

Herbert Schmidt continued to preach to Germans in America and founded the German Full Gospel Radio Mission in 1954. Then, eleven years after his safe return to the United States, he crossed the ocean once again in the fall of 1957. He preached in Germany for seven months until he suffered a heart attack while preaching in Heidelberg. He lived six more weeks and died on May 19, 1958. His funeral was held in Frankfurt, Germany.

Lloyd Christiansen, a Washington, D.C. pastor, heard Herbert Schmidt preach to a group of Potomac ministers. In 1991, he wrote that Herbert Schmidt regarded American ministers as "unacquainted with hardship and suffering." He added, "I have been haunted by the words of Brother Schmidt since that day over 40 years ago."

Part I: Memorial Journey

1. SPEEDING SOUTHWARD

OUT OF the realm of night a cloudy morning emerged hesitantly. The sun's rays seemed to be bound and muffled or the earth gone on a distant orbit. Absorbed in the depths of space they could not reach this shivering planet.

A chill gripped me as I stood with my suitcase in hand waiting for the streetcar to take me to the main railroad station. It was the beginning of October 1940. The trees had taken on the fiery red tinge of death. One by one the leaves dropped in their zigzag course to the damp sidewalk, to be trampled upon, and ultimately sink into dust and oblivion.

Their bright and cheery green was forgotten by those human beings, who with ecstasy observed their beauty before while enjoying their shade and coolness throughout the summer. These leaves that had clothed the trees with a beautiful wedding garment in the springtime, giving the fainting and weary-hearted wanderers new joy and vigor of life, were now being crushed and broken by those who had admired them before; their service done they were destined to die.

The giant lime trees were being unclothed. Some of the branches stretched their barren limbs like wrinkled hands in dismay toward heaven as if pleading for help and protection against the unseen enemy who deprived them of their beautiful summer garment.

11

The previous winter had been all too severe, biting into the very marrow of all tree life. The trees seemed weak and ailing, unable to hold their raiment any longer. Everywhere the forebodings of the icy winter were evident with its testings and trials for nature, man and beast.

Thus I mused until finally the streetcar came swayingly nearer and nearer. Little did I realize at that time how symbolic all nature was that morning. My meditations were prophetic in their character, for that journey proved to be the last one, and my return a sad and tragic turning point in my life, bringing the activity of many years to an abrupt termination.

The streetcar was squeaking and jarring noisily before it came to a hurried stop as if wanting to arouse some of the sleepy human beings who had waited too long for it, to rush them to their destinations.

I was glad to speed to the station, for as I stepped into my compartment the door closed. The locomotive was impatiently steaming, hissing and chafing, and was already hitched to the train. I was hardly seated when it began with a jerk, creeping out of the station, the platform vanishing in the distance and the train dashing into the mist of the morning.

My train was speeding southward toward Poland through autumn fields. Hard-working peasants were in the potato fields everywhere, and by the large and numerous heaps I judged that God had given a rich harvest. The abundant rains of August and September had been very favorable for this, the most necessary food of mankind. If later in the winter a great part of the potatoes froze and rotted because of severe frost and unskillful handling, it was not God's fault, but perhaps he shaped circumstances thus to show mankind that they need him after all in order to live, eat, and prosper.

The many very old mothers and fathers and all too young boys and girls, as well as the numerous women at work, reminded me that the grim war lord, Mars, was stalking over the earth again requiring the men in the prime of their years and grown-up boys to be absent and fight, bleed, and die on the battlefields of Europe. There another harvest was being gathered by the reaper Death. With bleeding hearts and troubled countenances folks at home were struggling and hustling to do the work alone, while their anxious thoughts were with their loved ones far away.

As the train sped on I asked myself how many of these people might know Jesus as their personal Savior, having learned to cast their cares upon him and seek solace at his heart. They have not been taught to surrender to Christ, nor do they know a Savior on whom they can lean during life's sorrows and heartaches.

Many of them in deep perplexity, sighing a sorrow and bereavement and with crushed hearts might ask God to whom they are strangers: "Why, O God, why!—if Thou art —why this bloodshed and the streams of tears in its wake?" Because you are estranged from God, and neither you nor your governments are ruled by the precepts of Christ and his Word. That is the reason you are at war, gripped by murder and cruelty, and being drawn irresistibly into the mire of despair and death.

Children of God, viewing all these calamities, have a double load and a severely aching heart. On the one hand they must bear the same burdens occasioned by the cruel war which brings suffering and sorrow. In addition they bear a crushing burden because of the godlessness of mankind and the antagonism to the only remedy which can bring the world out of the awful dilemma of war.

2. ON THE WAY TO FATHER'S VILLAGE

My first destination on this journey was Friedingen, the village where my beloved father spent his last years on earth. It was there I had joined him for a short period, when I had the joy of telling him the details about my salvation. The tears of joy sparkled in his eyes when he recognized that the love of Christ was burning in my heart, gripping and warming him as well.

In that village he was finally laid to rest in 1916, after his pilgrimage of seventy-four years on earth. I was thousands of miles away in the United States, and the First World War was at its height of grim intensity.

During the twenty-two years I had sped by hundreds of times in fast trains, almost within sight of the cemetery, but seldom taking time to visit the village. It necessitated a changing of trains and required much time for such a visit. I liked to picture my father up in glory where I should join him someday, rather than stand at his grave. This time, however, I boarded the local train which would stop in the station near my father's last home.

A strange, indefinable feeling made me realize that I was visiting that village for the last time—a premonition that something was about to happen in my life that would make me glad to have been once more in my father's last home.

Slowly the train moved on as if not sure of its way, and then hesitantly came to a stop. I heard the conductor call the name of the station, "Prust." That was also the name which he had called in 1908, when my father arrived from Russia. "Pruszc," I heard the Polish conductors shout throughout the years after the First World War when this province, West Prussia, was reclaimed by the Poles who had owned it in ancient times and had called it "Promorsze" ('Near-sea Earth'). Since the German armies swept over this province in 1939 they renamed the place. This reflected just a little detail of world-historic events during the past twenty-five years which contributed to the remaking of such an unstable map of Europe.

Thus the earth again drank the blood of the sons of this province. Eternal change, endless bloodshed and unceasing tears among Europe's people divided into territories which are bounded by so-called different races, each one laying claim to almost every square foot of ground, and several of them always having a just reason for claiming a certain patch of earth. They were fighting, striving, and struggling from time to time in wild madness until utterly exhausted. The survivor on the battlefield would then satisfy his claims and thereby create new hatred all around him. After some years or in the next generation the old tragedy of war and destruction would again be re-enacted.

As I stepped out of the train I beheld the same buildings, the same trees looked upon by my father 31 years before. In my memory I could picture that slightly stooped figure of my father stepping down from the train and passing the ticket-control gate where I greeted him, then walking down the station road toward the highway. It was long ago but very fresh in my memory.

Who of us has not some reminiscences of father and mother, visions which are forever indelibly imprinted in the shrine of our hallowed memories?

Thirty-one years ago I saw the tears of joy sparkle in my beloved father's eyes as he tenderly embraced me at the station for the first time after my surrender to my precious Savior. And how glad I am today, to have caused this joy in my father's heart, making him feel that the prayers for his son had been answered.

Dear reader, perhaps you have surrendered to your Master too late to bring that joyful news to your precious mother or your loving father. Sorrowingly they have passed on into eternity. You waited too long, but you will meet them in heaven's bright summerland. Yet, there are many whose father and mother are still desperately praying for the salvation of their beloved child, but you are still going the way of the world and sin, pressing tears of sorrow out of the eyes of those who love you most. How deep your remorse will be someday when you stand at the open grave. There will be no soothing tears that you weep, but tears that burn like fire.

Everything here was so young, beautiful and peaceable thirty-one years ago. Since then two terrible wars have swept over Europe like a devastating tornado, leaving destruction and ruin behind. It all seems so unreal, so distorted. There are crushed houses everywhere as if a giant hand had pressed them down to the ground or tossed them to one side.

Just over one year ago the German war machine rolled over this part of the country, smashing through the towns and villages. The contending armies were destroying what decades of toil had built and race hatred was at its zenith. The Poles had the death lists ready, preparing to dispose of that part of the German population whom they disliked and were considered the instigators of war. They were to be murdered as was done in scores of other places, but the enemies came too quickly. The Poles had to flee for their lives. The village mayor also fled, leaving the death lists in his desk.

That was a welcome find for the Germans, which intensified their thirst for revenge. There was no pardon given. The Poles had to pay very dearly in blood and tears. Cruelty begot more cruelty and sin.

In turn the inherent hatred against the Germans had been growing steadily until it became a deathly passion in the hearts of the Poles. The deeds of the conquerors are demanding retribution. Thus many innocent men and women on both sides had to suffer and pay the penalty for others.

But not only family memories and reminders of war held me under their spell. Walking through the little town, I remembered wonderful blessings of God which I had experienced years ago. There I had my very first experiences of testifying for the Lord after my salvation. When returning to Poland in 1920 it was here that I held my first meeting as missionary and was privileged to lead a number of souls to the fold of Christ.

In that gospel campaign my wife and I had a wonderful experience of the Lord's direct intervention by protection from diabolical attempts to harm us and thus bring the meetings to a stop. To accomplish these attempts, Satan stirred up hatred in the hearts of wicked young men to such an extent that they were ready to attack me.

Accordingly, they planned to throw a projectile through the window and hit the kerosene lamp on the table where I was sitting, whereby hoping to cause a fire. The liquid would have splashed over me as well and it could have become a very serious matter.

While the meeting was in progress and we were on our knees praying there was suddenly a terrible crash. The window had been smashed from a tin can filled with stones and dirt. Those who were looking around while others prayed, made the observation that the missile was actually flying toward the table and would have hit the lighted lamp; but just before reaching the objective, it made a right angle turn in midair, flying out through the opposite door into the corridor. God had held his hand over us and neither I nor any of the others were hurt, not even by glass splinters.

Those rowdies who had perpetrated the misdeed were not able to see what had taken place and thought they had missed the mark. They proceeded to concoct another plan to waylay us on our homeward walk and injure us by throwing stones. Equipped with a number of stones they went into position. Presently we came along singing, being very joyful at God's protecting care over us that evening!

Little did we realize what had been planned. Nothing happened however, and we reached home without incident.

After several days the leader of that band came to the meeting, repenting of his misdeeds and surrendered fully to the Lord. He received forgiveness and found peace with God. Then he told the story of that sinful plot, saying: "When we saw you coming on your way home that evening, we made ready to throw the stones but could not carry out our intention because our right arms were momentarily paralyzed. We then forgot all about the stones as we were greatly concerned about our arms. In consternation I realized that we had been up against a direct intervention of God in your favor. I, the ringleader, was seized by a mortal fear although my arm had become normal again after a few minutes. Later on deep conviction gripped me and finally brought me here today. Now the Lord has saved me for which I am very thankful. The enemy had planned to harm you through us but instead he lost one of his ardent servants. His plan backfired, and I am glad."

Now I was on my way to visit that house once more where the above mentioned meetings had taken place. On the way I observed familiar scenes which brought to me memories of the past. At last the house came into view and there the historic window aroused new praise and adoration to my precious Savior. Numberless times he has manifested his power and blessing in protecting my life since that memorable event.

There I stood in the courtyard. It seemed much smaller than before, and everywhere I could observe that many years had passed since I had been here last. The Lord had preserved it however from the devastation of war, and that was gratifying.

Suddenly a little girl came running along and an instant later a young woman approached, critically observing me.

"Good day," I greeted her and asked: "Are the Steinmeyers still living?"

"Yes," she answered, "they are in the field, digging potatoes. I am their daughter-in-law."

When I told her my name, she brightened up as I was saying: "I know the Steinmeyer family very well and have been visiting here many times and am anxious to see that brother and sister once more."

Many years had passed since I preached in this house and now I stood again in the very room. The son of my old friends, who is the father of the little girl, was at that time about the same age as this child is now. And the old parents were still working in the fields, gathering potatoes. The war had forced them once more into active farming to take the place of the son who had been claimed by war duties.

How true the Word of God is, when it states: "The days of our years are . . . labor and sorrow" until the hour comes to "fly away" (Psalm 90:10). A child of God is at least prepared for that great event, having made the future secure, but the masses of humanity live just for the enjoyment of the moment. They are wasting precious years only for this life's welfare and then suddenly face a dark and dismal eternity. How sad for one who has had nothing but labor and sorrow, sweat and tears, then to rush into death with a remorse which will burn as an eternal, unquenchable fire in the soul, with no return possible. Why, oh, why do people permit themselves to be deceived thus by Satan, the enemy of our eternal happiness!

In the meantime Brother and Sister Steinmeyer came home, and I could plainly see the marks of the twenty years which had gone over their heads since I had seen them last. The furrows in the shrunken skin of their faces betrayed the storms they had to brave and the struggles they had gone through. The years had begun to weigh them down as if an unseen load up their shoulders pressed them slowly to the dust.

There was however the same smile and the old light in their eyes when I spoke of the goodness and mercy of the

Lord in our life. This faith and confidence in the Lord are the greatest and surest riches we can accumulate on our pathway which is so full of toil, sorrow, and uncertainties. Nothing can deprive us of such wealth—our assets for eternity in Christ Jesus our Lord.

Looking around in the home, I could observe that the old neatness and cleanliness had departed. A digressing disorder prevailed. The young mother looked very sad and sickly. Seemingly she had lost her hold on life and was just drifting along aimlessly like a piece of wood on a stream.

A large tureen, containing potato and vegetable soup, was placed on the table and I was asked to join them at dinner. While we ate the young mother related an incident of eighteen years ago when my first wife and I had visited the village of her childhood to attend a harvest thanksgiving festival. Mrs. Schmidt took the little children together, teaching them songs and telling them Bible stories about Jesus. This incident was indelibly imprinted into that sister's heart and it became the means of bringing her to the feet of Jesus several years later.

How wonderful that such a small incident in that woman's childhood was leading her into salvation. It pays to let our love for Christ be active and make it shine for him. If we are prompted by the Spirit of God in our walk and work for him, something will touch the hearts of those with whom we come in contact, and blessing will flow which ultimately will lead someone into the light of the gospel. It also proves the importance of our children's being brought under the influence of God and his saints. Thus the seed of the Word will be planted in the hearts of the young, and some noble impressions about Christ will be turned into eternal blessings and happiness. "Cast thy bread upon the waters: for thou shalt find it after many days" (Ecclesiastes 11:1).

As I spoke about bygone blessings and our responsibility toward our children, I noticed tears in the eyes of that young mother. I asked her whether she had kept the faith she once had obtained in the hour of her surrender to God. She confessed not having been faithful to Jesus, and that the joy of the Lord had vanished entirely. As she thus spoke of the lost glory of God, she sank to her knees and cried out to God for pardon and mercy.

Those were sacred moments when we knelt in the presence of God and a backslider was brought again to the fold of Christ. The listless expression vanished and a peaceful relaxation overspread her features as she raised her voice in prayer: "O Lord, you sent Sister Schmidt to me in my childhood in order to plant the seed of your gospel in my heart. I thank you that you have brought that seed to growth and fruition. But I have forsaken you and your path of obedience. Now after so many years you have sent Brother Schmidt again in order to rouse me once more to live in obedience to you. I thank you for your great mercy. Amen."

The Lord had given me here the first fruit of my strange journey. The beginning of my missionary work for God was linked to the end, spanning the many years which had passed. In the heart of that sister God could resume his work anew, fanning into flame again that spiritual life which was about to vanish altogether. Though my wife had passed on from this earth long ago, her testimony is still remembered and effective. Praise his name forever!

3. On the Threshold of Long Ago

As the first day of my journey wore on, the sky cleared and a beautiful autumn day with its mild, fading sunshine enshrouded me when I set out to walk the three kilometers, separating me from Friedingen, my first day's destination. True to its name—Friedingen means 'place of peace'—this village had lingered in my memory through the years as that locality where I enjoyed the first months of divine rest and peace in the Lord as a child of the King.

Here I had also enjoyed the last months of fellowship with my father before my departure which proved to be the final parting in this life.

Although I have no relatives living in Friedingen, the place will always remain in my memory. There I looked into my father's eyes the last time as his hands were laid upon my brow when he blessed me after I had told him about my decision to give my life wholly into the service of my Savior. There also is the little mound which covers the earthly remains of him to whom I owe my physical life and my first impressions about my precious Savior.

This time I happened to take a field road which is used very little by the villagers who call it 'backyard way'. Never had I used it before, always having taken the larger road leading from Friedingen directly to the railroad station.

How quiet and serene the slightly rolling landscape was, spread out around me. There were cattle grazing on the pastures and here and there I saw groups of people busily digging and gathering in potatoes. As I passed they stopped their work, looking at the stranger walking along this unusual way.

A great company of songbirds were aroused by my approach and noisily took to flight. Led by instinct, imparted by their heavenly Father, they fly southward at the time when the sun loses its power and before the winter sets in. Prompted by something within stirring and causing them to congregate, they then make their getaway from suffering and death. There they were, ready to leave this autumn-chilled country and move into warmer and fairer regions until the storms and frost had spent their fury and given way again to the warm breezes of springtime. Then again these birds come into the smiling and blooming North to fill the air with their song and mirth.

There is one family in Friedingen whom I hoped to contact. In Brother Rucke's house prayer meetings have been held throughout the years. He was always the solitary representative of God, the hammer whom God used to knock at the conscience of the villagers, the stumbling stone of the scoffers. Although that family always had to remain isolated, none paying much attention to them, time was taken to ridicule them about their Christian life, proving that the people who knew them were compelled to weigh facts and consider questions of eternal value. They had their "Noah" to warn them and will have no excuse on the judgment day.

Just as persistently as they rejected his testimony, so tenaciously did Brother Rucke hold on to his faith in Christ. Without murmuring nor complaining, he stood his ground, leading a life of testimony for our blessed Master. He was a constant reminder that there is something in Christianity which they did not possess and which they slighted.

It was evidently the Lord who directed me in taking the little backyard road into the village. I had barely entered the locality and passed a few houses, when I faintly recognized the farm belonging to Brother Rucke. Passing the gate I came into the courtyard, finding the place without asking anybody and without arousing publicity in the village.

As the doors of the house were locked, the gates of the barn wide open exposing to view great piles of potatoes lying there, I concluded that they too were in the fields gathering in potatoes. There was nothing else to do but sit down on the doorstep and await their return.

Suddenly I noticed a chained dog coming out of his den. He looked at me intently but seemed to be undecided whether to sound an alarm or not. For a strange reason he did not give any sound but grudgingly and with bristled hair went back and lay down again, eyeing me constantly. When I told the owner afterward, he marveled that the dog did not get excited, for he is usually vicious, as I myself could notice while there.

As later became known, the police of Danzig tried to trace me and had I become known in the village as a stranger, I would not have been able to slip out without registering. This might have aroused questioning, being an American citizen, and it might have easily led to an untimely interruption of my journey. Thus the Lord led me into the village on the right street, and he himself kept me.

Viewing the buildings, I could recognize that many years had passed since I was here last. The barn showed plain signs of age and decay, reminding me of an old grandfather who has become feeble and was looking for the support of a cane, or a helping hand.

Presently I saw Brother Rucke hastily coming into the yard on a bicycle. He stopped, closely scrutinizing me. Time had left distinct marks in his face and appearance. He recognized me when I mentioned my name.

After conversing with him a while, I soon found that his spiritual life had survived. More of Christ was his desire, proving again that we can never come to a place when we are able to say, we have enough. There is always more to be had and our ideals as Christians are so high that, in a whole lifetime, we can never reach the top, for it is Christ himself who is our pattern and he is our goal.

Equipped with definite directions, I set out to visit an old grandfather, Graf by name, who had been intimately acquainted with my father. From him I hoped to obtain information. Graf was considerably along in years already when I had known him thirty years before and he was now at the age of seventy-nine. It was astonishing that he recognized me at once, calling me by name when I entered his house.

"Your father was the man who always said that he had no time to die," he began, "so when death came, he did not even have time enough to finish the shoes which I had ordered, but passed out of this life when only one shoe was ready, the other remaining unfinished."

"My father was a very industrious man," I replied, "and while busy he liked to jest and be merry, but he never feared death because he had prepared for eternity throughout his life. His accounts were always settled, ready for a sudden departure. That, I believe, is the wisest way to live."

"Knowing your father as I did, I can say that he was a very conscientious Christian," he proceeded; "he would not have done injustice to a sparrow. In fact he was too good-hearted to people. Quite a few took advantage of him and did not pay their debts for the work he had done for them. He could have left quite a bit of money behind when he went out of this life, but he could never press his claims for fear of being hard on debtors."

"It is better my father was poor and had peace with God and a good conscience, than being rich and losing his soul thereby."

"You are talking precisely as your father did," Graf assured me. "He certainly did not live for the sake of money, but he talked a lot about God and heaven. Sometimes I wish I had heeded his advice, then it would be better for me and I could be more satisfied with my own life."

Graf was one of those who always had something to talk about. He proceeded to describe incidents and conversations with my father in all detail which astonished me. His densely wrinkled tiny face appeared still smaller than it originally was because he had no teeth in his mouth. When he chewed as he did, between sentences as a matter of habit, his nose almost touched his chin. He looked quite grotesque when he inevitably smoked his pipe. Being completely covered with wrinkles, he appeared very old, but his little eyes were still sparkling like diamonds in the dark as he proceeded to tell me details about his friendship with my father.

25

"I have taken good care of your father's grave," he assured me, "and I always remember him with a feeling of friendship." Then he told me that he was the caretaker of the cemetery, living very close to it.

Presently we proceeded to visit father's grave. He led me through the old eroded gateway to the ancient part of the cemetery which was fenced in separately. Then we passed through another gate which led us to the new section. There we continued on an alley flanked with magnificent lime trees. In the center another promenade crossed this at a right angle, forming a cross and dividing the whole into four sections. Graf led the way to the upper right flank into the corner and at the second grave in the second row we halted; here I stood at my father's last resting place. Here was the terminus of his earthly pilgrimage.

The grave had been completely covered with evergreen plants which, however, had been frozen during the previous severe winter and dried up entirely. It made me think of a terribly scorching storm that might have swept over the brave plants singeing and leaving them withered. A solitary wild pansy freshly blooming in the center of the grave mound stood there like a sentinel of honor over the dead. It was the only living thing in that place of death. A pale autumnal sunray stole over the grave as if bringing a greeting to me from another and better world where there is no sorrow, no tears, and no death.

"Your father was a very busy and hustling man and he was very much liked in the whole village," said my old friend, "and when his death came so quickly by double pneumonia, he was mourned by many." Thus my companion went on, telling me things of bygone days as I stood at the grave, lost in reveries of the past.

Seventy-four years was his age when he was called up higher—a ripe age—and still "one shoe" remained unfinished. Unfinished is the life of most when the great call comes. "Teach us to number our days, that we may apply our hearts unto wisdom" (Psalm 90:12). Happy is he who has turned unto the only wisdom which will be recognized as such in eternity; the wisdom of working out our own salvation. How many souls must mourn their foolishness throughout eternity because they have failed to make themselves ready for that day when they shall be called to face the great Judge.

As I stood at the grave of my father, melancholy thoughts arose within me. I was thinking of my hurried departure to Berlin for business college in 1910, and then from there my equally hasty departure to Switzerland when in 1912 I had placed before me the alternative of entering military service or returning to Russia where I should have been dealt with as a deserter.

Without a goodbye to my father I had left Germany. It seemed to me then an easy matter, considering it unworthy of a true Christian to hesitate with a journey because of the necessity of saying goodbye to loved ones. Being quite radical in my views, I deemed it an unjustified delay in carrying out the will of God which for me meant leaving Germany without postponement. I rested on the word of Jesus: "My mother, my brother, and my sister are those who do the will of God" (Mark 3:35).

This attitude demanded of me not to have the slightest hesitancy to proceed on my way. I acted as if I had no father or relatives. Thus when I acknowledged a way as of the Lord, there was no halting nor tarrying. Equally firm was I with myself: "He who puts his hand to the plow and looks back, is not fit for the kingdom of God" (Luke 9:62). That was law in my life.

My hurry was in a way justified because I feared to be hindered from leaving Germany and be drafted to serve in the army which I would have considered entirely against the will of God. "I must serve the Lord my Master, therefore I have no time to serve the Kaiser." That was my strong conviction.

Now as I stood at the grave of my father, remorse filled my heart. Had I known that I would go on and on, always farther away from him until thousands of miles would separate us, I should have returned home at any cost to say goodbye. Now it is too late. The opportunities are gone forever.

When father lay on his deathbed in October 1916, he called night and day for me. In his delirium he would ask every few minutes whether "Gustav" had arrived. Then again he would stare at the door and say: "There you are, I knew you would come!" With my name on his lips in prayer he finally passed away while I was several thousands of miles distant in the United States. The World War was raging and communications were quite impossible. Not until March 1917 did a letter from my sister reach me, containing the news and details about the death of my beloved father.

All these memories pressed upon me as I stood there, looking at the mound and groping for some excuses. But I was not able to find any, and must only build on the grace of the Lord, for with him is much forgiveness. From father I can hear no "I forgive you" as he so gladly would have soothingly said to me while in this life.

Have you, dear reader, still a loving father, a precious mother? Don't offend them, do not slight them. If you do, you will someday feel the pangs of remorse and no soothing hand will be on your brow, no loving words of forgiveness will take the load of guilt from your heart. Be kind to your parents and do not add more to their sorrows and burdens than they already carry. Honor, respect and obey them. If they are serving the Lord, they seek only your eternal welfare.

4. FAREWELL TO HALLOWED GROUND

Sunday morning I quietly slipped once more to the grave of my father. An indefinable pressure loaded me down, forebodings of impending sorrow and trials, but I did not know then. I asked myself: "Is it the last visit you are making here? Are you saying goodbye forever to the grave of your father?" Then I knelt at the grave and pledged myself to God for complete faithfulness, come what might. I wandered around and passed the house where I used to live, lingering at the window of the room where my father usually slept and where he died. I walked over the ground which was hallowed to me and over the fields where my father had toiled.

In moments it seemed as if I saw his stooped figure, walking briskly as he used to. All is gone forever, only memories remain. The bright hope remains within me of seeing him, after I too shall have passed on into eternity, entering into the home above. There I shall see him again at the feet of my precious Savior.

There I shall also see my dear mother who had been torn from me when my age was only a little over four years. I am thinking of her as well, but I can never visit her grave in the little village of Annapol, in the Ukraine, near Novograd Volynsk.[1] Perhaps her resting place is no more, being eradicated by the years which have gone by. The plows of the Bolsheviks very likely pass over her grave, the plowman not being aware that he is passing over a hallowed spot. In heaven I shall meet her again, my beloved mother. I know she is there in heaven, as frequently I have seen her in my dreams, clad in pure white.

---

[1] Today Annapol is known as Hannopil, and Novograd Volynsk is known as Zviahel.

After having arranged with Mr. Graf to have the grave cared for in the future, I said farewell to Friedingen with a strong premonition that I should never see that village again, never again stand at the grave of my father.

Strange, that solitary little pansy on the grave gave me something tangible to rest my mind. It stood there as a symbol of life and hope. In my diary I find the following last comment about father's grave: "Little solitary floweret, you are the only living thing, standing guard on the mound. You will stand until you too shall bow your withered head and sink into dust. Thank you. You are to me a symbol of life and hope in Jesus, which I take with me on my darkening pathway through a sorrowing and bleeding world."

Once more I visited the family Steinmeyer in Prust and had the joy of meeting the son with whose wife I had prayed the day before. He too had lost the spiritual life which once he possessed. When I asked him about it, he proved to be completely indifferent concerning it. A cold chill ran through me as I sensed the dense darkness covering and filling that heart which once had been alive for the Savior and had received the wonderful blessings of the spiritual riches in Christ Jesus. Having seen such great works of God, I trembled for him as I thought of that Day when that son of so many prayers shall stand before his eternal Judge.

What tragedies are being enacted by the children of godly parents who are praying and agonizing for them— they who are trampling under their feet of disobedience the precious blessings once obtained from God? Oh, the tears and sighs of godly parents who see their offspring on the path of destruction!

You, son; and you, daughter. You love your parents but you are bringing infinitely more pain to them, pressing hotter tears out of their eyes than if you were their most gruesome and tenacious enemies. How dark must be your heart to inflict such sufferings upon your beloved father and mother. By that sorrow you cause them to wither and it ultimately breaks their health. You are hurrying them on to a much earlier grave by your indifference and sinful life. Come back to Jesus, surrender your life to him anew and bring that unspeakable happiness to them which they deserve; make the last years in which they are still with you, pleasant for them. You will be always glad and thankful for that.

5. My Spiritual Birthplace

Again I sped on in the train to my next objective, the city where my spiritual eyes were opened and my heart received the gift of eternal life. There too my wife and I settled down and made that city our headquarters from 1922 to 1925, living through the hardest years of my early missionary activity.

It was on Sunday when I arrived, and having become a complete stranger in the city, I obtained the necessary information from the pastor as to meetings, and attended the service at five in the afternoon. I sought out the same spot in the hall where I had been sitting on that eventful evening, thirty-two years before. A pitifully small number of people attended, and I was reminded about the mighty workings of God among the throng that filled the hall in 1909 when over eight hundred people were gathered. A number of souls were saved that evening when I surrendered to Jesus.

Times have changed since those bygone days. Great storms have swept over this assembly and over the city. When Pentecost came to Bydgoszcz, that assembly vehemently rejected the spiritual awakening; no wonder they were left to dry up. God has only one Holy Spirit and if his workings are spurned, there is no further possibility for such a church to prosper spiritually.

All those who have refused to fall in line under the Pentecostal outpouring have had to pay dearly. It is more expensive—spiritually speaking—to reject the Pentecostal workings of the Spirit, than to pay the price and fall in line to receive the blessings that come to us by experiencing the baptism with the Holy Spirit.

One brother who distributed songbooks in that meeting, appeared quite familiar to me, and looking from a closer range, I recognized him as my cousin whose whereabouts I had not known for years. By leading us together the Lord solved the question of my night lodgings. Had I had to go to a hotel, the police could have easily traced me, laying their hands on me before I had finished the journey. The dangers being unknown to me, God kept me secluded in the background. How wonderfully loving our Savior is in guiding us.

In that city I also again met the wife of my cousin who took such a lively interest in me before I was saved. Speaking to me very earnestly about salvation when I was rebuking him by saying that I did not want to hear anything about that subject, he replied in a touching way: "If you do not want me to speak to you about salvation, I will abstain, but you cannot hinder my praying for you, that God may give you light." That he did most faithfully, until I was gloriously saved after a few months.

Several years later he passed on to be with the Lord. His wife who had never taken a lively interest in spiritual things, did not remain faithful to God but went astray from the way of life. Through her backsliding the children have also suffered eternal loss. She came into poverty and the children suffered hunger, especially one of her younger daughters, Frida, who was greatly affected in her frail body. When married a few years later, she broke down altogether and at the time I met her again after many years, she was down with tuberculosis.

The Lord had sent me just in the very time of her greatest need and distress. Satan had driven her to the verge of despair. I talked to her about the great love of God and his forgiveness. While I was at her bedside she melted and with tears flowing, she reached up her hands to him who sticketh closer than brother when we are in sorrow, and exclaimed: "My Jesus, now I see your great love. I know that you will not cast me away but receive me to yourself." A wonderful peace came into her heart. She received the assurance that Christ had forgiven all her sins and accepted her as his child. Later she told me "You have been sent by the Lord, for I cried to God, saying, 'Lord, if you are living, you will send someone to me who can explain the way of life in a manner that I can grasp it.' Now you have come, and I have found peace in my beloved Savior."

Next I was very anxious to find an old friend whom I had known as a very precious child of God when we lived in that city. He had been a zealous witness for Christ, bringing quite a few souls to the foot of the Cross. After searching for some time, I finally learned that he had his own business and that he had prospered in his natural life but had entirely left the narrow way of obedience to God.

When he stood before me I saw the emblem of his political affiliation, the Nazi-party sign, and soon heard his defiant attitude concerning spiritual things. It pained me extremely to see how he had been ensnared and engulfed by a wicked anti-Christian political trend of opinion. Upon my earnest entreaty he answered: "I have learned to know that we can have religion—yes, Christianity, if you please— without unending meetings, without Bible and without pastor. As to the so-called earnest Christians, they are all hypocrites and do not believe themselves what they claim to own of God."

Alas, a ruined life, a destroyed child of God—the result of the inroads of Satan and his doctrines by the instrumentality of an aggressive political school of thought. How can such emptiness, presented by atheists, ensnare an honest child of God? That is the puzzling question I asked myself. God's Word however says very plainly: "They shall deceive the very elect" (Matthew 24:24). Again, as so often before, I looked up to my precious Savior, thanking him for keeping me true, and it is my earnest prayer that I may remain faithful to God unto the end.

It is a strange fact that the first sign of one's backsliding is his bitterness toward God's people. A backslider becomes a relentless accuser of the brethren, like Satan. Thereby he desires to soothe his own troubled conscience.

In the meantime Frida was brought to the hospital. "How I long to get well again for my three children's sake and in order to have a little time to live for my Jesus and serve him," she sighed. "My youth was so sad and I had had no encouragement. There was only poverty and wickedness around me. If only Papa had lived, then it would not have come to this, all would be different." She was carried downstairs and whisked away to the hospital from which she never returned.

Sadness gripped me as I meditated on the fate of my cousin's family. Back in 1924, while working in his field, the horses became shy and he fell from the wagon. The wheels went over his head causing such injuries that he died a few minutes later.

His wife was not worthy of the trust that fell to her. She let herself go and soon lived indifferently, neglecting her children. Little does she realize today what awful guilt rests upon her. Woe unto such who are a stumbling block to others, who cause offense to his little ones and are a snare of the devil to helpless children.

6. ON THE TRAIL OF WAR

From Bydgoszcz I traveled to Gostynin, a town near the district of my father's and mother's birthplace. Never before had I such a longing to see the place where my parents grew up. I was a puzzle to myself. During the twenty years of my travels in Poland, I never felt such a desire. It filled my heart with satisfaction that I was now on my way.

It was the first time I had visited that town. From the station I walked along the streets and presently came into Gombin Street. Gombin is a little town in which my father as a boy learned the shoemaking trade. How many times he must have walked on this very street sixty or seventy years ago.

As I went along I saw some neatly built houses, but others were in such condition that I wondered how human beings could live in such dilapidated shacks. Coming nearer to the heart of the town, traffic was becoming more lively. Among others I saw the Jews who conspicuously displayed their yellow David star on the left front of their clothes. The Jews were not permitted to walk on the sidewalk but had to go on the pavement. Thus I saw old men and women, young boys and girls, as well as children, walking very closely to the curb for it is not without danger to be found in the path of autos and wagons.

An untold sadness gripped me. What has mankind come to and where is wickedness and hatred leading them? They are tormenting their fellowmen; innocent children who have done no ill to anybody, must plod along as outcasts. Their faces emaciated, their looks full of terror, helpless and defenseless; they are delivered to the whims of wicked individuals who can treat them as they like.

My thoughts were directed to the precious word of God and I seemed to hear coarse voices there in Jerusalem, crying, "His blood come over us and our children." Alas, those men in the Holy City did not know what they were doing and what they were inviting upon themselves and their posterity. Fury of judgment came over the offspring of those angry men back there in Jerusalem, and today they are still plodding through the mire of judgment. "How long, O Lord, how long!" But judgment upon the persecutors of the oppressed always follows a divine law which does not only apply to the Jews, but to all nations who do wrong to the helpless.

The joy was great when I came into the home of Brother and Sister Jeske. He was pastor of the local assembly, one of the workers of the Russian and Eastern European Mission whom I had not seen for over three years. In the evening we went to the meeting and had the wonderful presence of the Lord with us. It was my joy to lead some souls to Calvary and they received pardon from guilt and sin.

Next day we started on a two-wheel horse-drawn wagon to visit Lwówek, the birthplace of my father. It was my privilege to ride over the only stretch of paved highway that Poland possessed—a magnificent road, leading from Warsaw to the summer seat and thoroughbred horse stables of the minister of war and dictator of Poland, Rydz-Śmigły. That highway had a length of 150 kilometers. Such roads should not have been built only to the summer residence of the chief, but to all sections of Poland.

Our way led us through very fruitful farmland and we passed through typically dilapidated Polish villages. Strange how peasants—not at all poor—can be satisfied to live in such poorly built houses. In the distance there came into view an imposing church, a Catholic edifice of the town, Gąbin.

Coming nearer to the place, we saw another church, but in ruins. Only the outer walls standing, an eloquent accusation against the devastation of war. The bulky tower was partly spared, fantastically pointing towards heaven.

One of the bells—which was still in place—leaned to one side as if it was caught in the act of chiming.

In the place of the altar the mosaic of the floor was still uninjured and gave the impression of having been part of a beautifully decorated house of God. As I stood there on the place of the altar I looked up to the clear sky, asking myself: "Why must this stately Protestant church be thus ruined? It has as little in common with war as John 17, and still, here are the ruins. We have here a picture of the fury of man who has strayed from God and has gone forth to destroy, not only objects serving war purposes but everything that stands in his path—symbolic of modern men and nations without God.

Examining the altar space, I carefully moved to a spot where I then paused, because here was memorable ground for me. In 1873 it was here that my father and mother stood as bride and groom and were wedded; here they gave each other their eternal, "Yes."

The parsonage was not destroyed. Above the main entrance I read 1828, the year in which this edifice was finished, the church being dedicated two years later. Until then all the baptismal, confirmation, and wedding ceremonials had to be performed by the Catholic priest; also for the Protestants, by decree of the Tsar which must have been unpleasant for both parties.

In sad reveries I walked through the streets of this town. Many houses lay in ruins and numerous Jews were busy removing the debris of devastation as well as tearing down unsightly buildings. The Germans are acting as if the last word had already been spoken in this world tragedy, but several hundred miles away, guns are still thundering that grim music of battle on a front of 1500 miles.

Were it not for the armed guards who are alertly watching the working Jews, one would think well enough that all is serene and normal. Shops are open and customers are coming and going. But under the surface there is a desperate hatred and thirst for revenge glowing in the hearts of the vanquished. At times I can see the sparks of hate flashing out of their eyes.

Will there be no end of slaughter and crime in this world? Is there to be an eternal circle of revenge, oppression and bloodshed? How peacefully and serenely the people could live together in this vast expanse of eastern Europe. There would be room for all and much to spare. But sin and envy does not allow any relaxation. There is no peace for the wicked. Mankind has very carefully chosen and deliberately dethroned God, so they also must shoulder the consequences. It is the law of life.

When they are in suffering and agony, they remember the Lord and say: "Why does he allow us to suffer thus? Why does he not punish the cruel enemies?" Simply because man must reap just what he has sown. He has sown wind and must reap the whirlwind. That is eternal law.

The next town, Sanniki, is only five miles from my father's birthplace. There we stayed overnight in the home of a Baptist family who had been brought from Volhynia, Eastern Poland, to settle here. They received a lovely farm from which a Polish family had been ejected to make room for the new settler. Cattle, furniture, all farm implements, linen and even some of the clothes, were taken over. I had a gruesome feeling when I retired, knowing that the real owners were somewhere destitute.

This I thought may prove to be a terrible setup for personal revenge and new bloodshed. But the new owner did not come here by his own wish but because of the policy of the German government, which compelled him to leave his own little homestead and settle here on the property of a stranger.

7. A GLIMPSE OF MY FATHER'S BIRTHPLACE

Next morning we made the last short lap of the journey. On the way into the village we passed the cemetery where my ancestors are buried. Then we drove into the village and finally I stood in the street where my father and his elder children had played as little girls and boys. In a house nearby, I met a seventy-year-old peasant who bore my name, who turned out to be a distant relative of mine. He led me to my grandfather's place where my mother spent her girlhood. The old house was in ruins, having been struck by an air-bomb.

Then I was led to the house where my parents used to live. In entering I had to bend low in order to avoid the lintel of the door. Here was the tiny kitchen which also served as an ante-room. Then we entered the living room which also served as the workshop and dining room. A door led to still another little chamber which must have been the bedroom of my parents. As there was only a clay floor it looked quite desolate.

This then was the rented house for which my father was responsible, but he did not earn enough to make ends meet. That was the reason he took his family and moved deeper into Russia, the province of Volhynia.[2] Thinking that conditions would be more favorable out there, he found a veritable wilderness and had to work hard to establish his family.

The untimely death of my beloved mother in 1896 brought a hopeful development to an abrupt end, casting a lasting shadow over my boyhood years and upon the whole family. Although we never had to suffer hunger we very seldom had butter on our bread. Cakes or white bread

---

[2] The historic Russian province of Volhynia includes parts of the present-day countries of Poland, Belarus, and Ukraine.

could be enjoyed only several times a year—at Christmas, Easter and Whitsuntide.

After visiting a cousin of mine who was seventy-eight years of age, we departed from my father's birthplace, returning to Brother Jeske's home. As I left, it seemed to me again that I was taking a final leave and that something would happen in my life which would bring great changes. I registered that thought however without alarm for I knew that my Savior would be able to take care of me whatever might happen. It filled me with satisfaction to have seen the home of my parents and the scenes of their childhood.

8. A HARVEST THANKSGIVING DAY

On Sunday morning, October 20, we drove to a place called Swiniary where a Harvest Thanksgiving Day was celebrated, and where they expected us to speak. The meeting was already in progress when we stepped into the prayer hall. It was crowded in real Russian fashion, every nook and corner and every square foot of standing place being occupied, even the empty places on the platform were sought out.

Brother Jeske preached in a way that seemed very strange to me. He reminded the people about the past blessings and the privileges enjoyed. He spoke about the sadness of our time and about the grave developments that might come upon us in the near future. It was a sermon which brought tears to almost every eye, a real farewell message.

The Lord also put a note of sadness upon my heart and I admonished the saints to remain faithful even though our days may be filled with pains and tears. Waves of blessings came over us in that meeting such as I have seldom experienced in my activity for the Lord in recent years.

Although we were entirely unaware of what transpired in my home in Danzig at that very hour when we were gathered on that Sunday morning, the Lord knew and His Spirit worked and moved in our hearts and prompted us to act and speak in a way befitting the occasion.

Just as we were gathered in that Sunday morning service, the Gestapo had come into my home in Danzig and searched it, holding my wife practically a prisoner in her own home for two hours. They took with them piles of my manuscripts, articles, correspondence and other purely personal matters, including diaries of my travels embracing a number of years.

On that Sunday the wires played from Danzig. A search was made to establish my whereabouts. This was not easy because the Lord had made me change my dates and itinerary, consequently my wife could give them no definite information concerning me. So it happened that when the police thought that they finally could apprehend me, I was ahead of them. All this seeming dodging of the police was done by God's leading while I was in a blissful ignorance of the threatening danger that lurked in the dark.

Had we known the seriousness of the developments, we certainly would have struck a similar note of sad farewell in the Sunday services, but even though we did not know, the Holy Spirit did, and he strove within us, guiding our thoughts and actions on that Sunday. This occasion showed me that the Spirit of the Lord is directing his children in a special way in times of danger and impending trouble.

On Monday, October 21, I went on my way to Płock and Brother Jeske turned homeward. For him trouble began immediately. The police charged him with having sheltered me and he was finally arrested and taken to concentration camp. That I learned only after weeks when I was in my prison cell.

The Lord led me on, evading the police for another ten days. It was very essential that I should have several meetings in other places where something definite was to be accomplished in the Lord.

Then I made a short trip to bomb-shattered Warsaw where I visited Brother and Sister Krakewitch, very precious children of God. Brother K. held a high position in the Polish government but now I found them destitute. They and their two children looked very emaciated, not having even enough dry bread to eat.

As I handed them some food which I had been able to get through the line, there were tears sparkling in their eyes. I had also some richly buttered rolls which I handed to them. They took and scraped the butter off, saying: "That is too much butter on these rolls, it will suffice for quite a few slices of bread for our two children in the coming days.

Brother Krakewitch continued to carry on a very blessed gospel work among the Poles in Warsaw and vicinity. Through the awful calamities which had befallen that nation, the people began to be open for the message of the Cross, and I am told that the hall is packed every meeting and that there is much crying to God and longing for the bread that comes from heaven.

Part II: A Prisoner of the Lord

9. SHADOWS OF COMING EVENTS

Returning from Warsaw, I stopped again in Płock in order to visit the birthplace of my mother. There I was scheduled to speak in a special meeting besides having an invitation to preach in Boriszewo, also near Płock, the place where some of my early meetings were held in the beginning of my missionary activity in Poland. In Boriszewo I spoke from the text in Hebrews 10:32–39, dwelling especially on the last verse:

> But we are not of them who draw back unto perdition; but of them that believe to the saving of the soul.

Even though entirely ignorant of the fact that it would be the last meeting of my twenty years' activity, my sermon took on the character of describing the development of the gospel work in eastern Europe. I spoke of the mighty revival and the outpouring of the Holy Spirit, then of the severe persecution and the wonderful victories that followed in its wake. I also touched upon the grave dangers threatening the assemblies in these last days. That was indeed my very last sermon after twenty years of preaching in eastern Europe.

Early in the morning of October 31, I returned to Płock. An hour after my arrival in the home of my friends, a man came in, asking me to follow him to the Gestapo headquarters. There I was ushered into a room and introduced to a little man who had a withered hand, and he questioned me in a very puzzling manner.

"You are not only preaching your religion but are carrying on political propaganda," he charged, "and we are going to put a stop to it immediately."

"Not in one sermon, preached in Europe, did I ever touch politics but confined myself entirely to spiritual themes."

"I would not expect you to say anything else, but we do not believe you and consequently must forbid you speaking at all in public," he replied angrily. "I will immediately notify the Gestapo in Lipno where you planned to speak, to have an eye on you, but if you do not register at the police, you will be arrested at once."

As I never before had been molested and no Gestapo man ever had come near with the object of questioning me, this new method seemed very strange, but I did not take it as seriously as it proved to be. I built on my good conscience and did not feel at all in any great danger. Nor did the thought of arrest ever occur to me. The Spirit within however, was warning, and the Lord prompted me to act according to the seriousness of the hour. I canceled the meetings which I was to have had near Lipno and decided to start for home the very next morning.

It was on Friday night of November 1, 1940, when I arrived at home. My wife gave me a full report of the transpired events. She assured me, however, that the Gestapo had not threatened to molest me, but merely demanded that I show myself at the Gestapo headquarters in Danzig as soon as I came home.

On the next day, Saturday, November 2, I went to the Gestapo to report my homecoming. Upon arriving, I was sent from one official to the other, but none seemed to know anything about me. In one room where there was a middle-aged man and two office girls working, they looked at me bewildered is if saying: ". . . and you have actually come, running into the den of lions?"

They directed me into an adjoining room where an official told me to go home and wait until I heard further from them. And I did hear in a way that I never should have thought possible.

10. PROTECTIVE ARREST

In the afternoon we went out with our children to visit my mother-in-law and early in the evening we returned home. To clear up the dishes quickly I helped my wife, after which we intended to eat supper. The children were put to bed and I kissed them goodnight, not knowing that it would be the last time in many months that I would hold them in my arms. I was still drying dishes when the doorbell rang at about half past eight that evening. My wife opened the door and a man in civilian clothes stepped in.

"Is your husband at home?" he asked.

"Yes, there he is in the kitchen," my wife replied.

"Call him," he demanded.

My wife opened the door to the kitchen and I stepped out and greeted him.

"Make yourself ready, you must come with me," he commanded. Glancing into his face I looked into ice-cold eyes in which there was no human feeling evident; they were riveted on me unmingled by mercy or consideration.

"What do you want of me, and where will you take me?" I demanded to know. There was a jerk in the muscles of his face, as if something had stung him. He disliked the quetion and the tone in which I asked it.

"That you will see later. I am not here to talk but to act." His words came out of a bitter heart like whip-lashes.

In moments of calamity the mind refuses to act logically at times. I went into my room as in a dream. I was unable to think of a thing I should take along but then I reached for my Bible and tenderly put it into my briefcase; the precious Book which had been my beloved companion for many, many years. Then I took several other things and came out again, facing my captor.

"Say goodbye to your wife," he commanded.

My wife was very frightened and began to weep, asking him sobbingly: "Will my husband return again?" It was a heartbreaking question of an anxious and terror-stricken mother of two little helpless children who would be left without a father.

"Whether your husband will return I do not know; I have orders to fetch him, that is all." He spoke the words as if he were flinging them at her feet.

The tears of a helpless and crushed woman were nothing to him. How could it touch him? Such, and more horrifying scenes are his daily routine. He is deadened to every human feeling.

"Can I say goodbye to my little children as well?" I asked.

"Yes, you may but make it quickly!" He snapped the words at me.

Quietly I slipped into the bedroom, went to the little bed, there lay my eight-month-old baby. She often cheered me with her beautiful smile, and now she reposed there, breathing deeply in sound sleep. For a few minutes I lingered, gazing at that sleeping, loving form, my flesh and blood. Tears did not come, they never come to me in moments of pain and calamity. I bent low and kissed my little Karin goodbye. In her sleep she reached up with her tiny velvety hand and faintly touched my cheek. Many times in my prison cell I felt that faint touch on my cheek; it was a great comfort to me.

I took her hand in mine and murmured: "How good it is, my little Karin, that you do not yet know sorrow; heartache has not touched you as yet. Neither do you know what this hour may mean to me, to you, to your future. Sleep little Karin, sleep, my heart remains with you whatever may happen, and don't forget Papa. Your crystal-clear blue eyes always seemed to me like an unruffled deep blue ocean. Your childish love has just begun to come into consciousness and you have just begun to smile at me. Now I have to leave you. I will miss your smile, I will miss your open look, your little hands stroking my face. Goodbye, my Karin, goodbye."

Then I went over to my little Ruth, five years of age. I tried to arouse her, but a sleeping child—especially in the first hours of sleep is not easily awakened. There she lay so peacefully as if the whole world was serene. I knew that she would not find me at home in the morning. She would ask Mamma for Papa and would receive an evading answer. I kissed her goodbye. For a moment she opened her eyes and looked at me wonderingly and just whispered, "Papa," then fell asleep again.

"Goodbye, little Ruth! You have always prayed for your Papa, you will continue to pray in your childish way, won't you . . ."

My captor became uneasy, entered the room and roughly urged me to get ready. To him my lingering at the bedside of my children seemed to be utterly out of place.

Now I had to say "goodbye" to my poor wife. She was young and did not have an easy married life. I was away on the Lord's errands most of the time and she had to struggle alone at home. She bore it valiantly, and now had to face this horrible ordeal. We did not know what this taking me away would mean. It could be prison but it might just as well be concentration camp. In that case chances would be slim to see each other again. It would mean unspeakable suffering for both of us.

I embraced and kissed her goodbye. A few steps away stood my captor, the personification of a bad omen. I could just whisper to her: "Look to Jesus for strength. Let him comfort you whatever may happen and let us remain faithful to him, our loving Savior. Thank you for all you have been to me, and take care of our precious treasures, our little ones. Goodbye, my Margaret. Let us meet often around the throne of grace, near the heart of our Jesus who will never leave us nor forsake us."

"Make it short!" our onlooker bellowed, standing a few feet away. He went to the door, opened it and said: "Now go, we have been waiting too long already."

A look into each other's eyes, a few heart sighs in prayer: "Lord, you see this heart-breaking scene. You alone know what it means and what will happen. I thank you that I am not being taken away as a guilty criminal or a perpetrator of evil. You, the Father of widows and orphans, take care of my helpless and frightened wife. It is much that you load upon her. Lord, let not the burden crush her but let her grow stronger through it, let her strike deeper roots in you through this awful trial."

My captor pushed me out through the door. Another lingering look of my wife and a sigh: "Now you did not even get supper!" as I descended the stairway and all was dark around me. I was led to a waiting auto, asked to enter and whisked away to the police headquarters.

A new horrible world—hitherto unknown to me —I entered: a world of terror and night, of humiliation and abasement. Into a dismal prison office I was ushered. The pale and doleful electric light disclosed to me a room with an officer behind a desk, and walls lined with shelves containing many bins.

"Empty your pockets of everything and lay it on that table," came the grating voice of the officer behind the desk. To him I was just, "The next one." There I stood before a little table which had only a few faint traces of once being painted and I began to take things out of my pockets and lay them on the table one by one: my purse, my pocketbook, the notebook, pencil, fountain pen and some other things which I happened to have along. When I had finished that mournful task, an officer came and went through my pockets once more, to make sure I had not slipped anything. I had not taken off my wristwatch, so he himself unloosed it, leaving me without a timepiece. My name and personals were recorded. All seemed to be so far away from me, so strange, so horrible. My belongings and my briefcase were put away and I realized that I was to retain nothing. "Can't I take my Bible with me?"

"No, you cannot have anything with you," he growled angrily.

"But I had the Bible with me all my life and this is the time when I need it the most," I ventured.

"And this is just the time when you cannot have it with you." Then to an attendant, "Take him away!" Promptly that man grabbed me by the arm and said: "This way, march!" He led me down into the basement, through a narrow and only faintly lighted passageway. We passed a few doors when he halted, unlocked a door noisily, opened it and pushed me inside, saying: "Here, it will be nice and quiet, none to disturb you all night."

He slammed the door, locked it, turned out the dim light in the passageway and I was plunged into a horrible darkness.

That was Saturday evening, November 2, 1940, about ten o'clock at night. The cell was unheated. A terribly foul damp air struck me, making breathing almost impossible. An open pail stood in the corner—as I found next morning —not properly cleaned, which made breathing a torture.

In complete bewilderment I stood there, stunned by the terrible turn events had taken. I could visualize my wife at home grief-stricken, not knowing what might be done to me. But we knew too well, what was being done to such

49

arrested persons. I again lived through the farewell scenes at the bedside of my little ones, of my wife. I could feel Margaret's tears still burning on my face. Then I came back to that bleak reality in that dismal and awful cell. Was it a terrible nightmare which was tormenting me, and was I to wrest myself clear of its grip in the next moment?

"It is impossible, it cannot be reality, I have done nothing that deserves this. My whole life, my health, my best years have been spent in gospel service for my Jesus, nothing else."

"Yes, and now you are getting the reward, your payment for it, your payment!"

There must be a terrible presence in this room. I am conscious of evil powers lingering here. I could hear that awfully grating and hissing voice distinctly.

Truly, there they are, one is visible in the darkness, and gloatingly he stares at me; triumphantly he challenges: "Where is your God, has he helped you from this? Where is he now, why does he let you come into this place?"

No doubt, this was a general attack of the enemy. Very viciously he challenged, and I had no answer, no way out. As one who is paralyzed and unable to turn his head, compelled to look in one direction, I stared at that apparition. I had no power within me to answer or resist. God seemed very far away, my heart was in an iron clutch of the relentless enemy.

Once before I had had a similar attack; in 1917, when I completely surrendered to the call of God for my missionary activity in eastern Europe. But there I was at once able to parry the evil attack and I saw the enemy recede step by step as I called out the name of Jesus; it was within the hallowed atmosphere of the Bible school. Here I was helpless.

"O God, have you not come with me into this horrible place; have you forsaken me? Oh, come to me and dispel these dark clouds." Thus I sighed inaudibly, staring into the darkness.

There seemed to be no answer—not the slightest breeze from the presence of the Lord. Yet the enemy was relentless in his attacks. This was the hour when he finally would get me down into the mire of despair, he thought—which would be very dangerous in a place like this—and he was very busy talking without giving me a breathing spell.

Alas, in such hours of extreme trials the devil pities us too, but for the sole purpose of planting bitterness against God's dealings and permissions in our hearts. Those are indeed perilous moments and sometimes children of God have given way to these awfully vicious whisperings, thereby poisoning their spiritual life, and giving the enemy free course to plunge the soul into psychic darkness or even derangement of mind.

Alone and yet not alone, forsaken and yet surrounded by grace. That is the answer as to the attitude of our God in such moments of great distress. He watches us like a mother her loving child in an hour of crisis, in sickness. Jesus my precious Savior was there all the time. He had come along with me into that dark and dismal cell and presently he spoke to me, interrupting the devil. . . . And how sweetly his voice sounded, when he said: "Now sing, 'He's a Friend of Mine'."

I was so deeply in grief that I did not catch the import of that voice, but Jesus has much patience. He spoke again: "Now sing, 'He's a Friend of Mine!'"

The third time his voice sounded in my heart as clearly as a bell: "Now sing, 'He's a Friend of Mine!'" I recognized that it was he who reminded me of my favorite song, which I had sung hundreds of times in meetings during the last twenty-two years and it was always a blessing to me and also to the listeners.

Once before this song was used by the Lord in a similar way to stem the tide of discouragement, back in 1918 when trials had gripped me, being without friends and without money in Minneapolis, Minnesota. Now after twenty years almost to the day, the Lord asked me once again to sing that song when I did not feel like singing at all.

Strange how the Lord deals with us at times. He demands us to do things that seem illogical, but there is always divine logic when he speaks to us. The Lord knew what was good for me in those moments and worked in my heart just the right way.

Slowly and faintly at first, I began to sing. It sounded to me as if I had put my head into a barrel. It did not ring well at all, but my soul listened and concentrated on the great and most wonderful Friend of ours, Jesus Christ our Savior. He thereby took my mind off the enemy and my ears from his evil whisperings.

The singing went better and better as verse by verse I was pouring out my wounded and troubled heart, and it soothed me like a healing balm.

> Why should I charge my soul with care?
> The wealth of every mine
> Belongs to Christ, God's Son and Heir,
> And he's a Friend, of mine.
>
> *Yes, he's a Friend of mine.*
> *And he with me doth all things share:*
> *Since all is Christ's and Christ is mine,*
> *Why should I have a care?*
> *For Jesus is a Friend of mine.*
>
> The silver Moon, the golden Sun,
> The countless stars that shine,
> Are his alone, yes, ev'ry one,
> And he's a Friend of mine.
>
> He daily spreads a glorious feast,
> And at his table dine
> The whole creation, man and beast,
> And he's a Friend of mine.

And when he comes in bright array,
And leads the conqu'ring line,
It will be glory then to say,
That he's a Friend of mine.

The last verse rang out in complete freedom causing the enemy and his whole cohort to flee, leaving me in contact with my precious Savior. My mind was serene and I began to investigate my cell. I found there was a cot, one end slanting upward and forming the head end, with bare boards the surface of which were rough and uneven as I felt over them with my hands. The reason of that roughness I learned only in the morning.

As I continued to make myself acquainted with that den, I found that I had about one foot width of space between the edge of the cot and the wall, and there were about two feet above the length of the cot. Because of the horrible odor issuing from that open pail—the only "sanitary improvement" of the cell—I wondered how I could manage to live in such a terrible place. Finally I detected the one foot square window which I managed to open just a little. It was indeed a very small and uncomfortable "bedroom" in which I was now called upon to spend the night. There was nothing whatever to put on the boards, no pillow, no covers, just the bare wood.

It should have been hard for me before, to associate such an inhuman cell with that modernized and clean city of Danzig, but here I had the gruesome reality and I was in the midst of it.

"He's a friend of mine," it kept on ringing in my heart. "Is this then really God's will for me to spend my time in this horrible place as a prisoner?" The Lord—as the true Friend—had protected me scores of times from greatest dangers, from prison cells, even when it was very threatening. Often the prison door had been ajar for me in the Balkan states as I was on my gospel trips, but I always skipped by. Would the Lord permit this to go on without delivering me?

In my heart a desperate cry rang out for deliverance, but I seemed to lack a strong grip in the prayer for my liberation. It was because the Holy Spirit did not back up that prayer at all—still I prayed and cried to God for my release. He however was not to deliver me but manifest his power and his great love which would transform my cell into a sanctuary. I was destined to learn to know my God from an entirely new angle.

It was certainly impossible to stand up the whole night through on one spot, being very weary and tired. I had not eaten supper and was now quite hungry. Presently I sat down on that wooden cot. In my heart there was a quietness and trust in God. I felt his presence with me and that was all that mattered. He, my Friend, was with me in this cell. Hallelujah! As I heard myself say "Hallelujah," I was startled.

Much I had read about the martyrs and their imprisonments and it was easy for me to realize that thousands of them were in much greater misery. They were thrown into dungeons after being maltreated, bleeding from many wounds, but here I was not in pain nor injured in body and with no dislocated joints.

Meditating thus I stretched out on those boards. Soon I fell asleep and slept through till the morning. When I awoke, a faint light came through the tiny window and I made the unpleasant discovery that the unevenness of the boards and the roughness had been caused by vomited matter which was dried to the boards. These cells in the basement were used to lock up drunkards who were picked up during the night in their drunkenness and left to sober up. In the morning they were released and the cell remained unattended. In a little tin basin, rusty, bent and battered, containing about two pints of water, I washed myself.

The awful desolation of the place again depressed me beyond degree and I felt forsaken and forgotten. I longed for my Bible and tried to recall the many verses and promises which I knew by heart, but they brought me no noticeable comfort. Heaven seemed to be brazen and the scorching sun of sorrow beat down upon me until I was stunned.

At seven in the morning an attendant opened the door. In his hand he held a great can and shouted at me to fetch my cup. Being unfamiliar with the "etiquette" of the place I could not see anything that resembled a cup so he shouted some more and finally pointed to an old rusty, battered mug into which he poured "coffee." He also handed me a piece of black doughy bread, equal to about three slices. That was to be my breakfast. That dark colored liquid was hardly suitable for drinking. It certainly did not taste like coffee, in fact, I could not associate it with anything I had tasted before.

11. Cross-Questioning

A little while later, a Gestapo man came, led me out of the cell, then through the streets of the city to the Gestapo headquarters.

In the registering office I was told to sit on a narrow bench which was very close to the wall thus not permitting a reclining position. At nine o'clock I was brought into a room where at the desk a hawk-faced man in a black guard's uniform was seated. I was asked to sit down opposite him in a straight chair.

After I seated myself as comfortably as possible, that man bellowed at me: "Sit down respectfully; don't you know whom you have before you! We are trying to treat you decently, but we can be nasty as well, if you give us reasons." I was not to cross my legs nor was I permitted to lean against the back-rest of the chair. The questioning began. He himself sat at the typewriter and wrote the answers down making seven or eight carbon copies. We were alone in the room.

"I want to know everything concerning your life, your activity and your travels just as it all happened," he told me as a preliminary enlightenment.

"Then you will have a great task before you, for my life has been quite colorful and active in every respect," I warned him.

"That is what I am here for," he countered. So the recording of my life history began more thoroughly than ever before.

Until two o'clock in the afternoon the questioning continued without any interruption. Then he seemed to be exhausted and made me sign the written pages and I was led into the registering office again and told to sit down on that same narrow bench.

Being extremely tired and worn out by now, I was on the verge of collapsing after sitting a while, so I cried to God for new strength.

After about an hour someone remembered that I had not eaten anything since that morning—"breakfast." A discussion followed among the policemen and finally I was led through the city back to the police prison and into my cell. There I found a dish of pea soup waiting for me but it had been standing in the cell since twelve and was cold and stiff. I tasted the soup but found that it was quite impossible for me to eat. Through the terrible pressure which my soul was subjected to and the plight I was in, no desire within me for eating was left.

Half an hour had hardly passed when I was brought again to the Gestapo headquarters. They did not care whether I had eaten or not, and nothing was mentioned about it. Again I had to sit down on the same bench and wait over an hour until five o'clock when finally I was ushered into the same room for continuance of the inquisition.

Now he wanted to know exactly what religious experiences I had gone through. So I related my salvation, emphasizing strongly repentance and the divine intervention in my life and the changes it had wrought. But we soon ran up against snags. He could not understand the language nor could he grasp the meaning of salvation. Much less was he willing to write such facts into the protocol. However he tried to describe it in his own way but that made it sound ridiculous and without sense.

"You mean to say that you left your Lutheran church and joined a sect," he began to argue.

"No," I replied, "it was not joining a sect nor another church but it was a repenting over my past sinful life and putting my whole being entirely into the hands of my Savior, beginning to live according to his holy will as it is revealed in the Word of God."

"What is 'his will'; who knows what that means?" he countered, "Has he who does not exist at all, come and told you what he wants? No, there is no such a thing, it is merely imagination."

"If you have a terrible disease and that evil is suddenly taken away and your body made perfectly whole, then it is not imagination but a positive fact. It was not imagination when my heart and life—diseased by sin and vileness—was changed in a moment and the love and craving for sinful things were removed from my heart. It is the Holy Spirit that is sent just for that purpose to convict us of our sins and put within our heart a desire to be freed from that curse. Then he instructs us concerning the way we are to take and the kind of life we are to live. He also puts an unspeakable joy into our heart and we know that we are children of God."

"What do you mean, are you beginning to preach to me here!" he shouted in anger. "Just answer my questions and no more. You ought to know very well that there are no such things as those about which you talk, and with this religious superstition we are finished, it is about time."

"With this 'religious superstition'—if you prefer in to call it such—anti-Christian man has battled nearly two thousand years. Whole empires have broken asunder in that fight, but Christianity stands today and is as powerful as ever. They have martyred millions of followers of Christ but Christianity lives, it cannot be rooted out and you will not succeed either."

"We do not want to root out Christianity but we shall see to it that it dies a natural death, as the children grow up under our supervision. Furthermore we do want to force a stop to such fanatical sects as the one you represent. There is no room for such in Germany as these so called 'movements' hinder our progress."

He abruptly stopped the discussion about salvation and put other questions to me. I could however see that he began to feel uncomfortable.

"You had returned to the United States in 1937. Why did you come to Europe once more, what was the object? Had your government a hand in your coming to Danzig?" Here he launched an attack against my Christian activity.

"God gave me a distinct call back in 1916, to work among the people of eastern Europe as well as in the Balkan States. I have been active under that call throughout the years since the close of the World War. When I was in the United States the last time, the desire for going back and continuing my activity was burning within me like a fire. It was the longing to preach and work anew among the people of those fields, and there is absolutely nothing that could have kept me back," I explained to him with emphasis.

"But as an intelligent person you should have known that war would come in Europe. You certainly will not claim such ignorance that you did not realize that," he replied.

"Most certainly I hoped that the main powers involved, would use their common sense and not let such a terrible conflagration burst upon the world which would ultimately wipe out all the wealth and achievements and throw all mankind into poverty and untold misery."

"There will not be misery but prosperity, peace and mutual understanding when we shall have wiped out those who disturb the peace of the world and keep Europe in disruption," he replied. To him as well as to the majority of Germans it was only a matter of time that the victory would be won, after which the grand plan of the *Neuordnung* ('New Order') in Europe would be put into realization for a thousand years of German peace and untold prosperity overspreading Europe.

"I am afraid that you are sponsoring utopian plans. As long as man is unregenerated, selfish and in sin, he can never succeed in such plans. Only God can bring justice, harmony, and lasting prosperity upon this earth," I replied.

"We are going to prove that it can be done and that the world can be managed properly by skillful men." For a little moment he had forgotten that he was the inquisitor and that I was his prisoner. He merged into oratory, but caught himself after a while.

While they had arrested me under the accusation of forbidden religious activity, they were evidently sure to find other motives for my sojourn in Europe. They hoped to discover such fact in my correspondence and papers which they had seized. Perhaps they could easily prove me guilty of spying for America.

Their contention is that every missionary of England and America is also a spy for his respective country.

Therefore the question of why I came to Europe in June 1939, was placed to me in all possible forms.

By now it was seven o'clock in the evening and I was led once more through the city into my cell to eat supper. Again a watery cold soup was waiting for me which I could not eat, having no appetite. By this time I had the greatest difficulty to keep myself upright and walked along as in a delirium. Mentally I was so exhausted that I could no longer think clearly, complete apathy having seized me.

That is just the way they want a prisoner to be, for then the protocol can be formed just as they like. None of them took notice of my condition, they were adamant and simply carried through the planned routine.

Once more I was taken for questioning and it lasted until twelve at night. When I was finally led back I just stumbled along as in a stupor. Deep down in my store of thought I remembered my precious wife and children and it seemed that my little Ruth was climbing up on my lap, putting her arms around me with her soft hands stroking my face.

A rough hand was grasping me and I heard a shout: "Watch where you are going, do you expect me to carry you!" The guard had caught me just when I was about to sink to the hard pavement.

Like a flash the thought shot through my mind: "When Jesus was carrying his cross, he stumbled too and fell, but he wore a crown of thorns; he was just as hungry but more emaciated, and bleeding from many wounds, and in pain because of many stripes.

"Yes, Lord," I responded, "a crown of thorns, hungry, bleeding, beaten, and carrying a heavy cross on your shoulder. Yes, Lord, I have it much easier and still it is so hard and bitter."

Like an electric current the warmth of his presence shot through me. I pulled myself together and walked on before my heartless guard. I knew an invisible form walked beside me. Oh, the wonderful and comforting thought that Jesus is with us in such trying hours!

Then suddenly I remembered my awful cell and the thought that I should spend the night again on those hard boards in that terribly foul air made me shiver, and I sighed: "My Jesus, you will surely not let me be put into that horrible place again!" Having said this to my precious Savior, I felt quite sure that he, who pities a sparrow, would not forget to take care of me.

The prison-gate was open and I was hurried into the building. We came to the door of my section and the key was turned to open another door. I heard the click of that lock again after we passed inside. The guard commanded me to go before him and we passed the narrow stairway leading upward. Just then a man came into view on his downward way. He glanced at me for a fleeting moment, then asked the guard: "Where are you taking that man?"

"Down into his cell again," the guard replied.

"No," he snapped back at him, "That which is impossible, is impossible. Give me that prisoner."

He took charge of me and dismissed the guard. Then he commanded me to walk up the stairs before him, to the second floor. There he unlocked the door to a cell, pushed me inside and locked it again while saying: "In five minutes you have to be in bed, then I will put out the light."

The cell—as I noticed immediately—was slightly heated. There was a cot with a mattress, two covers and a straw pillow. The air was more tolerable although similar sanitary conditions existed here.

Who was the man whom the Lord send to the right spot into our view in that fraction of a second, while I passed the foot of the stairway? He was a higher prison official. He seemed to know me at a glance and thus was used by the Lord to answer my heart-sigh there on the street, as I stumbled along inward my prison. What a wonderful Savior is Jesus my Lord!

In my semi-consciousness my heart's eyes looked to my Savior in love and thankfulness which could not be put into words, but my Jesus understood me. It was my first definite answer to prayer in my imprisonment, I registered it in my mind, while I sank into a sleep of exhaustion immediately.

And he, my precious Jesus, watched over me throughout that short night in a special way, to give me new stores of strength for the further ordeal that was to follow. Praise his name forever!

12. VISITORS IN DREAMLAND

My first day of questioning was on Sunday, the day I used to preach in my assembly throughout the years. Now the next day began, it was Monday, and I was taken again to be cross-questioned and it was carried on in a similar way as the previous day. My exhaustion was not much relieved because I had not eaten anything the day before and now, Monday, I still had no appetite, the prison food being such that it was almost impossible to eat.

My distress became limitless as the hours of the day dragged to a close without my hearing anything from my wife and children. In my cell again I was being tormented by the thought that my wife might have been taken into prison also, and that the children would be destitute. The most horrible pictures passed through my mind. I saw my wife in a dark cell, little Ruth running about the streets unattended, calling for Mamma, and baby Karin, eight months old, abandoned at home. Then I could see how little Ruth was struck down by an auto and was bleeding while lying on the pavement and none caring for her.

With a leap I charged at the door, trying to break it open, but those prison doors are built for the purpose of resisting such attempts. Utterly exhausted I sank down on the cot and fell into oblivion.

When I came to again, I felt a sharp pain in my shoulder and faintly remembered my foolish action of a while before and the word of Paul came to me when he says: "Ye have need of patience." I felt ashamed of myself, saying: "Lord, forgive me for displaying so little of your patience, but you see how I am being tortured under these conditions by the onslaught of the enemy. I ask you to undertake for me."

Presently I fell asleep. Still, it did not seem to be asleep for I was led away on a very dark and rocky narrow trail. It was an angel who was guiding me along that dangerous path until it widened out and I stood before the entrance of a cave. The oval opening, sharply declining, was about thirty feet high. The angel led me forward until I stood at the very brink of the entrance. As I looked down below, I saw the awful black darkness and I shivered, a great fear gripping me. Then I discovered before me a secure fence and was reassured.

Continuing to look downward I suddenly saw a man emerge out of the darkness below. He was not walking but floating above the ground. As he came nearer, he appeared very familiar to me. He was wearing a red vestment and as he approached I recognized him as I would a friend, whom I had known for years, and exclaimed: "Ah, the apostle Peter!" The surprise to see him here in this strange place, made me spellbound. I could only gaze at him. His reddish hair fell over his shoulders, he had a full red beard and a healthy-looking, even face. He gave me a penetrating and searching glance, then nodded slightly in a profoundly earnest expression as if saying, "All that has happened to me and much more than that which you suffer now."

Thus he floated past me and vanished in the distance.

Now I turned back and looking down once more into the cave and right behind the fence—about four meters away—I saw another man standing behind a pulpit, facing the right. In his hands he held an old scroll partly opened, but his gaze was into the distance, deeply absorbed in profound thoughts and meditation. He also wore a vestment but of slightly lighter color than that of the apostle Peter. His head was bald with only a narrow strip of hair around his temples and above the neck. He had a flax-colored, trimmed beard, his face very pale and ethereal.

As I beheld him, I exclaimed with equal positiveness as if seeing suddenly an intimately known friend: "That is the apostle Paul, how wonderful!"

My great surprise did not so much center in the fact that I saw the two apostles but that they were at the entrance of that cave and at this time.

Slowly the vision faded and it affected me so strangely that I awoke. It was not like a dream at all but like a real experience of seeing intimate friends. All the details of their features remain clearly in my memory until this very day. I can close my eyes and see them before me. Indeed I am convinced that I shall look upon them as seen here, when in heaven I shall finally stand face to face with them, just as they appeared in that dream vision.

When I awoke, my whole faculty of thought was occupied with these two representative apostles. Their life and their work; their imprisonments and suffering became so vivified within me that my own troubles faded and at times were forgotten. When afterward I was again reminded of the weight of my sorrow, the sting of pain was not so keenly evident. A deep peace filled my soul and I continued meditating on those two strange visitors, and with it came the opening of the channels of blessing, bringing me back into real blessed contact with God. I had gained a real fellowship with the Word of God in my heart, and many precious promises became a living power within me.

The dark and narrow walls of the cell did not look so dismal the next morning when I awoke to face a new torturous day because my Jesus had visited me in a special way. He led me forward on my dark pathway a good distance. When my heart began to pain in sorrow and loneliness again, I was immediately reminded that others of God's servants had had to go through infinitely greater sufferings and sorrow than I was called upon to experience now.

"How wonderful it is that you are not here as a thief, a murderer or robber, but that you are here for the gospel's sake," rang out within my heart from one day to the next, and I could say to my Savior: "You have permitted this to happen, and you who care for the sparrow and for the flowers of the field, will surely not forget me and my troubled wife and little children who are helpless there at home."

In spite of the distinct interventions of God and the deep blessings I received, the battle was not over. New crises came and despair lifted its head anew but with great love and patience the Lord met me always in the dark valley, lifting me up again and again to the mountaintop of victory and blessing.

13. UTTER HELPLESSNESS

The awful clicking noise of a big key, being thrust into the lock, was heard again. The door opened and the guard bellowed: "Out for questioning!" Not responding and jumping out of the cell in the very moment, brought scolding curses upon me. I was again led to the Gestapo headquarters.

The awful harrowing way and the ugly threatenings to extract facts from me and try to make me admit things which were not true, made the whole proceedings a farce. He was determined to construe an instrument just as he needed it in order to find reasons for holding me imprisoned.

Being an American citizen, there had to be a semblance of reasonable evidence against me. So there was art in the fiendish mode of his questioning to twist and wrest my own statements and explanations until they meant the very opposite from what I wanted to say. In moments I was plunged into the abyss of despair because there was nothing to relieve me from my helplessness.

For two days I had been led back and forth through the streets to and from the Gestapo building for questioning. In the mornings there were always several prisoners along, on the way to the Gestapo building. They had to carry over two big milk cans between two and two. It was evidently food that they carried to the special Gestapo prisoners.

On the previous days I had just to walk along with them but this morning I heard the guard call to an attendant: "We need only three more men this morning, he can help carry and do something as well," he said while pointing at me.

A stick was put through the top and I had to take hold of one end. My partner was a very tall fellow, consequently his end of the stick was higher, causing the can to slide over to my side and thereby giving me at once three-fourths of the whole weight of the can to carry. Being so weakened physically because of lack of nourishment in the last four days, I almost fell under the weight.

When the guard saw me falter, he shouted, saying, "Do you want me to help you? I have ways and means to make you go straight. Don't feign weakness. You are strong enough!"

Looking in that moment to the Lord, I asked for enough strength to carry my load.

Suddenly I saw in the spirit a man stumbling and then falling under the weight of a rough and heavy cross. It was Jesus, my Savior. On his head I saw a crown of thorns crushed into his flesh and he looked at me. I exclaimed within myself: "My Jesus, forgive me for complaining. My burden is nothing in comparison to yours. I am only threatened, but you have been cruelly beaten when your strength did not suffice to bear the burden that evil men forced you to carry."

The can was now pressing against my hand and almost the whole weight was on my side but it became easy. I did not feel it at all and reached the destination without any more strain on myself.

When we had put the cans down, the guard looked at me with a wicked smile, saying: "You carried your load easy enough, yet wanted to feign weakness."

"Someone who is much more merciful than any man, has helped me to carry my burden, thus it became very easy to carry. I wish you would know him, it is Jesus." I said it in greatest earnestness and for a moment he was nonplussed, staring at me.

"You don't know what you are talking about," he muttered, but the tone of his voice was not very emphatic. Then he shouted at me: "March through that door."

Thus he broke off the all-important subject, but I thought in my heart: "Ah, if you would know the sweetness of my vision; if you knew how Jesus touched me and how he lifted the load from my hand. Sweet mystery of the presence and the help of my Jesus!"

Again I was commanded to sit down on that narrow bench where I had to press my back against the cold wall in order to get as nearly as possible to an equilibrium, but relaxation was impossible. It was indeed a scientific fiendish contraption to make a human being miserable when sitting on that bench, waiting. Thus I had to wait helplessly until that inquisitor was getting ready again—at his leisure—to resume tearing up my nerves and harassing me to the very limit.

This was Tuesday, and not having had a shave since the previous Friday nor much of anything to eat, I must have been a pitiful sight.

Suddenly the leading official of the Gestapo headquarters entered and those present snapped to attention. He looked at me and then asked, "Who is that man?"

"Why that is Schmidt who was apprehended recently," came the reply.

Hearing that, he put his finger to his forehead and contemptuously exclaimed: "A preacher of the Word of God!"

It was certainly anything else but noble to ridicule me now, he himself being the instrument of my misery and pitiful condition. But there I sat as helpless as a worm and I was reminded of the prophetic picture of Christ when the Psalmist hears that great sufferer exclaim: "I am a worm and no man; a reproach of men, and despised of the people. All they that see me laugh me to scorn: they shoot out the lip, they shake the head" (Psalm 22:6–7).

"Lord, I am not worthy to be compared with you, but if they ridiculed and despised you, why should they not despise me!" Deepest thankfulness surged through my weakened body and a consciousness of pride welled up in my heart, for I was now permitted to live through an infinitesimal fraction of that which my blessed and holy Savior had to live through while he suffered in my stead, for me, for us all.

I realized more and more vividly how utterly helpless I was. I was delivered completely to the whim, mood, and passion of any upright or degraded human being who happened to be in charge of me. No appeal was possible. Without the will of the guard or attendant there was no possibility of getting in touch with the outside world or with a higher official.

"I am a worm," sounded within me and I repeated it often on that day when the questioning continued and page after page of typewritten matter was extracted from me, not as I willed to have it written according to facts, but as they needed it for their records against me.

But realizing that I was helpless as a worm somehow it was not causing me more distress. I was conscious of Jesus being present and if he desired to bring me some relief, he would most certainly find a way. If he willed however, that I should go through the bitterness to a finish, he would give me strength to bear it and it would ultimately mean a blessing to me.

14. Brought Nigh unto His Word

Not having had any news from my wife and children and not knowing what might have happened to them, it was easy for the enemy to plunge me from time to time into the abyss of despair. As long as the cross-questioning continued, I was preoccupied and my thoughts were forced into other directions, but when that was over, the situation began to weigh me down still more until at times I feared I should lose control over myself.

As I paced the little cell in utter helplessness and no Bible word that I remembered gripping my heart, I cried to God again, saying: "My Jesus, are you not near me anymore? Just let me have an assurance that you are here with me and help me to trust you incessantly." But there seemed to be no answer, and the enemy was hammering at my heart to bring darkness over my whole being again. I could only sigh and grieve and call upon him who is love and longsuffering.

Listening quietly within me, I could hear a voice, saying: "All things work together for good to them that love the Lord." I stopped my pacing abruptly and recalled in my mind how well I could preach on this text but now I had to realize how hard it was to apply it to reality.

"Yes, it is hard now," the inner voice went on. "It was easier to quote the passage while sitting in an easy chair or standing in a pulpit, surrounded by kindly friends and having all comfort around. Then it was easy to see that 'All things work together for good' but the 'All things' need to be tested in the roughness of vicissitudes; under the relentless onslaughts of the enemy and in life's worst adversities. Now suffer and triumph therein and you shall be made eligible to reign with Christ."

These lessons came forth to me in their relentless simplicity and clearness, and how did I behave now? I had to admit that my marks could not be called excellent. Neither could I rest in satisfaction when looking back into my former conduct. As soon as the sea of my life became rough I tried to get back into smooth waters instead of braving it and riding the waves.

That is why the Lord must compel us to battle it through instead of helping us to dodge the troubles and adversities; and that is also the reason why the Lord does not answer our frantic prayers for deliverance out of troubles at times.

It was new light which the Lord focused on my heart and life, although I was well familiar with that truth. I began examining my whole conduct and earnestly prayed that the Lord would help me to get the deepest possible blessing out of this trying situation and keep me in a serene spirit that I might not question the love of God and his wisdom in thus guiding my life.

But after all how did this cell fit into the "All things work for the good?" It was very difficult for me to reconcile the two. Within me a terrible conflict was raging, the worry for my family threatening to consume me.

Presently that inner voice continued admonishing me: "You are craving comfort in your soul, then look at the 'all things' in which you find yourself now. They are to become stepping stones which are leading nearer into my life and into my presence. I have been mindful of you and will care for you; no, I will not leave you alone in your troubles for a moment."

Again the Lord assured me of his presence and his help and I began anew to relax in his love. It was wonderful how tenderly he instructed me in my distress time and again. He always stepped in when the load was almost too heavy to bear.

Several days had passed since I was imprisoned. I had asked the guard a number of times to bring me the Bible but was told that it was now impossible. "But perhaps you'll get your Bible later on," he added not without sympathy.

Finally I thought, why not ask the Lord for my Bible. He could cause them to bring it to me. I definitely put the matter up to him and trusted that he would somehow make it possible that the Bible be available for me.

The next day the guard came to me asking whether I would care to go into a cell to join other prisoners. "Yes, I would, provided they are respectable men," I replied. He smiled as if wanting to exclaim: "Respectable men, here in prison!"

Soon he led me into a cell where I found two men. One was a Catholic priest, sixty-eight years of age, and the other was a former member of the Danzig Diet.[3] The latter was a tall and handsome gentleman in the prime of his years. Being opposed to the Nazi regime, he was too outspoken in his criticism of the party. Defending a friend of his who had been wronged by them brought him here into this cell for the second time.

In pre-Nazi days this cell was used for arrested persons of higher rank. Now this larger cell was simply used to

[3] The Free City of Danzig was ruled by the Danzig Senate (or Diet) from 1920 until it was annexed by Nazi Germany in October 1939, one year before the author's imprisonment.

accommodate several prisoners and contained just one cot. An additional two three-sectioned straw mattresses were piled up during the day on the cement floor in one corner. In the evening we spread them out side by side next to the cot, for sleeping purposes. Thus the whole width of the cell was filled. Before I came there were two other prisoners lodged in this cell, making four in all. Then three of the men had to sleep on the floor. To manage, they had to lie down the other way, putting their feet under the one cot, thus finding room for four men to sleep.

When we three were lined up for sleep side by side, the width of the cell sufficed—the priest on the cot and we on the floor.

In the corner of the cell was an open toilet, the flushing system of which was out of order. To offset that awful odor we took one of our covers and put it over the top.

The length of the cell was three and a half feet longer than that of the cot. There was a three-sectioned window which had dimmed glass, one and a half by three feet, and only part of which could be opened.

By standing on a little stool, it was possible to look out into the prison yard, and that was the only link between us and the outside world. We took turns in looking through.

Looking around the room, when I came in, I noticed a book and said: "Oh, you are quite up to date and even have a library at your disposal. May I look at the volume?"

"Yes, you may," the priest replied, "but it is only a New Testament; you may use it if you like."

"Only a New Testament!" I exclaimed. "It is the best book on earth and I have been craving for it ever since I was brought into this house. They have taken my Bible away and will not give it back. How did you manage to get yours?"

"Someone smuggled it in to me and the guard simply does not see it," he replied.

"I might tell you that this is a remarkable answer to prayer. I pleaded with God to send me my Bible but as the prison attendants are adamant in their refusal, the Lord simply did it the other way around, sending me to the Bible in this cell. Praise be to our wonderful God!"

Hearing me thus testify, the priest stared at me as if I had just emerged from another world, however he made no reply.

My other fellow prisoner did not hide his atheism, saying: "Now, Father, you have a very competent brother with you and should not feel lonesome anymore. As for me, I do not believe in such superstitions about answered prayer, and the less I will hear about this religious stuff the smoother will be our association in this 'Grand Hotel'."

"Concerning God and religion, you and the Nazis seem to tread on the same ground I perceive. I seem to hear my inquisitor talking. It is only to find out whether you are as intolerable as he, concerning views that are different from yours. Such complete negation of God as you are expressing, is often founded on bitterness over sore disappointments. We have plenty of time in here and no duties to interrupt, so it would be very interesting to learn details concerning your grievances about Christianity!"

"Disappointments, bitterness!" he retorted. "The whole church history contains nothing else so much as records of religious inquisitions, murders, and cunning."

"You are partly right," I admitted. "There is much of that in the records of church history but you must not overlook the fact that the Christian religions and Christ are not absolutely identical. If an economy with lofty principles is formed and the founder puts you in charge, you are duty bound to observe and enforce these principles. Supposing your co-workers violate these rules and you are compelled to withdraw, would it not be unfair to blame you for their misdeeds and failure?

"The critics of Christianity are unjust when they overlook the fact that church history is not a biography of Christ's work on earth. The Church began in fullest harmony with Christ in Jerusalem but later went her own way divorcing herself from Christ by introducing forms, laws, and rules which are grossly opposed to the principles laid down by Christ in his Holy Word. Yet, she is usurping the name of Christ and calling herself 'Christian' without living a Christian life.

"Instead of attending to spiritual matters and preparing her followers for heaven, the Church is going into politics, to influence or even direct worldly affairs and governments.

"If those so-called Christians, however, would have actually cared for Christ and obeyed his principles, exercising the 'love your enemy' rule of their Master, those terrible wars could easily have been prevented, neither would we have had that Nazi-nightmare in Germany to contend with. Instead of innocent folk being locked into these cells, those criminals, called Gestapo, who are tormenting their fellowmen, would be here in this 'protective arrest'."

"I see that we are getting somewhere. In a few sentences you have described the ugliness of the sore which is sapping life's vitality out of mankind," he replied.

"But still, you are making a great mistake," I continued, "the same that the Nazis are guilty of. Instead of diagnosing the disease, you stand at the sickbed declaring the disease proves to you that no physician exists. You are not going to the trouble of finding out whether the instructions of the physician—or, in the argument, God—have been obeyed."

"Hold on, now you are getting off the track. If there would be an almighty God, he could certainly enforce his injunctions, and not depend on the mood of a slothful follower," he countered.

"No physician can compel a patient to obey his orders. If good will is lacking, no government, however powerful, can compel anyone to obey the laws, but can only punish violations.

"God does not compel any human being to obey his laws or do his will. He says in his Word: 'If ye will obey my voice indeed, and keep my covenant, then ye shall be a peculiar treasure unto me above all people: for all the earth is mine.' And Jesus said lo his new followers: 'If ye continue in my word, then are ye my disciples indeed; and ye shall know the truth, and the truth shall make you free' (Exodus 19:5; John 8:31–32). The Lord does not desire forced service but he punishes violations and also unbelief. He has a right to expect willing obedience because he has created us, and therefore he is entitled to call to account every human being on that great judgment day concerning their behavior on earth.

"If the nations would have followed the injunctions of the Lord as laid down in the Bible, there would be no war today. They have refused to obey him; they cried as the Jews did in Jerusalem: 'Away with him! We do not want him to reign over us!' So they had to take the consequences and suffer the results of their attitude. So do the nations of today. They are in the mire of suffering as one nation punishes the other.

"It is grim humor when each nation prays to God for help to make them stronger than the other to destroy them. When it comes to subduing the neighbors, even the atheists feign faith in God and begin to pray.

"Then let me touch upon the other charges you make, namely, that church history is nothing but a record of crime and cunning. That you cannot substantiate. The first Christians in the Roman Empire used no carnal weapons against their relentless persecutors, who martyred many thousands, but they offered no physical resistance and yet only a little over three centuries after that helpless baby was born in the manger of Bethlehem, his followers were at the helm of the Roman Empire.

"And you don't want to insist that the apostles, Paul, Peter, and John, Polycarp, Martin Luther, John Wesley, Livingstone, Spurgeon, Moody and a host of other noble followers of Christ were criminals or even used any kind of force except charged by the power of the Holy Spirit—to reach their objective."

"Now stop a while, you are getting out of breath. I might admit that your arguments are partly new to me and worthy of consideration, but don't think you can convert me," he rejoined.

That ended our friendly argument. I noticed afterward that he was very careful not to make adverse statements concerning my faith. He refused to enter any more arguments about Christianity, but he became quite interested and asked many questions, and I had many indications that the Holy Spirit was able to find a foothold and knocked at his heart's door. If reports are correct which came to me later, he did not live much longer, having perished in a concentration camp. But I trust that he found his way to him who does not want anyone to perish but that each one be saved and have everlasting life.

As to the priest, he remained immovable in his silence concerning religious themes. He simply would not join in any conversation, but paced the cell by the hour. His hands he had loosely clasped in front and, as he told me, repeated his prayers by the count of his ten fingers, the police having taken away the rosary from him.

My heart was full of praise to the Lord for answering my prayers in such a remarkable way that I had the Word of God with me now, for which I had been craving so much, and for having other human beings present, with whom I could converse, taking away the sting of loneliness. So I was quite comforted.

15. FINAL ARREST

The police imprisonment was not a real arrest, the Nazis calling it *Schutzhaft* ('protective arrest'). The original reason for such an arrest was to shield an individual from the wrath of the masses when the Nazis came into power and when passions were running high. Soon however it took on another meaning and use. If someone was to get a severe reprimand or an unofficial punishment because of saying or doing something against the party, or having caused an offense against the Nazi regime he was taken into "Schutzhaft." Such an arrest was a preliminary "warning" that he was eligible for concentration camp. While a person had been locked up, it was decided whether he deserved concentration camp or to be held for regular court proceedings. Sometimes such persons were set free from "Schutzhaft" after a shorter or longer period of confinement. No arrest or sentence was pronounced.

Was a person to be held for court, he was formally declared arrested and brought into the regular jail to appear before the judge. In that case many months could elapse before such a case would come up in court proceedings.

In my case I was very confident that it could only be a matter of days before I would be released from the "protective arrest." Even my inquisitor assured me that at the most there would be a fine to pay and the incident would be over. What I should pay a fine for was a puzzle to me, but I admitted within myself that many weird things happen in the Nazi realm. So from hour to hour I was watching for the door to open, my name to be called and to be led into liberty. But I waited in vain.

My hope was further kindled when one day the priest was suddenly called out and released, as I was told but never able to verify. He might have been led into another place or into concentration camp.

By the priest having been taken away from our cell we lost a great advantage. He had received quite a bit of food which was smuggled into the cell by some of the attendants, and he faithfully divided it with us. Through his kindness we had some butter, salami, and some cheese which we could add to our prison food, and thus eating became tolerable enough. When the priest had gone, we were mourning his departure because now the extra flow of food stopped abruptly and we were limited to prison diet. It was our hope however that we should be released very soon.

On the thirteenth day of my imprisonment I was suddenly called out of the cell, trembling with joy and expectation of being released. However they took me into a police wagon with six other prisoners. Asking an attendant to what place we were to be taken, he answered: "You are going to appear before the judge."

We were whisked over to the courthouse and with another man I was locked into a tiny waiting cell in the staircase of the courthouse. After we waited an hour and a half the other man was taken out, leaving me alone in that cell which was only four by five feet in size.

After waiting another hour I was taken out and led into a little courtroom. There the judge—without any pre-liminaries—pronounced me arrested to be held for court.

"But why am I not released? What are the charges against me?" I asked in complete consternation.

The judge nervously took a folder on which my name was written and opened it, but it contained nothing but one sheet of paper—evidently instructions from the Gestapo to pronounce me arrested.

"But have you not the declaration which I sent from the police prison to the Gestapo in which I am giving explanations about my gospel activity in Europe?"

Once more he took the folder, opened it and then said: "No document has been sent to me from the Gestapo. I know nothing more about your case, and I have nothing to say but that you are arrested and that is all." How humiliating to a judge who is ordered to send someone of whom he knows nothing to jail and still be put in charge of the prisoner.

Again I was led out and locked into that tiny unheated cell. There in that dark and solitary place I stood and stared at the narrow walls. I was absolutely stunned and unable to gather my thoughts. It was impossible to grasp the significance of the situation.

It is hard for me to describe the despair that seized me. Once more I had to go through that excruciating agony of disappointment and despair as in the first hours after my imprisonment.

For two hours I waited until taken from that cell and marched into the receiving office of the city jail. There I was once more locked into an interim cell, but did not know why, as guards never gave any explanations or reasons for their actions.

Three hours passed when at last I was led into the registering office. Again I had to pass through the ordeal of emptying my pockets of those things which I had taken before leaving the police prison in the morning of that day. They thoroughly searched me now for fear that I might have concealed some instruments for violence.

All my belongings were again spread out on the table. There was also that precious New Testament which I had been given by the priest when he left. I pleaded with tears for that book, but the guards just laughed and said: "The sooner you learn to get along without such a book, the better for you and for the world."

"It might be that the time is nearer than you think, when you yourself will be in need of such a book and will try to get one. That day will be different from this one." He avoided my look as I said these words but did not reply.

A guard took charge of me again and commanded that I go before him. We went through several doors which he carefully locked after we passed through until finally he brought me into department three of the jail. After ascending an iron ladder to the third floor we walked along a narrow gangway, passing many dismal doors. Finally he halted and noisily unlocked a door. Glancing up, I saw above the door the number 44. "Go in," he shouted. Little did I realize when walking into that cell that it would be my abode for six long and weary months. When the sheet-iron-clad door of the cell was closed behind me and that awfully rattling key was turned, I just seemed to hear the death knell. All my strength left me and I would have dropped to the floor if there had not been a chair nearby. I sank on that hard and straight chair and faded into a swoon, hungry as I was. When I came to clear thinking again, my head ached from that mental strain of the whole day. I felt forsaken by God and man.

No comforting word from the Lord reached me. Perhaps he could not reveal himself to me then, because I had permitted myself to drift into darkness, and there was not even a sigh within me. Until now I had always hoped from hour to hour that I would be led out into liberty, now however I did not dare to hope any more. I was in the clutches of the court of a so-called highly civilized country, placed in the mill of their justice, about to be ground to powder.

After a long while of complete apathy I began to question, "Why does God permit this? Am I being punished for some past shortcomings? Is this to be the last chapter of my life?" Audibly these and many more questions came forth out of my heart's depth without receiving an answer. It remained dark within me.

As through an ocean of fog, my thoughts tried to press on into the distance. I sought to reach my wife and the little ones but it seemed that even my thoughts were bounded, imprisoned. I used all the mental powers of memory within me but it seemed impossible. Only dimly, as if thousands of miles distant, I could see their outlines. I whispered their names and I heard myself say: "Margaret, do you realize what has happened to me? Have you also forgotten me? Why must this happen to your husband, and why must this humiliating sorrow come to you? There you are with our five-year-old Ruth and with eight-month-old Karin. What shall become of you? Why have I not heard from you during the last two weeks?"

Again panic gripped me. Like a flash the thought struck me that my wife might be imprisoned too, otherwise she would have found a way of reaching me. The two-cornered terror, fear and sorrow now held me firmly in its clutches until it seemed that I must explode to atoms any moment.

. . . And once more there came that ugly influence of Satan, whispering to me: "It is no use, this is the end, therefore make a short end of it. They will beat and torture you and finally will send you to a concentration camp and give you the rest. Make an end quickly instead of wading through protracted agony."

Bewildered I looked around to discover some help, or get some argument to parry that awful onslaught of the enemy, but I was helpless. My mind did not work, it seemed to be the end indeed. I sighed and began to breathe the name of Jesus. I repeated that precious name a number of times. It was not a calling; it was pleading with the Infinite in a primitive way.

Faintly there came to me the memory of Psalm 130 and the words issued from the depths of my heart: "Out of the depths I cry unto Thee, O Lord. Lord, hear my voice. My soul waiteth for the Lord more than they that watch for the morning."

As I uttered the wonderful name of Jesus again, a strong love for Jesus seized me. I pondered over the temptation to do myself harm when I would separate myself entirely and for all eternity from Jesus my Savior, and that thought was unbearable to me. A great melting sorrow gripped me. I sank down on my knees on the cold cement floor and wept, asking forgiveness and saying: "No, I will never leave you, I will never cease to trust you, never be untrue to you. Happen whatever will, I love you, my Jesus, more than ever before. No prison can blot out that love for you."

Breathing the name of Jesus again and again, that name seemed to envelop me entirely. I had the sensation of a net being wound around me, string by string, stronger and stronger until that awful pain of my sorrow diminished and I could breathe freely again. I had the consciousness that Jesus was with me and that he was working in my behalf.

Such terrible acute attacks of despair can easily lead a prisoner to suicide, and the enemy truly tried it on me but Jesus was with me and he did not leave me nor forsake me, neither did he leave me comfortless. Jesus our Savior will, in one way or another, always bring us relief from our pain and sorrow. Very clearly and strongly I felt the tie of fellowship with my Savior and he poured oil into my wounded and troubled heart. I praised my wonderful Jesus!

Now I had recovered sufficiently, enabling myself to sing that precious song once more: "He's a Friend of Mine." That brought me back to an equilibrium in this new situation and I tried to get poised for the further battles that were bound to follow. They were bound to be very painful because I had no weapons nor arguments. The Bible was gone again.

I had no watch, no pencil or paper, no books and no friends whatever within reach.

16. My New Abode in Semi-Darkness

I now looked about and observed my new abode of desolation. The cell I found myself in was eleven feet long and six feet wide and had a cement floor. There was a cot which folded up against the wall, bedding consisted of a loose straw mattress, with a headpiece, two covers, but no linen. The straw headpiece was terribly soiled in many months of use by my predecessor. Then there was running water and an open toilet. There was a small table and a chair in the cell. Upon the wall was a shelf on which were placed: a little wash basin, an aluminum soup dish, an aluminum mug, a spoon and a salt shaker. Then there was a brush for sweeping the cell and one for polishing the cement floor. In the center of the door was the "Bull's-eye" through which every spot in the cell could be seen from the outside. Last but not least, there was also a towel which was similar to a burlap cloth. It was changed once a week.

This then was my cell, my world. Here within these narrow walls was my responsibility bounded, consisting of sweeping and polishing the floor every morning and dusting the cell every day. I also could open and close a window at will, two and a half by two feet in size. The glass was dimmed so that I could not see through. The upper part folded down half way and when it was opened I had a strip of a quarter of an inch by one foot in length to look through and see a little strip of the sky above the opposite building. It was barely enough to guess whether it was clear or a cloudy day. Because the window was near the ceiling I could not get close enough to look through.

The door of the cell was purposely made not to fit snugly, giving way freely to any sound within the cell. The window not being double, permitted a constant draft through the entire narrow cell from which there was no escape. At times that draft was so icy and penetrating that the bones in my body ached terribly. Not being permitted to have the bed down during the day, I was exposed to that draft from six in the morning until half past six in the evening, which caused very severe suffering and pain. In time it affected my hearing and brought chronic and terrible head noises which I am now always carrying with me as "souvenirs" of my prison days.

My cell window facing a narrow courtyard, with the court being flanked by six-story buildings on four sides, permitted very little light to come through those dimmed window panes. During the winter months the sky being mostly cloudy and the days very short, gave me only a very moderate light of the day from ten or eleven till three in the afternoon. The electric light was turned on, from outside the cell by the attendants from six till seven thirty in the morning and from five till seven in the evening. At other times the room was almost completely dark, making it extremely difficult to read even during daylight hours.

At six o'clock I had to rise and fold up the bed and at half past six in the evening was the time when I could take the bed down again. At seven I had to be in bed and the light was turned out. Thus I had to spend almost half of my prison time on that hard bed in the darkness of the night.

Concerning sleep the Lord performed a miracle in me. When I went to bed between six thirty and seven I seldom noticed the light being turned out, as I was already asleep. Usually I awoke between twelve and two and at times lay awake praying and reciting some Bible parts—especially the 23rd and 103rd Psalm. I fell asleep again and slept until the rising signal was given at six in the morning.

The mattress caused me some severe "headaches." I tried and experimented in every possible way but as soon as I began to stir and loosen the straw, it became more bumpy than before. Finally I had to decide on leaving it undisturbed and lay down into the same place until the curves of my body had been impressed very distinctly. That proved to be much better. After a time the place for my hips was almost down to the boards of the cot but it did not cause me very much pain or inconvenience. Thus I slept every night through the many months of my imprisonment, except the nights when I had to fight my battles.

During the first night I had a strange dream which gave me some comfort. Brother Rieske and my father-in-law visited me. Both of them had been called home into eternity long before that date. With Brother Rieske I had been associated in missionary work in eastern Europe for a number of years. In that dream my father-in-law said to me encouragingly: "Don't worry too much, you will be out very soon." With Brother Rieske I took a little walk and we discussed my imprisonment and then he became very sad, bursting into tears he said: "Oh, how I wish I could take this ordeal upon myself and; step into your place! But don't take it too hard, Jesus will not permit you to carry more than you can bear. Let him be your Friend and Comforter."

Every morning when dawn began to creep over the world outside, the doors of the cells were flung open and the prisoners led out into the courtyard for half an hour. When the guard came the first morning and opened the door of my cell, I did not know what it meant, neither did he explain anything. When I therefore did not move instantly to step out, he bawled: "Out with you, shall I bow asking you to come out!" When rushing out I saw the other prisoners—each one beside his cell-door—standing in soldier fashion, and when all were thus let out, the march of goose-stepping began along the gangway and down the stairways from the third floor. Each one had to keep four steps distance from the one before him and thus in the courtyard the prisoners paced on a circular narrow walk around and around, about 150 of them, filling the whole circle. Guards were watching that no word was spoken, not even a look of understanding between prisoners exchanged.

After half an hour all were goose-stepping back to their cells again.

"He was numbered with the transgressors," we read in Isaiah 53:12. Many times I had read that passage but now it was brought home to me in a special way. Here I was, thrown in with the transgressors of law. All shades of offenses and crimes were represented and I was one of these prisoners, numbered with them.

"What is your offense, what have you done?" the guard would ask.

"I have done nothing that I know of. My only offense is the preaching of the gospel for the last twenty years in this part of the world," I would answer.

"You better be careful what you say, they all claim to be innocent," he would scoff, treating me like any of the real offenders of the law.

At times when it seemed unbearable, I sank down on my knees and said to my Savior: "I praise you, my precious Lord, that I am not here in this awful place as an actual law-breaker, guilty of a criminal offense. It is your grace and love which has kept me, otherwise I might have been in one of these places long ago." Thus praise and thanksgiving welled up in my heart to him who saw me and who was my companion even in that place of horror.

Slowly I adjusted myself to the life of the prison. In the morning at half past six the door was opened and out of a giant kettle "coffee" was dished out, for which I had to stand ready in the door of the opened cell with my mug. A piece of bread was handed me, equal to about five slices which was for the whole day. The black coffee was as "neutral" as that neutral buttermilk my wife and I obtained once some years ago in a little town of the wild West on our way to California. It simply had no taste, not even of water.

The bread had to be divided carefully in order to have something later in the day. I allowed myself at the most two slices of dry bread and a cup of that "coffee" for breakfast.

A PRISONER OF THE LORD

Naturally it did not still the hunger at all. Thus the waiting began for the "dinner" that was brought at eleven-thirty. It consisted of rather thin and watery soup containing peas or beans, and sometimes vegetables. Again it did not satisfy for it was not enough and nothing else with it. Hunger then stared at me, tormenting my physical being. At times I seemed to see those proverbial wolves snapping and sneering at me, gnashing their teeth while they circled around me.

Supper in one evening consisted of a flour-soup of blue milk and some groats in it, and the next evening tea was served. With it was brought fifteen grams of margarine and also a slice of blood sausage about one inch in thickness. As there was only very little bread left, the supper did not by far satisfy, leaving me again in a state of hunger and craving for food. As supper was served at half past five, hunger began to gnaw before going to bed, making me feel quite miserable.

The next day came and dragged on while I was in an eternal waiting for something to eat. Having no watch and being so much in darkness together with the uncanny quietness of the place, many times brought me to the verge of utter collapse.

In a little pamphlet of rules and regulations which was found in every cell, the introduction ran about thus: "The treatment and whole life in the prison is to be an ordeal for the prisoner which he should remember his whole life as an experience that he must avoid by any means." That it is an ordeal as horrible as is humanly possible, cannot be denied. And if an innocent person is dragged into such a prison life and subjected to just as horrible an ordeal, it is utterly unjust and will make out of the most devoted follower of a regime, an enemy of the same.

Being completely cut off from the outside world, and not permitted to talk to any person as well as being bawled at by the guards and attendants who refuse to give any explanations or answers to tormenting questions, drives a prisoner to the very verge of despair. That a number of the inmates are committing suicide in spite of the rigid control, is no wonder.

Often I thought of those poor prisoners who have no God, no peace in their soul and a guilty conscience to contend with. What a horrible torment they must endure. How my heart went out for them as they marched around that circle in the courtyard every morning. In the faces of some I could see utter despair and hopelessness. But there was no way of getting a word of comfort to them.

Religious services were not allowed, nor could one have the comforts of a personal consultation with a clergyman. Thus there was absolutely nothing to break the monotony of the dreary and destitute life in that prison.

17. FROM DEPTHS OF DESPAIR TO HEIGHTS OF JOY

Like a hidden fire the concern for my wife and children smoldered within me hour by hour, consuming the very marrow of my being as the days dragged on. At times I could not even eat the scanty food that was served. My physical strength diminished visibly but I did not give it a thought. I really did not care. Separating me from the outside world, the narrow cell walls stared at me. At times it seemed they were animate, laughing and sneering at me. At times again they seemed to close around me, threatening to crush me to death.

Above the little table a previous prisoner had scribbled the following words on the wall: "Vengeance is precious and sweet." "Vengeance, what?" I asked myself. "No, that craving does not tempt me; hate would only intensify the suffering."

Evidently the writer of those bitter words was a prisoner who had become a victim of injustice, and he breathed longingly to revenge himself for the wrongs suffered from those who were in the places of power.

Prayer for those who had brought that misery upon me, and talking to my Jesus about it helped me in a wonderful way, easing the sorrow that weighed me down. I often spoke to him aloud as to a present, precious Friend, telling him my troubles, explaining to him the deepness of my sorrow, concern and fear for my wife and the children as if he could only learn by my telling and explaining everything to him. Thus always another day came creeping upon me. Every moment I suspected my captors would come, open the door and take me out of the cell and subject me to the ordeal of beating and ill-treatment. This kept my nerves always on edge and in a state of excitement.

In the courtyard below I heard a sound of sawing and chopping of wood. It was something neutral, a sound which my mind could dwell upon without misgivings, as it suggested human beings doing something useful. So this world here was not only concentrating to make men miserable but to let them create some kind of values— means to an end. It soothed my overstrained condition. I liked the sound.

Suddenly that horrible clattering of a big key thrust into the lock and its turning startled me. The cell-door was flung open and an attendant shouted: "Out with you!"

Out I went, taking my stand beside my cell door according to instructions, until he had locked the door again. Then he led me away and another guard commanded me to go before him. Another prisoner was joined to us and we were directed along corridors, through doors, in a zigzag until I had lost all sense of direction.

Presently we went down a flight of stone steps into a cellar. In a narrow and dark corridor I was told to stand quiet and wait, while he and the other prisoner went on further into the cellar. Here I stood now in semi-darkness all alone.

Glancing to the right I saw another corridor turning to my right and on the wall I saw an inscription and a pointer toward the right; it read: "To the punishment cells."

A panicky fear seized me and my imagination played havoc in my brain. I saw myself ushered into a large room and men getting ready to beat me. I fairly cringed under the lashes of the tormentors. Cold sweat oozed out of my pores and a deathly fear crept over me. Never in my whole life had I experienced such an awful agony of fear.

Then I heard steps again. The guard returned and commanded me to go on, pointing to my left. I was surprised when he did not direct me into the horrible passage which was the cause of my awful fears. Along we went through another passageway and up a stairway through another door.

Now I found myself at the end of a high, stately corridor with large arched windows. The sudden flood of daylight caused me to close my eyes, until I became used to that much light. I was now in the courthouse. As we started to walk along the corridor, I looked ahead and saw a lady some distance from us walking in the same direction. She appeared to me like an apparition. Furthermore she appeared familiar. When we came nearer she turned around; I looked into the face of my beloved wife.

Flung out of extreme fear a few moments ago into supreme joy so suddenly, could have had serious consequences. The reaction was devastating. I had lost my speech, and could only stare at my wife. She in turn must have been terribly shocked at seeing me in such a haggard state. There was no talking, it was not necessary. We were then led into the room of the judge's secretary and there, seated at the table. We could spend twenty precious minutes together.

It proved that the old tempter had just lied to me in suggesting that my wife had been arrested and that more terrible things had happened while I was imprisoned. Here she was within reach.

I held her hands tightly, hands which came out of the world of freedom; held them so as not to let them go again; as if they could take me along into liberty.

"Ruth sends her love to you," my wife said. "She wanted to come along, held on to me and cried, but I thought it better if she did not know where you are.

"It was very hard to locate you," she continued. "None seemed to know where you had been taken. From police they sent me to the Gestapo, and from there to the prosecutor. Some of them said you had been taken to another city. Thus I went for days from office to office until I finally was told, that you were in the police prison. When I came there, they said that under no circumstances could I see you. No remonstration helped, they remained adamant. On my last call at the police prison office they informed me that you were not there any more.

I had to start my search anew as they refused to tell me where you had been taken, and it took days until I finally was directed to the judge who handles your case. And he told me that you are in this jail, but it was impossible to procure the permission to get in touch with you until through the kindness of the judge this meeting was arranged."

Again the Lord had intervened, moving the heart of the judge and caused him to make it possible for me to see my wife in his office, instead of looking at each other through those humiliating bars. From the Gestapo strict orders had been issued not to permit my wife to visit me at all.

It was not common that through the initiative of the judge such contact with the prisoner could be arranged, but I take it for granted that the judge himself did not agree with my arrest, but had to act under orders from the

Gestapo. Therefore he had pity on me, permitting my wife to visit me in his office.

To me personally it was a wonderful intervention of God in my behalf, thereby answering my heart cry, relieving me temporarily of a great load of sorrow. I praise his name forever!

But even this joy did not remain without bitterness. When I was led out from that precious time of meeting my wife, I was not taken right back into my cell but locked into one of those small dens in the staircase of the courthouse with which I had been already acquainted. It was not heated or ventilated. There I had to stand and wait for two hours before an attendant came to take me to my own cell again.

18. REMEMBERED BY A REAL FRIEND

The solitary and monotonous life continued. One day after another wore on without a ray of light penetrating my darkness. It was a very welcome break of the dreariness when after some days the attendant asked me whether I cared to write a letter to someone.

"Yes," I answered, "is that possible? I have wife and children in the city and certainly should like to write to them as often as I can."

Only then I learned that a prisoner was allowed to write to his blood relations once every week. The scope however was very limited as only strictly personal matters could be written and nothing was to be mentioned about the cause of imprisonment.

A sheet of paper as well as pen and ink was brought and I sat down to write to my wife from the prison cell, on prison stationery. With great eagerness and delight I wrote the letter, for by writing I could talk to my wife for a little while and I could hope that a letter from her would reach me as well.

Unknown to me the Lord worked for me in a further miraculous way. It was through a friend with whom I had had contact months ago. A little less than a year before my imprisonment we had considerable difficulties concerning our support from America. The German authorities simply would not give us permission to receive the money sent to us. Accordingly the money remained in the bank in Germany or it was returned to the United States and we remained without funds.

My wife and I cried to God but no change for the better was in sight, yet the Lord was working in our behalf. One day someone rang the doorbell and when I opened the door, I faced a stranger who said: "Perhaps you will not remember me but in 1922 I met you in Warsaw and heard you preach several times. I have never forgotten you. Recently I heard your name mentioned in our Baptist church and obtained your address. As I am passing through this city today, I take this opportunity of visiting you."

After hearing his explanation and learning his name, I remembered him and we had a precious renewal of friendship.

He then asked me: "Do you have any troubles, and can I be of any assistance to you? I have influence in my position and have friends who can reach still farther. Being a member of the Baptist church, we are always ready to help children of God wherever possible."

This encouraged me to tell him about the conditions we were living in, and our vain attempt to secure the money which was coming to us from the United States, and went on: "As I am not in Europe for pleasure but obeying the call which the Lord laid on me many years ago, and being yet able to do a definite work by helping the children of God in eastern Europe in this time of distress, I do believe that it is God's will for me and my family to receive the support which is sent to us from the United States to keep us from suffering. This gives me the evidence that the Lord has sent you to us and I trust you will be able to help."

After a few weeks time we received the notice from the bank that we should apply for a permission to receive our money. The Lord had undertaken by the offices of a friend whom he had sent our way in the time of need.

Following my arrest, my wife informed him of what had happened to me. He was quite shocked and rushed to our city at once. He went to my prosecutor, in whose hands lay my case, and he very likely succeeded in making them a little shaky concerning my guilt either in espionage or secret and unlawful religious work.

Soon after my arrival in that city jail, I had sent petitions to the judge asking for permission to receive my Bible but received no answer. After the visit of my friend these were reconsidered and who can measure my delight when the guard came into my cell, delivering a package. Opening it I found the most precious of all books, the Bible. I clutched at it and kissed its pages, tears of thankfulness trickled down on the open Book as I hungrily read just where my eyes fell first. It was Psalm 56, a message from God to my present need. Then my eyes fell on Isaiah 53 and the words stood out: "He is despised and rejected of men: a man of sorrows, and acquainted with grief: and we hid as it were our faces from him; he was despised, and we esteemed him not."

"Lord," I cried, "I will not despise you. If ever I loved you, my Jesus, it is now. You understand me, for you are acquainted with my grief. Again you hast visited me in mercy and grace. Hallelujah!" Oh, how wonderfully the Lord refreshed me! I raced back and forth in my cell, praising the Lord for his precious and wonderful Word and I pledged there and then that I never would neglect his precious book. The windows of heaven were opened to me and I drank in the message of the cross. Waves of glory flooded me again and again.

Dear reader, has your heart ever been touched by the precious Word of God? You have not touched the best this life can offer you, if you have never had a taste of the sweetness of his wonderful and living Word, for it is indeed sweeter than honey, more precious than any other book on earth.

And you who have learned to love the Bible: never neglect that Book of God and never cease to praise him for that blessed volume. It will uplift you and give you the food which strengthens your spiritual being for this life and for eternity.

But that was not all. I unpacked a writing block, a pencil, a pillowcase and a bed sheet, a towel and some other things. My joy knew no bounds. And it became all the more precious to me because the guard who brought the package, had said: "Your wife has brought this for you." I knew that with her own hands she had lovingly packed all this into the package and carried it herself to the prison office. All that counted for me very dearly and I felt the tie of friendship in a double sense; I felt myself so near my family, I was very happy.

All this joy and blessing came to me because of a noble friend who really proved himself a true friend in time of trouble. While it is proverbial that friends become rarer and rarer as our troubles increase, here was a friend who was not shied away by my adversity. With what thankful love I was commending him to the care of God, when I learned later on, about his acts of kindness and concern.

Then and there I asked the Lord for the grace that whenever I should come out of this prison, I should deal kindly with anyone who is in trouble and in suffering. How noble it is, to pour oil into the wounds of suffering ones. They are doubly thankful and we have the promise so beautifully expressed, "What ye have done unto one of my least ones, ye have done unto me" (Matthew 25:40).

Words can never describe my thankfulness to God for having received permission to write. Now I could sit down and meditate, and write about my thoughts. Many an hour I have whiled away, lost in thoughts and writing. To my precious Savior be praise and honor forever!

19. NEW DEPTHS OF TROUBLE

When I had been brought into the city jail, I learned through the "Rules and Regulations" that, if a prisoner thinks he has been arrested without sufficient reason, he may send a written protest to the investigating judge and state his case. I made use of this privilege and protested against my arrest. After several weeks my protest was rejected.

That blasted my last hope of a speedy release and the last vestige of confidence in German justice. Now I had to realize that I was here to stay irrespective of the merit or demerit of the case until they would see fit to bring up my case in court proceedings. That they would not hurry my case was made evident by learning the story of other prisoners. My neighbor had already waited a year and a half for his case to be taken up.

From time to time grief and depression took hold of me like a mighty tornado and threatened to uproot the moorings of my faith. Such struggles often left me quite exhausted and listless, but each time the Lord stepped in and imparted new life and faith.

Then one day I had the happy surprise when I was again led to the judge's office and there found my wife. Again we had a few precious minutes together and, learning that my children as well as my wife were secure at home, I was very much relieved and comforted.

After parting I was again locked into that tiny interim den about half past twelve. I waited and waited without anybody coming to lead me into my cell. Not having a watch, I was unable to know the time but realized that hours must have passed. I began to knock and pound the door with my heels. Then I called and shouted but there was no answer. The unheated cell in the cold of winter stifled me. Evidently the guard had forgotten about me and had gone home from the courthouse at the close of the office hours, leaving me in this terribly cold corner. Many hours of standing up had left me without physical strength and I had to sit down on the floor, reconciling myself to the necessity of spending the whole night in this horrible place. In a crouched position I sank into a stupor while I had the sensation of being naked and an icy sheet being spread over my body.

Suddenly I heard a faint noise which seemed to come from very far, then rattling of keys and unlocking of neighboring doors. I was aroused and tried to call. Then I heard steps near my door; finally it flung open. The attendant of my department and a higher prison official had come in search of me. They were highly relieved when they had me in their custody again.

That was one time when I was glad to be back in my cell where it seemed warmer than ever before. A glance at the table warmed up my heart for there I saw my Bible reposing.

Six hours I had spent in that icy cell only thinly clad and without overcoat. It could have been my death but the Lord my God graciously kept me. To him be the glory and praise.

In the last days I had been praising the Lord very much and was quite near heaven many times, which did not fit in with the calculations of the enemy, therefore this incident gave me a severe blow. Once more the enemy's plan to plunge me into despair was defeated.

A week passed by after this attack. The promised visit of my wife was not realized, and the enemy succeeded in throwing me into special misery by his whisperings, saying: "Now Margaret has also been arrested and you will not hear of her again. Your children are destitute and your home deserted."

I was helpless for I had no arguments to ward off these subtle attacks. Since my arrest I had heard of a similar thing happening which had a very tragic ending. So I gave way to worrying and grieving. From day to day I waited to be called and led over to the courthouse, but in vain.

At last I was led out of the cell and rejoiced that now I would be brought again to see my wife. Instead, I was ushered to the door of the visitors' room and lined up with other prisoners during the hour set for visitors.

Presently my turn came and I walked into the visitors' room and there stood my wife. Bars separated us while we talked to each other, a guard watching at my side. It was quite a humiliating ordeal which lasted ten minutes. However, I was extremely thankful to God, because my tortures concerning the safety of the wife and children were dispelled once more.

A rather pleasant intermezzo took place when I was again called and led to the courthouse to see my attorney. A lawyer was to be present at a certain hour but, as it happens frequently with busy gentlemen, he did not come at the appointed time, making us wait for a whole hour. I do not think that a delay ever was more happily accepted and made use of, as our awaiting the arrival of that lawyer enabled us to sit together and chat for over an hour. It may be that the lawyer had delayed his coming on purpose, or perhaps the Lord caused some delay in his affairs in order to give us that special treat.

Severe frost had set in and my cell was not warm enough. The cement floor proved unbearably cold and the icy draft through my cell became a breath of death. But the Lord stepped in again, this time before I called. He caused my wife to bring warm houseshoes and heavy woolen socks to the prison office, and surely I did praise the Lord for his wonderful love and care for me.

Even when I had donned these socks and the houseshoes I still felt the sting of draft, but it did not pain my bones as before, enabling me to endure it more easily.

20. CHRISTMAS GREETINGS FROM HEAVEN

Margaret had struck upon the idea to send a petition to the judge that I be released for a few days over the holidays to spend Christmas with my family. I had bright hopes and rejoiced in the anticipation of enjoying home and family at least for a few days.

On December 18, I was called to a special physician and told that he was to examine me for my health and determine whether I needed relaxation at home over Christmas. He however did not even look at me properly, much less determine the state of my health. I feared that his report would not make the outlook brighter for me.

I waited from day to day without hearing anything more about that matter, neither did my wife visit me. Thus Christmas eve approached without my even receiving a letter or a Christmas card from my family. On top of the disappointment of not having been released for Christmas, I remained without word from my wife and children and the enemy began tormenting me anew, saying: "Your wife has been too aggressive, offending an official, and has also been arrested and now the children are abandoned for

99

Christmas." The despair that gripped me again and again was as cruel as death. I was hardly able to breathe at times.

Christmas is the time of family reunions and here I was cut off, being without even a word of greeting. I gave way to my grief. I could not pray, neither could I read the Bible. I just sighed and brooded over my calamity. Thus the Holy Night wore on without my having any comfort. And the Lord seemed to be silent.

My little Ruth had drawn an advent card with the picture of a burning candle on it and, long before Christmas, my wife had sent it to me. That was the only visible indication of Christmas and the tie with my family. I put it up before me and stared at it, then wrote the following words on that little card: "Christmas Eve 1940. 6:00P.M. This is my only Christmas token in this dark cell. My little Ruth has drawn it for me. And though there is no visible sign of Christmas in this dreary cell, I have the Christ-child within my heart. He stills my sorrow and heart-ache in my loneliness. He is precious and real to me."

Christmas day dawned. I felt the loneliness more keenly than the evening before. Thoughtlessly I turned the pages of a book which the attendant had brought the previous day from the prison library. It was a novel and did not interest me. Suddenly I noticed a little card between the pages which I thought was a bookmark and did not pay attention to. Finally it dropped out on the table and I picked it up to put it back into the book again.

As I glanced at it fleetingly I thought: "A strange bookmark." Looking at it closer I noticed a little drawing of a Christmas tree branch and it somehow aroused my interest. Turning it over, I read the following words: "Hearty Christmas greetings to you. All the brothers and sisters of the church are praying for you. Family M. . . ."

My heart gave a leap and I was electrified. Tears melted out of my eyes. I sank down on my knees and exclaimed: "O my precious Savior, you have not forgotten me after all, and I am not forgotten by my brothers and sisters. They are praying for me. Thank you, Jesus. You have sent me this greeting directly from heaven. I praise you for it and I thank you for my friends who have remembered me thus."

Only after I was released did I learn what way the Lord had chosen to bring this card to me. I just rejoiced in the Lord's visible care for me, and a new and deep love and trust in him filled my heart, dispelling all the loneliness and sorrow which had enshrouded me.

An acquaintance of members of my church who was also imprisoned did some service in the prison library. He was asked to get that card to me, and at his own peril placed it in the book which was then delivered into my cell. Had this been discovered it would have meant severe punishment, but the Lord protected him and all concerned, bringing me great comfort.

Greetings from heaven had been sent to me and for a long time I was praising the Lord and thanking him for the many true friends he had given me, and those who were constantly praying for that lonely and suffering child of his in the cell.

A channel of blessing was opened to me and I continued rejoicing all day. I felt new contact with heaven and the sweet fellowship of the saints. The Word of God was precious to me and the communion with my Jesus very real. Again he had proved himself a true Friend who never forgets his own.

21. GOD CHANGING MY DIET

The prison was gnawing at my physical resources. Slowly but surely I was sinking to the rock bottom of my reserves. Until now my body was adding something from day to day to that which was lacking in my daily food, but my weight had gone down alarmingly: I was sure of that. There would be an end of the reserves very soon. I felt weakness creeping over me, and my suit became looser from day to day.

Something was wrong in my body for I felt spasmodic pains in my abdomen and it seemed to be the appendix which was ailing. "My God, if appendicitis has set in, I am lost," I cried to God. "I can die in my cell without anybody taking notice as things function too slowly in this place. You must protect me, O Lord. I believe you wilt not permit me to perish."

Greatly distressed and in violent irregular and interrupted pains, I cried to God for help and protection. Thus I waited for him to undertake, but although the pains would stop for a day or two, they would begin again with renewed force. I decided to comply to the rules of the prison and report it to the attendant.

"Let me see, whether it is that bad," and he mockingly looked into my eyes, saying: "Not unto death, half as bad as you think." He then said that he would take me to the prison physician.

Said but not done. I waited two days but the matter seemed forgotten. Thereupon I reminded him again. He then shouted at me: "1 have other worries, your fake pains can wait!" Against such insults I was helpless, so I did not say any more about it. The next morning he led me to the physician.

The doctor scrutinized me, then asked: "What are you here for, what have you done?"

By this time I had been asked the same question so many times that I began to be tired of it. I answered: "Very, very much I have done, perhaps too much. I have been preaching the gospel in almost every wild and forsaken nook and corner of Europe. I slept in beds, on benches, on clay floors with a bit of straw as a mattress; I fought evil powers, flies, fleas, lice, bedbugs, beetles, etc. I have eaten almost every diet under the sun: dry or doughy bread, hot pepper-seasoned meals in Hungary and the Balkan countries, scalded maize dough in Romania, sour buffalo milk in Bulgaria, and sometimes ate nothing but dry sandwiches for days. In one year I slept in over two hundred different beds or their substitutes. All that has gone on twenty years, only with some pleasant interruptions in the United States, England and other countries where I was treated like a king."

"Without examining you, I can say that you are suffering from chronic indigestion and you have to be mighty careful about yourself. This is no place for you in this condition, you had better try to get out of here. But you did not tell me why you are here."

"I thought I did, but to be more precise: I have done nothing else than being active in the gospel ministry in eastern and southeastern Europe. Although nobody has told me why I am here, I can gather from the questionings that I am suspected of propagating a forbidden religion and of spying for America."

"Have you received no paper of accusation from the prosecutor? How long are you in here?" he wanted to know.

"I have nothing which would show me why I am here or what I am accused of, although I am in this prison over two months."

"You are just the average. All come here more or less feigning innocence but when the records are turned on, they are as black as night. They surely would not treat you thus if they had no reason. You better be careful about claiming your innocence. It might be worse for you in the end. You have a good chance now to prove the power of prayer. Therefore pray, pray, pray!"

This he seemed to have spoken in ridicule but he must have had a warm feeling for me. In later visits he asked me time and again whether there was any new development in my case. I always had to answer in the negative. None seemed to remember me. I was forgotten as if sunk into the depths of the ocean.

For three days I had to be without any food on order of the physician, but at every mealtime a hospital attendant brought me a giant mug of some kind of tea. That I had to drain to the last drop. The pains vanished and did not recur again, but the hunger was torturing me unspeakably as the tea intensified my appetite.

After the days of forced fasting I was called again and the doctor told me that I was to get diet food. Mornings, noons and evenings I received a fairly good milk soup for which I was infinitely thankful, being delivered from that horrible coffee in the morning and the indefinable tea in the evening. After a few days I returned to the regular dinner soups.

Had the Lord answered my prayer immediately and taken away the pains, I should not have become acquainted with the physician, neither would the food have changed or improved. Now, however, a sick-diet soup was brought me in the morning and evening for a long time.

This experience made me realize more than ever before that at times the Lord does not answer our prayer in our way because he plans to accomplish another phase of need which is better than an immediate answer of our prayers.

At times the Lord has to deal with us in special ways in order to call our attention to some lack in our spiritual life, or a grave fault in our character. In such a case an immediate relief would defeat God's plan and purpose for us. What we need is explicit trust in him who never fails to be mindful of us. The Lord did not only plan a relief of my pains but wanted to cause me to get a change of diet, and he managed it in a wonderful way. Praise his name forever!

22. Dinner Out of God's Kitchen

On January 11th, I was led out to be weighed. The scale tipped at 68 kg. The last time I had been on the scale shortly before my arrest I weighed 86 kg, and I realized that I had lost 18 kg, nearly forty pounds in 70 days, which meant that I had lost an average of over half a pound a day. It dawned on me that, if this would go on a little longer I should certainly collapse.

Although I had been granted to receive the special soups every day, it was evident that it would not have stopped my losing weight. Having become so weak already that my knees were sagging when I walked back and forth in the cell, I could plainly see that unless the Lord did a special thing I would not survive very long.

There was only one recourse open to me, so I went to him who is full of compassion and who would listen to my plea. I cried to him: "Lord, Thou seest my plight and misery, how the last bit of physical energy is slowly being consumed. Unlock the door of this prison and lead me out, or if I am appointed to linger on in this cell, then you must bring me relief from this prison diet. Do not let me perish here."

Saturday evening, Sunday, and Monday morning, I was pleading before the Lord. Suddenly the burden was lifted, and I had the assurance that he to whom all the resources of the world belong, would do something for me.

A few weeks before I had made petition to the judge to grant me special meals from the outside world but that was refused.

"What do you think," a higher official of the prison said, "hundreds of thousands of our soldiers are out on the front, staking their life every minute and often having to be without meals, and millions of German hard workers have to be rationed and you, a foreigner, want to have special meals. That is preposterous. You would be the only one in this prison to get such privileges."

I could very well realize that in this time of war and the awful scarcity of food in Germany, I was expecting much to have special consideration. However, I knew the Lord would not let me perish. He was bound to do something. How it would be done was beyond me.

Monday noon there was that characteristic rattling when my cell door was unlocked and in came an attendant. Putting a three-section dinner tray on the table, he turned and walked out as usual, giving no explanations in the matter.

The cell was locked again and I was alone, gazing at the table. I was bewildered and for the moment did not realize that this was the answer to my fervent prayers. The thought came to me that the attendant might have made a mistake in bringing this into my cell which had been intended for someone else. At second thought I decided to wait a while and if no one should come to claim it, I would investigate what it was.

Later I had to smile at my being so stupid in my faith. I surely deserved Jesus' telling me: "O you of little faith." I also had to think of the time, when the apostle Peter was led out of prison by the angel and came to the door to find the maid so surprised that she forgot to open the door, letting him stand outside.

At last I felt on the outside and I noticed that the containers were quite warm. Then I began to take it apart. On the top there was a little dish, covered and wrapped in paper. I unpacked it and found a nice pudding in it. Then I took the first section off and, lo and behold, there were potatoes. The second section contained a noodle soup and the third held an appetizing piece of meat embedded in gravy and vegetables.

As I looked at the table with all the food on it, I had a feeling similar to what Elijah must have had when the angel, under the juniper tree, touched him and said, "Arise and eat."

A full meal was spread out before me. After not having had a real meal for 72 days, it was a strange sight to behold. Perhaps never in my life did I thank my precious Savior so heartily for a meal as I did while seated at that table, which was spread by the Lord himself. While eating, tears were coursing down, dropping into that food which had come down to me out of God's kitchen. The Lord had indeed remembered me; he had heard and answered my prayer. How wonderful the food tasted, I cannot tell. For the first time in 72 days, I ate with appetite and real joy, I was really satisfied, and my hunger was stilled.

The whole afternoon a prayer and praise service was held in my cell, undisturbed by anybody. To me it was the most wonderful experience I could remember. It was God's doing, for I knew how belligerent the prison officials were when I turned in the petition for extra food. The Lord however, had overcome all the resistance and had brought it to pass.

Toward evening the tempter came, saying: "It will be only one time, you will not get it tomorrow or any other day." I asked the guard but he did not give me any light on my question. So I just had to wait patiently. The next days would disclose the truth. I trusted the Lord that he would send these dinners continually. And so it was.

Where the dinner came from and who brought it, was still a puzzle to me, so I accepted it just as from the Lord's kitchen. Weeks later my wife asked me on one of her visits, whether I was receiving the dinners and she told me the whole story of how it all came about.

The Lord says in his Word: "Before they call, I will answer." This literally happened in the above case.

Days before my weighing which caused me to be alarmed and pray desperately, my wife was suddenly reminded in her heart that she should try in some way to get extra food to me. She went to the prison office and asked, but they flatly refused to consider such a thing. She then went to other officials, but with similar negative results.

The thought kept burning within her and she went to a higher official, pleading for me. Finally he told her: "Go back to the prison office and ask them to name some restaurants which are eligible. Then go to these places and, if you find one of them willing to deliver a dinner to the prison each day, you can come to me and I will arrange all that is necessary."

My wife rushed back to the prison office and told them of her desire. "Are you here again?! I told you that such a thing is impossible. And furthermore, it is not desirable in this time of war. We do not want to bother with such a thing."

When she mentioned the name of the official to whom she had just talked, they immediately stopped their opposition and grudgingly looked up their old records and gave her the names of a few restaurants.

Equipped with these, she rushed to the restaurants. But one after another refused and her heart sank again. Then she came to the last on the list and the manager said to her: "If you can find someone, who will come and fetch the dinner every day and carry it to the prison gate, then we will do our part, otherwise it is impossible."

On the next Sunday morning my wife told the brethren about this need and a sister volunteered to be the dinner carrier.

On Monday the first dinner was brought to my cell, and thereafter every day the dinner came, sometimes at one, other times at two or three o'clock. At times the man at the gate forgot about the dinner and let it stand in his guardhouse. When it finally was brought it was cold, but all the same it was a message from the outside world and I enjoyed it doubly.

Thus the Lord relieved me of one terrible danger and concern, that I would break down in my health and succumb in that cell. That this could have been the case and that it happened with others, was proven by my very cell-neighbor, a Swiss citizen. He had been imprisoned for a longer time and gradually became nothing but skin and bones. To him no special consideration was granted. Shortly before I was released, he had been brought to a prison hospital cell. His feet were swollen, his heart worked very feebly and he was unable to stand. An attendant whom I asked concerning the whereabouts of that prisoner, said to me pointing to one of the cell doors: "In there he lies; he will not live much longer; he is done for. It is undernourishment, poor fellow."

When I heard that tragic story, I was all the more thankful that I have a Savior whom I know and who cared for me so wonderfully there in that dreary cell. I knew him who died for me on Calvary and I became acquainted with his excellent kitchen and have been eating his food.

The blessed Pauline word was proved to be true when he says: "Godliness is profitable unto all things, having promise of the life that now is, and of that which is to come" (1 Timothy 4:8).

23. HEAVENLY ORCHESTRAS AND CHOIRS

New waves of agony and sorrow swept over me when I did not hear from my family for several weeks, and there seemed to be no end to my imprisonment. I was haunted by fears anew and pictures of horror passed through my mind. I saw my wife with a bloody face and ugly wounds, and the children sick unto death. Night or day such pictures would suddenly flash into my mind and I would start as if hit by a bullet.

In such a pitiful condition I went to bed one evening. My strength was sapped and I was weary of life. A deep longing for heaven gripped me: "Take me home, my Savior, I am so tired and weary. In this world there seems to be no more room for me but this cell, not many times larger than a grave. I long to be in the land above with you, my only Friend who visits me in this prison."

With this prayer on my lips I fell asleep. My precious Savior did not answer my prayer to take me home into his glorious heaven, but he gave me a taste of heaven; brought it near and permitted me to hear sounds of the heavenly spheres. I learned to know the loveliness of my precious and wonderful Savior as never before.

"Yea, he loved the people," it is said of God. His unlimited love enveloped me in a special way when my heart was weighed down beyond endurance. That night he put me to sleep very quickly as so many times before, when I was weary and distressed. It reminded me of a mother who sits at the bedside of her little one and sings softly until her loving child falls into slumber.

That night the Lord visited me, for he lifted his child that was so downhearted, into his heavenly regions and opened my ears to hear heavenly music; mighty orchestras that sounded like overwhelming thundering billows of harmony, such as is impossible to describe in human words. I was not able to define the character of the instruments but the music resembled mostly the sound of thousands of harps playing together. I heard them in all shades of tones from the lowest to the highest pitch, in marvelous turns of harmonics and in volumes of softest tones to triumphant ecstasies of exultation, such as never can be produced on earth.

Into that wonderful music, mighty choirs were blending at times, singing the most magnificent anthems and psalms. The Lord on high was exalted and worshiped. Then they were singing about the reward of the redeemed in their glorified state. They were singing some songs that I recognized, but most were anthems which I had never heard. Heavenly songs, heavenly music!

While I heard that music and the mighty singing, my body seemed to be stripped of its earthly properties, and I began to vibrate in a strange way like a musical instrument while it is being played. I became part of that harmony and I took on an ethereal constitution. Such immense volume of joy surged through me as I never could contain or endure in my natural being. I joined in the singing with a voice altogether different from the usual. I sang the praises of the Lamb of God, singing of him on the throne of glory. All was so real I seemed to belong to the singers and had always been in the environment of that music.

Finally I awoke hearing myself singing in other tongues, and my sorrow and heartache were gone, swallowed by the glory that surged through my whole being.

After a while I fell asleep again and that heavenly music and singing continued. The celestial concert and choirs were bringing forth music and song which could never issue from the store of the fantasies of a human brain. I know they were real heavenly musicians and their music and song an occurrence of heaven above, not a mere dream.

The Lord had lifted the curtains, and opened the door permitting me to hear what is actually going on in heaven. I expect to hear such music when I get there, and I long for that fair land above more than ever since I heard the actual sounds of heaven.

When I awoke in the morning after that memorable night, I was floating on the wings of the glory of God. For hours I paced the five steps of the length of my cell back and forth, worshiping the Lord and singing his praises in songs of the Spirit and in tongues. It was glory and radiant joy which filled my whole body, in real harmony and union with heaven. Never would I have thought it possible that

111

such volumes of bliss could surge through our earthly frame.

Since that night I have often had similar orchestras and choirs within my reach, but I never actually saw them. It was always as if I were standing in space with a bluish mellow light surrounding me and the sound coming from beyond the reach of my sight, as far as I could see.

It was as if a channel was cut during that night, and a streambed formed in which that heavenly music and song came to me. From that night on, whenever I was very lonesome and very downhearted, I had the floodgates of blessing opened and heard that marvelous music and song and awoke while floating on the crest of that heavenly harmony.

The whole day long after such nights the echo of that heavenly music rang within me, and I had sweet fellowship with my Savior. Some hours it even made me forget my cell and the surroundings as I kept praising the Lord.

One day I asked the Lord to give me expression in song to describe those visitations of spheric music and song, and the following words were given me in the Spirit. Whenever I sing this little anthem, I get a measure of that heavenly glory into my heart:

> In my dreary cell at midnight,
> I can hear the angels singing;
> Joined by mighty harp orchestras
> I can hear God's anthems ringing.
> They are rocking me to sleep,
> Sacred vigil o'er me keep
> In the cell, oh, so dreary—
>   In the nighttime.

Often when I waited and waited for a visit or a letter from my wife, and day after day would pass in loneliness and despondency, my precious Savior took me up again in the nighttime, to listen to those heavenly orchestras and choirs, and they refreshed me beyond measure, washing away, as it were, the sorrow that had been weighing on me until it was about to crush me. Oh, how I love my Savior! How I loved him in that dreary cell!

Why did he not speedily free me from that prison? Because he wanted to show me his love and sweetness in the shadows of sorrow. It seems he can only then reveal himself in that glorious way, and give us his choicest blessings when we are in suffering and great sorrow. In our everyday life, when we live and move under the power of our own volition, we are too preoccupied and often too "busy" even in "God's business" to really concentrate on the heavenly spheres, to get the heavenly touch on us. It happens that we fail to take time enough for prayer and quiet waiting to give God a chance to reveal his sweetness unto us. Therefore it is his grace that compels us at times to become quiet enough to be solely occupied with him, our wonderful and precious Savior, Jesus Christ.

Ah, how much blessing we lose, because we are not getting near enough to heaven; not into hearing distance of that music, that singing in the heavenly spheres. Yes, many of us, even spiritual preachers, are too shallow and too superficial in our spiritual life, to get a real personal touch of God, until finally we become satisfied with imaginative blessings which are no blessings at all, but only words and empty phrases. Such was the case with the church of Ephesus, which had lost the first love, and from Ephesus to Laodicea is only a very short distance in the Christian life.

Then we wonder why we are dry and out of touch with God, but we are too busy, praying only a few minutes in our private life without power and unction. And when the Lord does not at once satisfy us, we get discouraged, indifferent, or even hardened and say: "The Lord does not want to give it to me; I cannot help it." But he always is ready to reveal his sweetness and beauty to us if we only get quiet enough to draw near to him, our living Savior. Then he draws nigh unto us with blessing and his sweet fellowship.

Since I have heard that heavenly music and singing, everything that I hear below here, is falling short, is unsatisfying. Often I had the privilege of sitting in the Philadelphia Church in Stockholm, listening to that magnificent music and the singing of their splendid choir. But at times tears of longing welled out of my eyes, for it was only a breath compared with that which was my joy to hear—the heavenly choirs and orchestras. Yes, it made me homesick for what is awaiting in heaven.

It is not possible for me to give utterance to what I feel within. There is a fire burning, a fire of longing for heavenly things, for heaven itself. When I happen to be with people who are too shallow in their spiritual life to appreciate the value and what it means to suffer for Christ, I would take wing and fly away—to heaven.

Praise God, for he is willing to sweep away all hardness of heart and all indifference and bring every one back to his bosom and to his fountain of blessing; the real and original Pentecostal blessing.

24. SIGNIFICANCE OF PRAYER AND INTERCESSION

While secluded in that lonely cell, I had much occasion to meditate on various phases of our spiritual development and on our Christian usages. It especially was prayer and intercession which arrested my attention, that being the only unhindered and uncensored means of my contact with the outside world beyond my narrow cell walls.

It dawned on me very forcefully that I myself had fallen short in my prayer life as a child of God. First, I tried to argue with that voice within my conscience in order to press down the debit side. I tried to excuse myself with "much work, much travel and much responsibility" but all that did not lessen the account but made it still larger, for these points cited as excuses should have caused me to pray all the more because I was in need of more grace.

Then I faced the issue and opened my heart wide to the reproving influence of the Holy Spirit whose interest it is, to reveal Christ to us and make us more conformed to his will.

Valuable lessons were then conveyed to me in this respect, and I had to acknowledge that while in our ordinary spiritual life we consider prayer both as a necessity and also as a privilege, most of us do not examine ourselves very carefully, but take for granted that we are faithful in our prayer life. We pray before meals, even if it is often only pitifully perfunctory. Some of us have the commendable usage of also giving thanks after the meals: then we also pray every morning, after rising, and in the evening before retiring.

Family worship is not generally practiced, but we might make a fair guess when we state that one third of the Christian families are adhering to this kind of devotion. It is more seldom that the whole family can be united for that noble exercise.

It must be said however that many more Christian families could easily erect such a family altar if they would not permit some excuses to overrule. One of these excuses is that they cannot get the whole family together because of the daily routine of the several members which cannot be co-ordinated to allow all of them to be together at the same time. It might be suggested however that the above excuse does not always stand honest analysis. In many families a time could be reasonably found either before or after one of the meals, or in the evening.

Another excuse is put forward by claiming that some members of the family are not saved and consequently have no desire to attend such devotional exercise. To this excuse can be replied that most of the unsaved members of such families would not be so belligerent if the family altar would be a fixed institution and as inevitable as the daily meals.

Neither of these two reasons or excuses should however hinder family worship with those members who can and care to attend. Daily honest prayer and trust at the family altar can finally remove many obstacles and even bring obstinate family members to the feet of Jesus.

Let no child of God take the matter lightly and perhaps offer the above-mentioned excuses to cover the neglect of daily worship in the family. It can be safely said without passing harsh judgment that those who neglect the family altar, are also far below the mark in their own personal prayer life.

It is still more difficult for a child of God to get the vision and burden for a real service of prayer, and an urge to intercede for other saints and for the work of God in general. One has to live close to Jesus in order to come under the burdens of prayer and intercessions that go forth from the Holy Spirit to the saints. Those who are "tuned in" on the Holy Spirit, hear the message and get under the burden of prayer. The others do not notice anything and are ignorant of any special need within the body of Christ.

Those children of God who live close to Jesus, are familiar with many prayer needs in the household of God, and are often under burdens of prayer. Thus they are builders of the house of God and co-workers of his in a real sense of the word.

The Holy Spirit has mustered a host of saints for intercessory service in our day when there is such tremendous distress in the world among the children of God. But some of the saints are naively ignorant about the distress within the body of Christ. They are lacking prayer material even for their daily prayers and are far away from any real burdens which they should bring before the Lord. It is just as sad when one observes some frequenters of prayer meetings who are also deplete of any intercessory burdens. They never get beyond their family—their relation —and assembly interests.

People who lack real intercessory burdens, are often leaning toward spiritual gossip. They have no special intercessory prayer ability, but they have a "gift" of criticism and will not carry their burdens to the Lord in prayer but convey critically, what they know, to others. The listeners to such tales are also being defiled, therefore we must not lend our ears to them, but rather pray.

Intercessory prayer is mostly concerned with the members of the body of Christ. The Holy Spirit is the invisible director of the band of intercessors. We might best designate them by making use of a newly coined word "global," thus the band of intercessors are a perpetual global prayer meeting that never ends, and the attendants are spread over the whole earth. It is not a localized prayer meeting, but the Holy Spirit "broadcasts" the prayer needs and prayer requests, and the hearts of the members of that band are very sensitive receivers and pick up these messages out of the spiritual "ether." Followers may be received into that order for intercession in the United States, England, Australia or any other country, to intercede for a child of God in great need somewhere in a hidden part of Europe or China. There someone is going through a very severe trial, perhaps in prison or in banishment; it might be a child of God in utter despair because of being separated from loved ones.

Simultaneously while that trial is on, that global prayer band is interceding in the different parts of the world, and new trust and faith is imparted to that lonely suffering member of the body of Christ.

To this wonderful truth I can testify myself. There in my dismal cell, when the claws of despair threatened to embrace me in their deathly grip, and when I was not able to pray anymore, I heard a soft, loving and pleasing voice within me, saying: "The saints are now praying for you. You are not alone in your grief; others are burdened for you."

Actually, the Holy Spirit had sent forth an urgent "broadcast" to his faithful members of that global prayer band, and they are praying and interceding for me. There in my dreary prison he brought this fact to my notice, thereby giving me the needed comfort.

When I heard that voice within, it invariably electrified me. A warmth surged through my tired and weary spiritual being, and also through my emaciated body. I began to thank God, for I knew that my precious and faithful friends and saints in the United States, and those in a number of other countries were now in prayer, breathing intercession for me somewhere, in their places of work, in the kitchens, on the field, wherever they happen to pick up and receive that message of the Spirit.

Thousands of miles away, I felt the fellowship of the saints. I was alone like a solitary figure there in that dark cell, but realized that I was in the midst of that noble band of intercessors who live very close to Jesus.

O friends, let us join that band, that global prayer meeting of intercessors, that we too may have a part in the glorious accomplishments of those prayer warriors.

Someday the members of this great band shall have a reunion before the throne of the Lamb, and you will see that their crown will be shining with more stars than others.

For that day let us work and prepare.

25. BATTLE WITH DARK MARAUDERS

Although the Lord gave me those glorious waves of blessing, I had great battles to fight with intruding evil powers from time to time—marauders who are always diligent to carry away with them the stores of blessings we have obtained in the presence of Jesus. Usually we go weakened out of such a battle and have to struggle a good deal to get back into his presence again.

For a long time I was aware that my cell was infested with some evil powers and I began to pray definitely that the Lord would drive them out, but the more I prayed the more they disturbed me. A prison is the place where Satan has a special power to interfere, for it is his ground. My struggle went on for weeks and became more and more desperate until at times I was about to give up the fight.

One night the climax had come and they attacked me so viciously that they were about to overpower me. An icy fear crept over me as an impression within me became so strong that I almost had to utter it audibly. "We will kill you this night." These words kept on ringing within, in spite of my constant resistance and prayer. Cold sweat oozed from my pores while I kept on claiming the blood of the Lamb and rebuking the enemy in the name of Jesus.

The battle became so intense that I jumped up from my cot and my hair stood on end. I continued to claim the covering of the blood of Jesus my Savior and kept on believing God for complete victory. Finally, the resistance was broken and I had the consciousness that the evil powers had fled, and that Jesus was completely filling the room with his presence. The glory of God was flooding me and I was praising the Lord for that great victory. Now I began to feel at ease and I sensed that the room had become a sanctuary of God.

From that night on I never again had such struggles with evil powers and no more interference in the trend of my thinking. It was also much easier for me to pray and often the glory of his presence overshadowed the awful loneliness which crept over me from time to time.

Strange as it may seem, only when we are more completely filled by the spirit of God and surrounded by spiritual atmosphere, do we sense the proximity of evil powers very keenly. There are some rooms and houses which they infest and attack more viciously. That is the reason why Spirit-filled saints have more struggles in their prayer life and they must contend with these evil powers that challenge them almost any time. Children of God who live in the presence of Jesus, are a menace to these dark powers and consequently warfare follows when they approach. (See Daniel 10:13–14, Ephesians 6:12.)

Of this we have examples in the life of Jesus our Lord when he walked on this earth. The demons were aroused whenever he came near, causing them to cry out. That did not happen when the disciples approached. Paul also had the experience that evil spirits cried out when he came near. He knew of that warfare and therefore often spoke about it. He says: "We wrestle not against flesh and blood, but against principalities, against powers, against the rulers of the darkness of this world, against spiritual wickedness in high places" (Ephesians 6:12). "Fight the good fight of faith, lay hold of eternal life" (1 Timothy 6:12).

If evil powers become restless when we draw near them, it is a good sign that we are in the Lord; but it is a dangerous sign when all is quiet around us. May God help us to be good soldiers for him.

26. A Peculiar Communion Service

Until now I had not had the Lord's supper in my cell. No preacher was admitted. I sent a petition for a minister to visit me but that was rejected.

As much as was possible for me without a watch, I observed the hours of the meetings. One Sunday morning I had an irresistible hunger for the communion but saw the futility of such a longing as I could not get into a meeting.

Suddenly the thought flashed through my mind as I read in my Bible, "Why not have the communion right here in this cell by yourself? Jesus is here and so there are two of you, you are not alone."

This thought was brand new to me, in fact it must have come from the Lord. I looked up from my Bible and said: "Yes, Lord, you are here and if you sanction such a proceeding, I surely will be more than glad. But what shall I have as the visible token of your supper?

Sure enough, bread was in my cell, but wine? "I have none and cannot secure any. It is water that I must use and if Jesus will, he can even turn it into wine." I uttered those words aloud and as I continued to develop the thought of the Lord's supper, a great joy in the Spirit gripped me. It gladdened me beyond measure to realize that I could take part in the Lord's supper, even though alone in this cell.

It was communion Sunday in our church, so I awaited the time when I thought they were partaking of the table of the Lord. Then in prayer and supplication I tuned up with the Lord and read the portions of Scripture, especially the one where Jesus says to his disciples: "With desire have I desired to eat this passover with you before I suffer" (Luke 22:15).

These words gripped me mightily and I realized that now my Savior desired to eat this supper with me. I began to praise him as loud as I could without arousing the always-alert prison attendants.

Then I put my hands over the bread and the battered and dented tin mug and prayed. After that I partook of the bread, and when I took the cup of the Lord, I noticed that the water had a wine color. The Lord had turned it into wine. It did not taste like water at all. Jesus was with me, he wanted me to partake of the Lord's supper and surely it was an easy matter for him to give me real communion wine.

It tasted sweet and lovely and the presence of the Lord overwhelmed me, and his blessing surged through my whole being. I felt wonderfully invigorated even in my physical frame. Surely that was the most remarkable and peculiar communion I have ever taken part in.

From then on I always observed the communion Sunday and celebrated the Lord's supper. Only that first time, though, did I have the wonderful experience of water becoming wine. However it was always blessed, for I felt the presence of the Lord in a special way on such occasions. I was with my Jesus in that lonely cell. To him be all the praise forever!

27. A GOD-SENT VISITOR

Whenever I had experienced special blessings, it was a signal that some extraordinary trials were ahead. This was also to be true after that wonderful communion service.

Invariably was I alarmed when news from my family failed to be forthcoming. Often my wife desperately tried to reach me but was hindered by the prison authorities. I did not know what was going on outside of my cell and groped in the dark as to the reasons for not hearing from her. There came a period again when for weeks my wife was not permitted to visit me and even some letters which she had written were held back by the censor, which resulted in complete isolation from the outside world.

Once a week my wash was changed. My wife usually came to the prison office on Thursday, left the laundered things and took the soiled wash with her. When that package was brought in to me I knew that my wife had been there and was still alive and in health. This indirect contact was always a personal greeting from home and family.

When I had waited several weeks in vain for a visit of my wife and had failed to receive a letter from her, I became desperately alarmed, thinking that something had happened to her or the children.

Just to do something, I signaled the guard and after an hour and a half of waiting, he came, asking what I wanted at such an hour of the evening. Falteringly I asked: "Has there no package come for me this week?"

"No," he replied angrily, "if there had been something for you, I should have brought it to your cell, you know that very well. Don't you bother me about such things in the future or you will be due for punishment as you are signaling without cause." He slammed and locked the door and I was alone again.

There I was in the darkness of that cell, being consumed by fears and forebodings, by loneliness and sorrow. I shivered violently. "O Lord, don't let sickness come over me. Don't let me get ill in this horrible place. Give me strength to endure. Friend of the forsaken and helper of the helpless, come to me now for I am in deep misery. Let a spark of light come into this tomb of despair."

When that cold fear crept over me and my whole body was trembling I feared that I would utterly break down, which I feared the most. I knew what happened to those who were getting sick in the terrible prison. On my knees I tried to gather my thoughts and get into quietness and trust before the Lord, but did not succeed. The awful strain and pressure of the situation kept me in a near delirium.

As I was kneeling thus before the Lord, I felt distinctly a hand softly touching my forehead and remaining there with a slight pressure, and that awful gnawing pain and sorrow subsided perceptibly. My heart became peaceful. It was the hand of my precious Savior, coming again to rescue me from a spell of despair.

Oh, the touch of Jesus! How many times had he come to me. Now in the hour of this sore trouble he was there again and smoothed the turbulent ocean of my sorrows. Again the words of Paul crowded into my memory: "All things work together for good to them that love God, to them who are called according to his purpose" (Romans 8:28).

Am I called of God? Do I love God? "Yes, Lord. You have called me, I have come to Calvary and you have spoken forgiveness to my sinful heart. Since then I have loved you, always. Deep down in my heart this love is rooted and anchored. But why the senseless suffering in this terrible cell, drawn out endlessly, making my life a nightmare without end?"

"My child, I have brought you back to the scene of your call and work, and you are required to accept in suffering that which is yet lacking in your mission. Your co-workers are in safety, but you are to bear afflictions for my body. You are not yet valiant in suffering and this is your school to become patient in adversity." Thus spoke my Savior to me in that hour of grief.

The passage in Colossians 1:24 came to my memory where Paul writes concerning his ministry and suffering. He says, "Who now rejoice in my sufferings for you, and filled up that which is behind of the afflictions of Christ in my flesh for his body's sake, which is the church." Then I was led to Romans 8:17, where Paul writes: "And if children, then heirs: heirs of God, and joint-heirs with Christ: if so be that we suffer with him, that we may be also glorified together."

This then is the meaning of my present ordeal of any suffering for Christ. The Lord touched a theme, a phase of spiritual development which is known well enough but much neglected in the teaching of the church of Christ, and less practiced. It is however the final stage of preparation, the baking, the seasoning by fire; the process of unpalatable dough becoming tasty bread.

"O Lord, then I am far from being a willing disciple of yours. I am writhing and fretting so much in my suffering.

Make me quiet and help me to submit to the heat which you must put on in order to season me for your use."

As I was listening to my Savior, a truth was vivified to me which I had touched upon in my teaching and preaching, but it never gripped me as it did now. I looked back into my life and into the life of other children of God. There I found that we are always trying very desperately to avoid any inconvenience and suffering. If possible, we fight and talk and argue until we have slipped out of it or until we have come "on top," having the right of way and satisfied that we have vindicated ourselves. Friendships are broken and hearts wounded just because we insist on having our right. This may be carried on to such an extent that we forget at times to "live and let live."

While I was meditating thus, I heard the noise of a key being shoved into the lock and turning, but this time unusually careful as if not wanting to be heard. In the darkness of the cell I saw a man coming in like a shadow. He quietly greeted me, then asked me how I was feeling.

"To tell the truth, I am not at all feeling well," I answered. "In a place like this it is vain to ask how one feels. Furthermore I have not heard from my wife and children for a number of weeks, neither have I received a letter. That makes me unusually uneasy and troubled. Something might have happened to them and here I am locked in this cell, condemned to helplessness."

"I also have a wife and children and can guess in some measure, what it means to have no contact with them and how you may feel. We cannot alter anything for you as we are just called to do our duties in this place, which is bitter enough at times, especially for one whose heart is not petrified as yet. If I can help you in any way, I am willing to do so. Let me see, supposing you write a note to your wife —but strictly personal matters, not touching anything which concerns your case—and I shall see that your wife will still get it this evening."

His words overjoyed me and he had to admonish me to remain quiet as I exclaimed: "A message to my wife, why that is wonderful but it would only reassure me partly, I still would not know anything about her and the children."

"That we can take care of," he replied. "I will bring the message to your wife myself and ask her to write a reply which I will bring along and see that you get it tomorrow."

This was a marvelous turn in my hopeless situation of a few minutes ago. I knew however, to what perilous danger my visitor exposed himself as it would mean imprisonment for him if detected.

"As far as I am informed, you expose yourself to the greatest dangers and are liable to severe punishment if you are found out," I warned him.

"I only dare to do this for you because I trust you, and am convinced that you are innocent. Furthermore I do not believe that anyone should be persecuted for his belief. That is why I feel a very strong urge to help you."

"Do you realize that you have been sent directly by the Lord into my cell at this time?" I told him then about my struggles and fears concerning my family, and I explained to him how the Lord had come to my rescue a number of times, and this evening again. As I thus spoke I noticed that he was greatly moved. Indeed God must have been in his heart and prompted him to give way to such an urge to come and help me in my distress.

He went out again, turned on the light in my cell and I began to write a letter to my wife. How wonderful it was for me to realize that these lines should be read by her that very evening, I can hardly describe. While I was writing, my heart was flowing over with praise and thanksgiving to my Savior who again was performing a miracle in order to lift the awful burden from my heart.

A new proof was given me that a living God is ruling over our life and he is with everyone of his children every hour and every minute. How comforting it is that he always

126

finds a way to help us. While I was writing, my heart was singing: "He's a Friend of mine and he with me doth all things share."

Later my visitor came back and took my letter but not before he had turned off the light. He did not want me to see him distinctly. Loaded with greetings to my wife, he departed and I was singing and praising the Lord from all my heart for having so wonderfully undertaken for me again. While he taught me a deep spiritual lesson, he did not forget to help me out of my deep distress.

On Sunday evening the same man slipped into my cell and handed me a letter from my wife but extracted a promise from me that I should immediately, after reading, destroy the letter to keep on the safe side.

My fears and seeming forebodings of ill concerning my family proved to be unfounded again, and I realized more than ever before that I should be on my guard against my own imaginations which can so easily be used by the enemy to make me miserable. Now I had peace and quiet in my heart for the Lord once more had stepped down on my level, bringing me comfort and assurance. Praise his name forever!

28. MY WATCH RETURNED

Every day and every hour I was in greatest discomfort to be without a watch. Four months I had been without it. The short winter days as well as the small window with its dimmed glass, made the days all the darker and shorter. Even during the three hours when it was supposed to be daylight I was hardly able to read. Only with great strain on my eyes was I able to read and write. My eyes were greatly weakened during my imprisonment. Being so much in darkness without a watch, made life all the more miserable.

One day when I was lamenting again in my mind about not knowing the time, I asked myself suddenly: "Why haven't you yet spoken to Jesus about it? You have prayed for all kinds of things but never that your watch be returned to you." Sure enough, I had overlooked this matter entirely. I really felt ashamed of myself, complaining about it for months and never definitely telling the Lord about it, although he promises to hear our petitions whatever they may be.

Immediately I went before the Lord, telling him of my great need and asking him for his intervention. While I was in prayer, the thought came to me very clearly that I should write to the judge, asking for the return of my wristwatch. I was now quite sure that I would have my watch returned and that it would be only a matter of time.

The petition to the judge was handed in. To have action on such petitions usually took two weeks and I had myself ready to remain without my watch during that period. How great was my surprise when the guard came in after three days and put my wristwatch on the table, going out again without saying a word.

There my watch lay on the table. I looked at it for a moment, then tenderly kissed it as a good old friend who had been absent all too long. Praise and thanksgiving arose again to my precious Savior who had shown anew that all power is his and that he can sway the thoughts of men.

Feeling my watch on my wrist again, I seemed to be dreaming. So many weeks I had been without a timepiece and completely helpless as to the progress of time. If one has the sun to go by or the light of a regular day outside, one can judge approximately, but in a dark cell where I did not see the sun nor any real sunlight during four months it was indeed a wonderful change to be able to observe the progress of the hours by the means of a watch.

This answer to my prayer was also a further great lesson to me as I realized how wise the admonition of Paul was, when he said, "Be careful for nothing; but in everything by prayer and supplication with thanksgiving let your requests be made known unto God" (Philippians 4:6).

29. A SOLITARY PREACHER

At times I had heard that animals in some way sense the sorrow of human beings and like to linger around as if desiring to be a comfort to them, but I could never verify such assumptions. However, I had a strange experience during my dark hours in that dreary cell.

In the morning at daybreak a little sparrow came to my window, sat down on one of the iron bars, looked into the cell and sang his doleful, melancholy song. Sometimes he sat ten minutes, at other times up to twenty. He seemed not to be scared when I came near him. Through the dimmed glass I could not see him very distinctly, but at times he shifted so that he could have a glance at the cell through the open part of the window. Then I could clearly observe him.

That little visitor was often a real comfort to me and I talked to him. He was a living reminder to me of the words of Christ:

"Are not two sparrows sold for a farthing? And one of them shall not fall on the ground without your Father. . . . Fear not ye therefore, ye are of more value than many sparrows" (Matthew 10:29, 31).

The solitary visitor thus became to me a living sermon from the word of God and was a mute messenger from the Lord, causing me to remember the faithfulness of God. When I think of it now, it appears much more wonderful than when I was in the cell. Ordinarily a sparrow will hardly choose such a dark corner for a resting place. I am convinced that the Lord sent him there to preach a sermon over and over again about trusting him, and confidently leave my case in his hands.

That solitary preacher reminded me about the sweet tenderness of my precious Savior who would not forget to keep me, even in that dark and dreary cell.

30. THE FIRST SUNRAYS

Since my imprisonment I had not seen the sun or its rays. Day by day it changed from semi-darkness to blackest night. Only a very narrow little slit enabled me to peer through and see the sky above the opposite building whereby I could determine whether there was a clear or cloudy sky. In March however the sun reached lower and lower down over the roof of the building across the courtyard until on the fifteenth of March early in the afternoon the sunrays struck my little window. Because of the dimmed glass they could not penetrate. Only that narrow little slit enabled some of the golden rays to find their way into my cell.

In my daybook I made the following record of this occasion: "Today for the first time the rays of the sun stole their way through that little crevice into my cell and rested on the wall. They are the first messengers of spring and— of my liberty. It caused a feeling of bliss within me. In half an hour my dark cell was beautifully lit up. Thank God that the Sun of righteousness is always shining within my heart."

My eyes flooded with tears as I watched that strip of light on the wall slowly moving toward the right until the angle of the sunrays prevented their getting through any longer. Then again the semi-darkness slowly took possession of my little cell.

When looking at my abode while the sunrays lighted up the cell, it seemed more horrible and desolate than in the semi-darkness. I was shocked when I glanced at the walls, how besmirched they were. I looked at the folded-up bed and the shiny surface of the burlap-like cloth, shiny with the dirt which had accumulated, perhaps through years of use. So after all, the darkness of the cell was mercifully covering up the horrid reality.

A lesson was brought home to me through that experience. The cell is a fitting picture of the human heart being in semi-darkness, which prevents a human being from seeing the real condition of his life. As one comes in touch with God and his word, some sunrays of his grace strike that dark cell of the heart and a shock comes to such a person. If one is honest, he will repent and cry out for the cleansing blood of Calvary. But others deliberately withdraw into their semi-darkness again, refusing to come under the reproving word of God, for they do not desire to be disturbed in their way of sin. They feel much better in the darkness because then they do not see the ugliness of the heart and life; they love darkness more than the light.

Someday they will have to move into the light of God. His light will be mercilessly turned on them in full strength and the judgment of God will strike them. It is better to come into the light now, instead of waiting until that great judgment day.

31. My Defender

A very strange system of prosecution is being employed here. My wife had made arrangement with a lawyer to act as my defender and a petition was sent to the judge that the lawyer be authorized as my defender. After weeks had passed, the lawyer finally received the permission.

When my wife informed me, I asked my lawyer to visit me. He came and we discussed my case at length. After that visit, I did not hear from him for a long time. Again I wrote him to call and he came. Naturally I wanted to know whether any progress was made.

"There is very little to do," he answered. "There is war and the law authorities have many other duties to perform."

"But if they have so many duties, why do they bother about me? Why don't they let me go and dismiss the case? It is impossible that they can have any serious charge against me because there is nothing wrong in my life. I am now imprisoned over four months and not a word of real accusation has been leveled against me. I should think that they had had time enough to look through my correspondence and papers which they seized. Furthermore they must have investigated my movements, my friends and contacts. If they had found something amiss, they surely would have confronted me with the acts. Have you been able to look into my case, and did you speak to the prosecutor?"

"Until now I was not allowed to look into your case, as I received no permission to see the documents or the results of the investigation at the prosecutor's office. Four months is not a long time in such a court case. There are prisoners here, held for court, who have already waited over a year and there is no end in sight as yet. It is better for you to exercise patience, for if you bother them, they might take you to another place, compared to which this prison is a comfortable hotel. If the war closes you will be released automatically."

"But why don't they release me and restrict my movements? I surely could not run away against their will, and I would not if I gave my word," I contended.

"They very likely suspect you of something which they keep a secret. Evidently they believe you to be a spy, and that you camouflaged yourself so thoroughly that they cannot get at facts. That is evidently the reason why they hold you in prison."

Conversing with my defender, I realized that he talked very guardedly and that he had very little leeway to be a factor in speeding up my case. It was extremely discouraging to realize that he too favored silence, and advised me to wait in that cell until the war should end, a very disheartening prospect.

After this visit of my defender, a few weeks again passed and I did not hear anything from him. Once more I wrote, asking him to come for consultation. He did not come, neither did he answer my letter. I was quite distressed about it. When I asked the guard, my only link of contact with the outside world, he simply shrugged his shoulders and confessed ignorance as usual, leaving me in my hopelessness.

My wife was not permitted to see me anymore. Some of her letters to me and mine to her were held back by the censors, thus my isolation was complete. It remained a puzzle to me why I did not hear from my defender anymore. Only after my release from prison did I learn that the permission to defend me was withdrawn, but I was not to know about this turn of events. That made it evident that their charges against me were flimsy and would not have stood scrutiny of a lawyer before the judge.

Being entirely ignorant about developments and my imprisonment protracting endlessly, I became very desperate. The fear constantly haunted me that they would come anytime and take me to a concentration camp. A convenient way to make it unnecessary for them to produce charges to justify my arrest. The only way left open for me was to turn to the Lord in my helplessness, which I did, calling upon him in my deep sorrow.

And so often before when at the breaking point of despair, I fell asleep while praying and sighing. Again I heard the marvelous heavenly orchestra and choir. This time several voices wove a song into the music of the orchestra and the singing of the choir. The chorus of that song was several times repeated. When I awoke after some hours of sleep, I heard myself singing that melody and words. Part of the words of the chorus I remembered in the morning and made note of them when the light was turned on. They were as follows:

In patience and in trust there is your safety,
Until you'll wear a crown of life,
A crown with many, many stars.

That experience in the night flooded me again with supernatural joy which lasted throughout the day, and the music was ringing within me for several days. It helped me to overcome the keen attacks of melancholy and the awful monotony of the cell life.

"Patience and trust" were the salient words of that heavenly song and I placed myself anew entirely into his care as I prayed: "Lord, it seems that I am being deprived of a defender, but you have said that your Spirit is to be our Advocate, our Defender, and I take him as my Counselor in this my trouble. I will not worry about it anymore, if only your presence and your glory fill my cell as it has been from time to time. You do all things well."

The attack of the enemy was diverted and I had peace in my soul as the Lord was very near me.

32. In the Sanctuary of God

Ever since my arrest, my main burden of prayer was that the Lord should release me from this awful imprisonment. The more the winter wore on and spring approached, the more restless I became and all the more desperately I prayed for my release. Having had so many wonderful answers to prayers, I desired to exercise such strong faith that the Lord would have to step in and undertake for me. But there seemed to be a closed sky. I could see no indication whatever that things were moving forward. That caused me keen disappointment. Temptations, doubts, and struggles invaded my prayers.

As no news from the outside reached me, I again felt completely forlorn and at times bitterness threatened to creep over me. But "patience and trust" kept on ringing in me and I realized that I had not learned the lesson and struggled into a state of looking to the Lord and waiting for him to move in his time.

Thus meditating, I fell asleep one evening and I distinctly felt myself lifted up by an angel and being swiftly carried through space. Presently I heard a faint sound of faraway music which became more distinct every minute until there was an overwhelming sound of orchestra music similar to that I had heard so many times before. This time however the sound came from a direction where the whole horizon was aglow with an indescribable flood of light that blinded me. I sank down on my face and out of me poured a spontaneous praise and worship to the Lamb of God.

Again a mighty volume of song mingled with the orchestra music, and I felt myself melting into the harmonies of adoration and praise which issued from the music and song of thousands of voices. Faintly I sensed that a change was coming over my whole being and I floated up into an upright position again. I saw that I was surrounded by an indescribable light and my chest heaved with praises in song which issued from within.

An angel touched me and softly said: "Now go back, it is not your time to remain in this kingdom of light, music, and song. You shall come later and remain through eternal ages." Thus I was led back again and awoke, an unspeakable joy and bliss filling my whole being.

Those blessed dream visions when I heard the mighty music of harp orchestras and choir singing recurred quite frequently and the floods of joy were replenished as new blessings were poured upon me. The whole cell became aglow with the glory and presence of God. Day and night I was praising the Lord and I worshiped him by singing in the Spirit.

He gave me new songs and melodies which I wrote down and which became a source of further blessing to me as I sang them daily during those weary months. They were born in the night of sorrow and trial and were sung in the night of affliction.

One of these songs especially proved to be a permanent source of encouragement to me, for it expressed the progressive feeling of my heart throughout those months, depicting the various stages of emotions which had swept over me from deepest despair to the quiet and faithful trust in my Savior as I rested my case in him. That song is as follows:

> In the nighttime there is weeping,
> When pressed by sorrow's pain;
> When the tempest's rage is growing,
> And prayer and hope seem vain.
> Am I of God forsaken?
> Hath he gone far away?
> My faith and trust are shaken,
> I'm left in sore dismay.
>
> My child, when grief is mounting,
> I'm very near to thee;
> Thine every tear I'm counting,
> Thy pain is known to me.
> Thou art My valued treasure,
> So cherished in My sight,
> And out of sorrow's pressure

Shines forth My heavenly light.

O Lord, to Thee I'm turning,
Thy favor I desire;
When sorrow's heat is burning.
Watch Thou Thyself the fire.
The task of my refining
Needs heating sevenfold,
Till Thou, in splendor shining,
Thine image canst behold.

1 bring Thee adoration,
Thou blessed Lamb of God;
For joy, for tribulation,
On life's path that I've trod.
Thy cords of love are binding
My being close to Thee;
Thou art my place of hiding,
My rest, my victory.

As day by day passed in unbroken fellowship with my
Jesus, there seemed to be only one wish unfulfilled in that
cell, namely to have my autoharp or guitar. I was quite
happy, so much so that I was surprised at myself, saying:
"You puzzle me. It seems you are becoming reconciled to
this cell altogether."

Waves of overwhelming joy and glory came over me and
at times I exclaimed: "Lord, I have no more wish; I am
satisfied. You are with me and you are my world. This is my
sanctuary and I don't desire anything else, even if I have to
stay in this cell my whole life through, it is all right, IT IS
WELL!" I exclaimed these words scores of times as the
floods of blessing were rolling over me.

The volume of God's glory became so great at times
that my chest heaved and pained from the exertions and the
necessity of holding in to avoid too much noise.

One day after a new attendant had taken charge of our
department, he suddenly opened the cell door, looked at me

intently and then remarked: "You act strange. It seems at times as if you have someone in your cell and are conversing with that person. Is there something wrong with you?"

"No," I answered. "There is something altogether right within me. I am indeed not alone in this cell, I have a very pleasant and distinguished companion with me—Jesus Christ my Lord. His presence is making this place entirely tolerable for me."

"I cannot see your companion," he replied, making an attempt at joking, but then he gave me a very puzzled look and went out again. Through the "bull's eye" however he watched me repeatedly as the days wore on, very likely thinking that my mind had snapped.

The glory of God within me and the sweetness of his presence often became more intense than at the time of receiving my baptism. I felt that the whole cell was flooded with his glory and thus I raced back and forth worshiping the Lord. He dwelt there with me.

"Patience and trust," complete abandonment unto God allowed no more agonizing to have my state altered. I was completely satisfied in Jesus and his love. That was the culmination of my imprisonment. God had proved to me and within me that he can satisfy a human being irrespective of prevailing circumstances.

The strange behavior of martyrs, who could smile under the most excruciating pains and tortures, were not puzzling me any more. My wife had brought me *Fox's Book of Martyrs* and I read it with delight and understanding. It was perfectly clear to me how they were able to stand those awful pains. The glory of God flooded and enfolded them, consequently they did not feel the tortures and pains; they did not feel the heat of the fire, because they were enshrouded by the fire of God's presence which neutralized every pain and anguish. Praise be to our great Savior!

In patience and trust is our safety. Let us get near to the Lord: let us be enveloped by his presence and his glory, then all that which is hard to bear, will become easy. Even the painful yoke is easy when he is present.

33. NEW QUESTIONINGS

One morning, after having been flooded with his glory for quite a few days, the door was unlocked as noisily as ever but it did not shock me as it used to. I now seemed to be fully composed and immune. The guard summoned me as roughly as ever and led me into the building which houses the prison offices.

"Are you taking me to see my wife?" I asked the guard as expectancy seized me.

"No," he replied, "you are going to meet the prosecutor."

He ushered me into a spacious room where I looked into the face of the man who handled my case.

"Sit down there on that chair," the prosecutor said not at all unfriendly, pointing to a chair at the right end of the desk.

"We are going to go through your case once more from beginning to the end, and I want you to answer all my questions candidly, and it will mean very much if you cooperate with me to clear the case speedily." Thus he admonished me to tell him all, and exactly as things stood. "There are phases which are not solved through your first questioning," he continued.

"I can unreservedly promise to answer all your questions in perfect honesty for I have nothing to hide. There is nothing shadowy in my life; and anyone, searching for nothing but the truth in my life, will have no hard task to obtain it. Since I was seventeen years of age and throughout my life until today, I have had one main interest: to live for God and serve him. The last twenty years I have been solely preaching the gospel of Jesus Christ and I mean to continue to do so exclusively until the end of my days."

"You will have to cut your statements shorter or we shall never get through, and you will remain in your cell the rest of your days," he rejoined warningly.

"I expect to be in that cell not one hour longer than God will allow," I replied.

"Don't be too sure about that. Why does God then want you in the cell at all, and why has he not gotten you out long ago?" This he snapped back at me in some embarrassment.

"For the same reason that he allowed Peter and Paul, as well as millions of others of his servants to be imprisoned. Perhaps one of the main reasons was to show that no human instruments of cunning and persecution can persuade true followers of Christ to give up their faith or grow weak. Great persecutors and mighty empires have fallen and are forgotten, but Christ and his church are standing today as firm as ever."

"There is one thing that you must remember," he assured, "we are not persecuting the church nor any religion but we are endeavoring to root out sects which are destructive and are demoralizing the people. If you are swamped with them in America, we have nothing against it but as soon as you try the same thing here, you run against a snag."

"Then you should not have put me in this cell and kept me here for nearly six months because I am not demoralizing the people. On the contrary, through our preaching the people are liberated from destructive and demoralizing habits such as drinking, smoking, thieving, robbing, murdering, revolutionizing, etc. I can give you proof of my statement in this very city that such is the case."

"You belong to the Pentecostal sect, don't you?"

"Yes, I do, with the exception that I deny belonging to a sect, rather, I belong to that body of believers who are incorporated in the body of Christ which is the only true and competent Christian church. All regenerated men and women the world over, who have surrendered their life to God and are willing to obey the injunctions of the Bible, no matter what their affiliation is, are members of that church, and the Pentecostal movement is part of it."

"Movement, movement! There is only one movement in our country and that is the NSDAP, all the other 'movements' are illegal."[4]

There he refuted his former statement of not persecuting the church. And indeed, they don't like any Christian movement: they don't want people to be saved, they don't want revivals because they take measures to have Christianity die out in one generation.

"The youth belong to us, we are going to train them according to our principles not yours," he snapped angrily.

Changing the subject, he began, as my first inquisition, by asking me why I had returned to Europe in 1939 when there was such a turmoil in Poland. I explained to him that I came to continue my religious activity. I said, "Dangers never keep me from doing my duty as a minister of the gospel, and therefore no trouble which threatened Europe could deter me for a moment. I should have felt like a coward, if I had refrained from coming because of trouble brewing in Europe. Those who needed my ministry in times of peace, need me a hundred times more in days of calamity."

---

[4] NSDAP stands for Nationalsozialistische Deutsche Arbeiterpartei, German for 'National Socialist German Workers' Party.'

"Explain to me with what organization you are affiliated," he continued.

"I am one of the founders of the Russian and Eastern European Mission, with headquarters in Chicago, Illinois, and I hold ministerial and missionary credentials with the General Council of the Assemblies of God who have their headquarters in Springfield, Missouri. The main aim of our mission is to work and spread the gospel among the Slavic people, but we also carry on an extensive religious activity in the Balkan States and in the Baltic countries."

"What positions did you hold in your Mission?"

"From the founding of the REEM until today I hold the position of Field Superintendent. I am a trustee of that organization."

"Why do you call yourself 'Editor' in your passport?"

"I am the founder of *The Gospel Call*, first issued in the year 1926, and when the REEM was organized, the paper became the official organ of the mission, and I was the editor of that paper for years. Besides that, I was also associate editor of a monthly paper called *Wort und Zeugnis*, published in Milwaukee, Wisconsin. In Danzig, I issued a Russian monthly paper named *Primiritjel*, which was stopped in 1939.[5]

"The reason for designating myself as editor in my passport was to arouse less suspicion in the European so-called Christian countries when traveling as a preacher or missionary. In some backward countries of Europe the authorities suspect a missionary to have horns concealed under his hat and horse feet in his boots."

---

[5] *Wort und Zeugnis* (German, 'Word and Testimony') was begun in 1915 for German Pentecostals in the United States and became the official organ of the German District of the Assemblies of God. *Primiritel* (Примири́тель, Russian, 'The Reconciler') was begun in 1929, and Schmidt's co-workers also edited papers in Ukrainian and Polish.

"You cannot very well deny that most of the Anglo-Saxon missionaries are spies for their countries," he snapped back.

"Those are most unjust charges and cannot be proven. Although every missionary has a right to love and stand up for his own country and to speak good things about the homeland, I do not believe that missionaries are spies for their respective fatherland. No one has ever approached me in any way whatsoever, suggesting that I do any kind of secret service for my country. I should have flatly refused because I don't believe that a Christian minister should meddle in political matters. I adhere to Christ's principles as he stated them to Pilate: 'My kingdom is not of this world' (John 18:36). I am not working for my country, America, nor even for any denomination, but solely for Christ and for the rescue of perishing souls."

"Did you get that?" he turned to his typist.

"I wish that the 'foster parents' of Christianity— the Jews—would adhere to that famous utterance, 'My kingdom is not of this world,' then we would not have to fight this war," he put in sarcastically.

"It seems that the Jews and the National Socialists are in the same category, they both hate the Christian faith," I said.

"With the difference," he interposed quickly, "that, while Christians were busy exercising the graces of humbleness and self-abasement, the Jews were amassing riches by deceit, by cheating and grabbing until the Christians had become their slaves. It must be taken for granted then that the Jews like to see others to be good Christians for it makes their own task all the more easy to become the masters of this earth."

"According to your logic there should then be no more cheating, grabbing and stealing in Germany because, the Jews having been eliminated from places of responsibility in your country, there are only political and religious offenders in this prison. But I am not aware that I find myself in such a worthy company. On the contrary, I suspect that the majority of the inmates of this prison are here because they have too freely exercised the same characteristics you accuse the Jews of."

The typist had stopped writing as the conversation went on without interruption and the prosecutor did not indicate a desire to repeat anything for her to record. He abruptly switched the subject and asked: "Who is Gustav Kinderman and where is he?"

"Rev. Kinderman was secretary here at field headquarters but left Europe in May 1939 when our office was liquidated."

"I am truly sorry that he is not here anymore, we should be very much interested in him."

"Very likely it is the same interest that you have in me, but I hardly believe he will be disappointed not to comply. He is in the United States, his homeland, with his family and is quite happy to have put distance between himself and this city."

"Do you know a Pastor Steiner of Bern, Switzerland?"

I was astonished at the mention of his name but then remembered that they had my correspondence and likely found letters from him to me.

"It is my privilege," I answered, "to know Pastor Steiner since 1912, when he and I together were immersed in water baptism in Zurich, Switzerland. He is one of my most highly respected friends."

Next he asked me about Pastor Barratt, against whom he seemed to have a special grudge. He wanted to know whether I spread his writings. They had found some of his tracts among my papers and consider him as the father of the Pentecostal movement in Europe.[6]

Pastor Pethrus was not forgotten by him. He wanted to know whether I was in contact with him. I answered that I knew Pastor Pethrus since 1919 and that we more or less kept contact throughout the years.

Suddenly he broke off the questioning and told me that on the next day he again would call me for the continuation of the hearing.

"Will that—for me so tragic—ordeal of imprisonment come to a decision soon?" I asked him in parting.

"Yes, it will not last much longer. I will do what I can to speed up the proceedings," he replied.

The guard took me out and led me back into my dreary cell. I realized however that now things were moving forward and I felt very hopeful. His attitude was entirely different from that of the man who quizzed me in the beginning of my imprisonment.

The next day came and I waited hour by hour to be called again but in vain. I waited the next, the third, fourth and fifth day but heard nothing more about being questioned. I then asked the guard about the matter but as usual he gave no definite reply.

My hopes had been revived again and those daily disappointments and waiting caused me new struggles. I had to wrestle for new patience which was very hard to obtain. For fourteen days I had to wait until the cell door opened for me again to be led into the same room to the prosecutor.

---

[6] Thomas Ball Barratt (1862–1940) founded the Oslo City Mission in 1902. In 1906, he visited the Azusa Street Mission and was baptized in the Holy Spirit at the Holiness Mission in New York City. After his return to Europe, he trained Pentecostal leaders in various European countries.

He plunged right into the questioning. He accused me of having been the driving force in merging the Pentecostal assemblies with the Baptists for the purpose of gaining access into the Baptist churches in order to infest them with the Pentecostal faith. A rather lengthy discussion followed concerning Christian doctrines and methods of carrying on Christian work. He confessed that he did not know much about differences in Christian doctrines and that he wanted some enlightenment.

He professed surprise when I explained to him the doctrines of the Pentecostal movement and how we conducted our meetings. He went on: "I strongly suspect that you are giving your sect an attractive rosy coloring to impress me. If the Pentecostal churches would be as sensible as you describe them they would not be so disliked in the world," he argued.

"Every godly person and every spiritual movement and revival in church history was first disliked, shunned, and slandered. The same as happened to Christ and his apostles. When those churches became worldly and lost their spiritual life, they themselves began to fight the work of God every time a new revival of spiritual life occurred. Christ explains the reason very clearly when he says: 'If ye were of the world, the world would love his own: but because ye are not of the world, but I have chosen you out of the world, therefore the world hateth you. Remember the word that I said unto you, the servant is not greater than his lord. If they have persecuted me, they will also persecute you; if they have kept my saying, they will keep yours also'" (John 15:19–20).

"Well, there you are. Why are you then complaining when you are put into prison? To be really true to your religion, you must be put into prison, that is what you must then want," he replied sarcastically.

"Indeed we are not seeking imprisonment, neither do we seek the friendship and good will of the worldly-minded people in order to avoid trouble or smooth our pathway. In fact we are alarmed if everybody likes us and pats us on the shoulder. The church of Christ is flourishing in the purest and richest way when she is persecuted, because it is the refining process she then is passing through and is being moulded in pure gold after the pattern of Christ. In my imprisonment I have learned to know Christ in a new and marvelous way and I will leave this prison with deeper and stronger convictions in my faith than ever before.

"Although those who inflict suffering upon the saints will be punished for their deeds on the judgment day if they do not repent in this life—yet their unjust deeds against the children of God are means to bring the saints into closer contact and greater likeness of Christ their Savior."

"A strange doctrine this is. You truly seem to be beyond recovery," he replied. "If everybody were that way this world would be a curious place."

"It would be a Paradise, for everybody would strive to please God and one another. Wars and strife would not be possible nor necessary. There would be no prison and no state prosecutor known," I replied.

The best trump in his opinion he kept to the last when he suddenly flung a charge against me, saying: "You received and accepted missionary money, did you not?"

"No sir," I returned, "since we closed our mission office, I did not receive any mission money whatsoever."

"Yes, you did, and I have proof thereof. You received an amount of 600 Reichsmarks, and other amounts were announced as on the way," he insisted.

"Very well, the 600 Reichsmarks arrived but when I received the letter of explanation I sent the money to the Baptist Union and wrote to the donor that I could not accept any missionary money and that they should send all money to that office in die future." As a foreigner I was not allowed to accept any kind of gifts or donations according to Nazi law.

When he claimed to have further evidence concerning money, it developed that they had mixed me up with a leading official in the Baptist Union by the same name.

Mentioning the fact, the prosecutor did not say another word, closed the protocol and sent me back to the cell without giving any further explanations or prospects of an early decision in my case.

34. BATTLES ON THE MOUNTAINTOP

It was impossible to guess whether anything would follow the new questioning. Only after I had come out of prison, did I learn that my friend of influence had made another visit to the prosecutor and after a lengthy talk was promised that he, the prosecutor himself, would go over the whole case with me once more. That had now happened and they worked on the case, evidently with the aim in view of finding some tangible offense in order to convict me.

Usually when the sunrays came in more boldly and stayed in my cell longer, lighting up the darkness around me, my loneliness and homesickness gripped me with irresistible force. There were my two children at home, and I pictured in my mind how I was taking them out for walks and playing with them in God's wonderful nature. But here was the reality of my walking back and forth five steps endlessly, as the hours crept on slowly.

Then I had an orchestra night in my dream again and it was more beautiful than ever. When I awoke, the whole room was filled with music and it seemed that I was mingling with my voice and joining the multitude of the choir, singing and praising the Lord in other tongues. I again fell asleep, the music and singing continuing. When the music and singing finally stopped I heard a loud voice, saying: "First Corinthians 1:2, 8, 9, 18, 19 is for you." As I awoke I still heard the ringing of that beautiful male voice, and I looked around in the room for I actually thought that someone was present in the cell. I scribbled the passage as well as I could in the darkness. When the light was turned on in the morning, I read the message, realizing that the Lord wanted me to meditate on these passages and derive some spiritual food for my soul under the circumstances to which I was subjected.

As I meditated, the Lord gave me additional light, as the truth was unfolded to me. It was to be the concluding message I received from him and a truth indeed which always stayed with me as very essential.

In the second verse there are the three stages of development in the life of a child of God. First, the sanctified saints or those who have advanced far into holy living and surrender to Christ. Then there are those who have not yet taken that step but have heard the call or understand from their Lord and Master that spiritual life is not only salvation but a steady progress and an ever deeper cleansing, to be transformed in his image. And finally those who have just heard the message and have surrendered to God and are calling on him without having an ear for spiritual growth and development into Christ-likeness.

The eighth and ninth verses give us the wonderful assurance and promise that he himself is responsible to take us through into a holy and blameless life in Christ.

Verses eighteen and nineteen give us the statement concerning the value and power of God in the cross of Christ to all who will submit themselves and lay their own wisdom of the world on the altar of God.

There is a progression and a steady flow of wonderful unfolding of truth hidden in those passages, and I did praise the Lord for giving me such precious promises to dwell upon. They occupied me so much that I did not have time to think about my suffering and struggles. My path was a more even one and I could trust him explicitly that he would fight the battle for me.

There was a spontaneous singing in my heart and it was really heaven on earth for me.

Later I was plunged into a new severe battle when suddenly one of my teeth began to hurt. The pain grew rapidly and became so intense that strong fever seized me. At intervals I was shivering violently.

I notified the attendant and asked to be brought to the physician. A few hours later he returned and told me that the dentist could only receive me after five days. That was terrible heartlessness because the tooth should have been pulled immediately. However I could do nothing to cause them to give me earlier attention. He went, closed the cell door and I was alone with my pain and anguish.

How wonderful it is that we can flee to our Jesus in such hours. He does not send us away, saying we should come after five days, and he is always ready to help us.

In my desperate plight I went to the Lord and he touched me so that the pain subsided, the swelling went down considerably and I could sleep.

After five days I was led to the dentist. On the way over to the other building the guard remarked scoffingly: "Well, you did not die yet, did you, and after all it wasn't as bad as you thought."

"It is not as bad as it might have been because I have a living God who answers prayer," I replied. "If you would have looked at me closer, you would have seen how my face was swollen. The pain you could not have felt but I had to suffer very much. You were too heartless to trouble about it but I went on my knees and prayed for help and the Lord heard my prayer and took away the pain. That is my story about the tooth."

He unlocked the door to the hospital and led me in. That stopped the conversation but I trust that the Lord brought home the testimony to the heart of that guard.

The two weeks in May were glorious in many respects. I was reconciled about the state I was in and the showers of blessing were flowing day by day. In dream visions I attended wonderfully blessed meetings. I preached the word of God. Under the 12th of May I have the following note in my daybook: "The blessing of God is marvelous. I am lifted into heavenly regions. I feel that I am carried on wings of prayer and intercession by the saints. The cell has become a real sanctuary of God for me. Hallelujah!"

35. INTO LIBERTY AGAIN

The night from the 15th to the 16th of May was again filled with heavenly music. I felt that I was lifted into regions beyond. Then I found myself in a meeting where I testified about the blessing of the Lord and how loving he is to us. I emphasized his watchful ministry over us in the following words: "His eternal eyes are on us every day, every hour, every minute, and it brings joy to his heart when he can do us well." I went on speaking of the greatness and goodness of our blessed Savior.

Then one out of the audience stood up and said to me: "We have a special song that we want to sing for you; it is an Easter song. The whole audience will sing it because it is your resurrection day and a special joy will be yours today."

They sang then a marvelous song in the German language, every verse of which ended with a triumphant "Hallelujah!" The heavenly orchestra was accompanying the singing softly, producing a perfect harmony.

When I awoke, the room was full of the glory of God and I thought: "This is indeed the culmination of joy and glory, the music and singing could hardly be exceeded in harmonious beauty. I wonder what it means."

The song and music kept ringing within me and I was full of the blessing of the Lord as I went about performing the little duties which filled my morning hour: sweeping and polishing the floor of my cell, putting up my cot, reading my morning lesson in the Word.

Breakfast came and I ate my soup and the piece of dry bread. Everything seemed as on other mornings and still there was an indefinable difference within and around me.

Suddenly at eight thirty the cell door was noisily opened. I did not have that electric shock that it more or less always caused within me. The head captain of our department came in and handed me a lengthy document and also a single sheet of paper. Without saying a word he went out again.

As I sat down and glanced at it, I found that it was a legal description of my case. The charges were named and I was summoned to appear before a special court at ten o'clock that very morning.

So I held in my hand the paper of accusations for which I had been waiting so long and had been asked about repeatedly by the doctor. This was the day that I had been waiting for so many months, the day of decision.

Bewildered I exclaimed: "A lawsuit after all!" They were suddenly in a great hurry and gave me a bare hour and a half time to make myself acquainted with the contents "but my defender will do all that is necessary," I thought.

The charges, stripped of their technicalities, were simply the accusation that I, being a Pentecostal preacher, had been active within the jurisdiction of Germany and, as the Pentecostal "sect" is prohibited, I had broken the law of the land and was to be punished for it.

It took them six months to find out that I am a Pentecostal preacher, although the police knew it for years and I had been pastor of the Pentecostal assembly in Danzig which I founded years ago. I had also freely told them when questioned and never denied it. They also had taken my papers including sermons and articles as well as correspondence which showed very clearly that I was Pentecostal, and still I had to wait six and a half months for this hour. What a senseless and cruel method!

What would they do with me? Anything could happen. They could at the best set me free. But it was also possible that I would go to the concentration camp. At any rate the day of decision had come. It would be a new beginning whatever was decided.

These contemplations concerning the possibilities, left me strangely serene, as I was so enveloped by the presence of God that the whole matter seemed to concern another person, or a person that did not exist.

Peace like a river flooded my being. It washed away all the concern and fear. Calmness reigned within me. No matter what happened, the Lord would be with me and that is sufficient.

Before ten o'clock a court attendant came, led me into the courthouse together with another prisoner who was charged with robbery. We both were locked into a little waiting cell near the courtroom.

The other prisoner's case had been called first and he was led into the courtroom. I had to wait until his case was finished and it took over an hour.

After I had been in that tiny cell for well over two hours I finally was summoned.

As I was led up the stairway into the courtroom, the guard remarked: "Your lawyer sends you greetings and wants me to tell you that it is not necessary for him to be present in your defense, because the case is so simple and clear that it can be just as well handled by the court without a defender."

Strangely enough, when later I spoke to the lawyer he denied having sent me such a message, as he had nothing more to do with the case and had not been notified concerning my appearance before the judge. Evidently the

Gestapo surmised that I would demand my defender; and to prevent that, this message was conveyed to me.

The formalities were gone through, the prosecutor read the paper of accusation, the same that was sent to me an hour and a half ago. He wove in some of my arguments that I had brought forth when being questioned. I was asked whether I admitted having been in the Pentecostal church and whether I held the Pentecostal doctrine. I affirmed.

Then the prosecutor stood and recommended to the court that I be sentenced to six months of imprisonment to have retroactive force of the time I was held for court.

The court withdrew for deliberations and after half an hour reappeared. Having accepted the recommendations of the prosecutor, I was sentenced to six months of imprisonment to have retroactive force.

I was asked whether I would accept that sentence. Not being willing to spend another six months in the cell to be held for another court proceeding, and also realizing that an appeal in almost every case brings a stronger sentence, I accepted. This was in fact the only logical procedure, because no actual offense was involved but that I, being of Pentecostal faith, was accused of carrying on Pentecostal work. That was and is true. I had only one desire—to get out of the clutches of the Gestapo and have enough time to put Germany behind me.

In accepting the sentence I said in essence: "In all my activity since the beginning of the war I never allowed myself to do anything which could offend the laws of the lands in which I preached. I always undertook gospel trips with proper permissions to travel as a preacher and have never gone to any local church which had trouble with the police.

"Since some of our churches joined the Baptist Union, I have worked in harmony with them as there was no essential restriction imposed upon me by the Baptist Union.

I am also convinced that I did not harm the state in any way by my preaching the Pentecostal truth. In the whole civilized world such preaching of the gospel as I have carried on, is not resented, and in my country it is honorable to be a preacher of the gospel."

"You are free," the judge pronounced. The agonizing ordeal of being a prisoner was at an end.

The guard led me back once more into my cell and I began to gather my belongings in preparation for my departure.

Free! I had been praying and pleading for it throughout these months, but it was not realized. Then I became reconciled to my state in the cell and had gained victory over the feelings of my body and soul. God had flooded me and filled the cell with his glory until I was satisfied. As soon as I had reached that stage, the Lord began to move and shape circumstances for my liberation. Then I was pronounced free, to walk out into liberty, to go where I pleased.

When I craved for liberty with all the passion there was in me, it was denied; now when I felt heaven within me and the cell had become a sanctuary, I became free to leave this place.

Strange world, mysterious life, unfathomable pathways! My Jesus does all things well.

Once more I sank down on my knees on that hard cement floor of the cell to pray. The lessons I had had to learn here were just as hard as the cement on which I had been kneeling so many times and for such a long period. I asked myself: "Have you any complaints against God; would you have it differently now?"

"No, my precious Savior, you have done all things well. All things are well. If you had answered my desperate prayers months ago, I would not have been enriched with that marvelous blessing which came to me in this cell. I would not have tasted that sweetness which comes of suffering. I never would have thought it possible that such volumes of glory could flood a human being. I never should have guessed how a dreary cell could become a sanctuary with such a heavenly atmosphere, with so much of heaven in it. Indeed, I would not have taken part in that heavenly harp orchestra music and mighty choir singing. I am satisfied, my Lord, and my fervent prayer is that you keep me enveloped in your presence, with your blessing, such as I enjoyed in these last two months.

"These months of trial are a preparation, O Lord, for the greater trials and sufferings which will meet me in the future and also shall come upon a host of your faithful followers."

When I passed through that cell door the last time, I turned, looked back and lingered, as if hesitating to part. I took the whole cell in with one eager look. "Goodbye, you good friend. I kiss the rod that has smitten me, I bow before the innumerable sighs that passed to the heart of God from this cell. The tears of sorrow, and the tears of joy that have flowed here throughout the six months, they are gathered and remembered in the presence of God. They are precious in the sight of the Lord. Goodbye, school of suffering! By the marvelous grace of God I have been able to graduate. I have the certificate in my heart. I am satisfied. Goodbye."

Storms of sorrow and suffering are due, which will sweep over the little flock of Christ before he finally comes, gathering in his saints. I will not be a novice in the coming times of suffering. I shall be equipped with knowledge of the mode of battling against the inroads of despair. I know how Satan attacks and will be able to meet his onslaught with more certainty.

"Thank you, my Savior, for this school. It is perhaps a preliminary training I have received enabling me to go among the members of your body and give them some of the results of my experiences and transmit to them the knowledge obtained which will awaken and arouse those who are too complacent in their comfortable life. Lord, help me to redeem the time and cause your people to be more alert in these days which foreshadow the coming grief and sorrow."

Slowly I walked along behind the guard. He turned and said: "You don't seem to be in a hurry to get out of here."

"I don't get out of anything. I prayed that I should be able to stay, to remain in the sanctuary of God's presence which I enjoyed in that dark cell."

This I said more to myself than to the guard. He looked puzzled but made no further remark.

I came into the registry office. All the contents of my pockets were now placed before me on the table. I was invited to put them back into my pockets. One by one I took and placed them into the proper place—almost automatically—I had not forgotten where each one belonged—the power of habit. Then I asked to leave my books and other belongings there, to come later with a suitcase and fetch them. My wife had brought me books and other things which had accumulated in the cell and I had no way of taking them now.

Then I had to wait in another office for a while in order to receive the papers of leave. A number of the prison attendants and officials appeared, one after the other, and passing by, shook hands and congratulated me on my liberty. I did not think they had noticed me. I did not know some of them, but it proved to me that my case had gripped their heart's interest after all. In some eyes I could read more than they would dare tell. It made me glad. My heart was singing. I had a proof that their heart was not always in harmony with the harshness of their behavior. I also had confirmation of my impression, that most of them are not in agreement with the Gestapo system. One of them had remarked to me once: "It seems the only way our cruel Gestapo can be harnessed is by the forces of England and the United States."

The lovely sunshine poured through the great windows. I had to blink, not being used to the brightness of God's nature. How lovely God has created this physical world! But what misery follows when sinful and corrupted man takes the law into his own hands, forms laws and rules with his darkened mind and then imposes punishment upon his fellow beings who are in reality much better than he who sits over them in judgment.

So often in my dark cell I thought of my Slavic brethren in eastern Europe who had come under the heels of despots and under the wheels of the war machine. My suffering is nothing in comparison to theirs.

Thousands of miles away from their loved ones, not knowing anything about them, they languish until they are freed from their pain and sorrow when passing from this life into the presence of Jesus.

So after all, I was favored by the Lord. I could now sit here and anticipate walking out onto the street, and home to my wife and children. I began to praise the Lord for those privileges.

Out of these reveries I was aroused when my name was called and a paper handed to me on which the dates and duration of my imprisonment were mentioned. I walked out of the office, down a stairway and out on the cobblestones towards the prison gate and liberty.

The gate swung open when I showed my paper. I stepped out onto the sidewalk into God's free world. Several dozen steps down the street I passed the Baptist chapel. No more uniformed men shouting at me viciously. I could now walk by my own volition where and how I pleased.

How wonderful it is to be free, to walk and act in liberty; and still more wonderful to be free from sin and the servitude of Satan.

Free! Serving the Lord, living and breathing for him and him alone.

36. FREE AND YET NOT FREE

I walked through the prison gate as in a dream. Everything appeared very strange to me. The sunshine, the budding trees, the people that passed. One might have a similar feeling if he suddenly came into possession of a million dollars.

The 126th Psalm came to my memory; I had to recite it as I walked along:

> When the Lord turned again the captivity of Zion, we were like them that dream. Then was our mouth filled with laughter, and our tongue with singing: then said they among the heathen, The Lord hath done great things for them. The Lord hath done great things for us; whereof we are glad.

Strange too, there was no hilarious gladness within me. My heart somehow was sad after all. Was it a premonition of other impending sorrows and heartaches which awaited me?

A chorus crowded into my memory which always had gripped me throughout the years, and I hummed it as I walked to the streetcar stop:

> But oh, 'tis weary waiting here:
> My prisoned spirit would be free.
> Upon the bars of earth I press
> And look and long, dear Lord, for Thee.

True it is that we are captives in our vile body. The real triumph will only then come, when the portals of glory will swing open and we will march into our precious Savior's

159

presence: "Lord, that is what I was thinking of, when I walked through the gate of that prison into liberty."

Again the 126th Psalm came to me, and I recited the rest of the words which were so fitting to the occasion and my heart's mood:

Turn again our captivity, O Lord, as the streams in the south. They that sow in tears shall reap in joy. He that goeth forth and weepeth, bearing precious seed, shall doubtless come again with rejoicing, bringing his sheaves with him.

"Lord and Savior, I am longing to bring in more sheaves, to be yet useful for you, even if it will bring many more tears of sorrow. Count me in, count me worthy, O Lord, to work for you some more, and lead still more souls to Calvary. Let my life count for you once more, precious Savior and Lord, before I finally march through the portals into the liberty above."

37. HOME SWEET HOME

A fifteen-minute streetcar ride to my home is not a long time, but now it seemed endless. I stood on the rear platform, took in the scenery, saw familiar streets and objects.

Finally, I stepped down on to the street, and walked along the sidewalk toward my house. I ascended to the second floor. There I stood and looked at my name on the door. After a fleeting moment I rang, pressing the tiny button. I heard the bell ringing inside, then the familiar hurried steps.

The door opened, my wife stood before me. She did not know anything about the developments as it had all happened just that morning. There had been no indication on the previous day that such a sudden turn would come. Therefore when she opened the door and looked into my haggard face, she was utterly taken aback.

"Where do you come from?" is all she could manage to exclaim. In the next moment we were in each other's arms.

There stood my eldest daughter, she was six years and nine months of age. "Papa!" she exclaimed under her breath. I folded her into my arms as a precious treasure and kissed her. What a feeling of joy surged through me when she put her little arms around my neck and quietly held on to me.

In the dining room stood my little Karin. She was one year and three months old. It was impossible for her to take in the significance of the scene, but when I entered the room she had stopped short in her newly acquired ability to walk, held on to a chair and gazed at me.

When I tenderly took her in my arms, she scrutinized me with her big blue eyes, then put her little head on my shoulder and reposed as if she was very tired from long waiting. How glad I was that she recognized me and was not shy. There were tears flowing in that wonderful hour of homecoming, and they also trickled down on the fair hair of my little Karin who does not know of sorrow and heartache, does not feel the awful pangs of my separation.

Home, sweet home! Only those who have once been deprived of their home know the sweetness of home and family, and can feel with those who are torn away from their loved ones.

Those who have never suffered separation do not know what it means to be deprived of family life, and they are apt to make it more difficult for those who are suffering a separation. A little more of Christ's love changes that at once.

It is usually sad for those who are away from their home. They have not only the sorrow and longing for their loved ones, but must feel the strangeness of their surroundings, and sometimes are dependent upon people who are not able to feel another's grief.

Visitors and guests are usually treated kindly, but when they are compelled to stay they are likely to be considered a burden. It is more tragic still when they are slighted by those who never have had to miss their homes and family and do not take the trouble to think of what homelessness means.

It is well for such children of God who have opened their heart and are called upon to deal with homeless ones, to strip themselves of every vestige of selfishness in order to fulfill the injunctions of the word of God to be hospitable and loving, especially to those who are suffering for Christ's sake.

In the Word of God a good deal is said about this, and the most amazing words are given by Jesus himself when he says:

"And whosoever shall give to drink unto one of these little ones a cup of cold water only in the name of a disciple, verily I say unto you, he shall in nowise lose his reward" (Matthew 10:42).

"For I was hungered, and ye gave me meat: I was thirsty, and ye gave me drink: I was a stranger, and ye took me in: naked, and ye clothed me: I was sick, and ye visited me: I was in prison, and ye came unto me.

"Then shall the righteous answer him, saying. Lord, when . . . ? where . . . ?

"And the King shall answer and say unto them, Verily I say unto you, Inasmuch as ye have done it unto one of the least of these my brethren, ye have done it unto me" (Matthew 25:35-40).

This is a very timely admonition because sorrow and trials among the children of God will increase as the shadows of the Great Tribulation are cast more strongly over us. The saints will then be called upon by the love and Spirit of Christ to exercise that noble duty in a very extended way; therefore, it is time to practice it now.

In my life of much travel and work in God's vineyard, I have had occasion to taste the sweetness of hospitality given in the Spirit of Christ, and I also have been privileged and enabled to exercise and extend hospitality to others, and know therefore how the Lord smiles upon us when we, prompted by his Spirit, are obeying the injunctions of his precious Word.

It is a strange fact that I found the purest and sweetest expression of hospitality in regions where the saints were poor and deprived of all comforts of life. With tears of joy they received me and were ready literally to give their all to show brotherly love. But I saw indifference, ugliness and unchristlike behavior in some homes where wealth and comfort could have made it easy to exercise hospitality and brotherly fellowship.

To sum up: suffering and poverty make children of God draw closer to the Lord and into more expressive fellowship with each other. In times of sorrow and pain a child of God is more able and willing to give up selfishness and obey the injunctions of Scripture under the promptings of the Spirit.

———————

It was a hallowed moment when I was permitted to kneel in prayer with my family after such a long time of longing and loneliness, after that long ordeal of separation.

"O Lord," I sighed, "keep my home and family, and let me not be deprived again of my loved ones." That was my tearful plea.

I walked around in my precious home from room to room as in a dream. It had been my lot to be away from my home often and for long periods in gospel work. But this homecoming was different. Untold suffering lingered in my memory and made the reunion all the more precious.

Then I sat down at my own table, opposite my wife and between my two little daughters. It was lovely beyond words —to eat food again, prepared by loving hands, eat as I pleased and choose the kind which suited me and take as much as I desired. All this is so normal to the average person but to me it was a new privilege.

If God has given you a home and a loving family then do not cease to thank God for them. And to show your thankfulness to God, be kind to those who are without these blessings, treat kindly the ones who are deprived of their home and family. Remember, it can also happen to you that these blessings and privileges could be taken away.

As I looked closer at my wife, I saw lines of sorrow in her features. The shadows around her eyes showed that she had had an abundant share in the sufferings which I had to endure. Her numerous attempts to visit me or to bring some kind of relief and also endure such rough rebuffs by the officials, were great humiliations. To be the wife of a "prisoner in jail" was a heavy weight to carry and she could only endure all by drawing closer to the pierced side of her Savior.

The few letters received from her were a lasting blessing and uplift to me in that dreary cell and they are precious tokens of memory. The Christmas card which I received from her eleven days after the holy night, were loving words of comfort and I read them hundreds of times: they shall remain a living message to me. It read as follows:

Dear Herbert: May the light of Bethlehem even in these Christmas days illumine your dark little room, and may the song of the angel, "Behold, I bring you good tidings of great joy," fill your whole heart. At this Christmas season I am not able to bring joy to you, as much as I have tried. But in thought we shall lie together, and let us remember, "He

became poor, that we through his poverty might be rich."
Let us be really brave, as it behooves an honest Christian to
be, and even in the darkness of suffering we must let our
light shine. My wish to you is that richest blessings may be
yours in these trying days.

Your Margaret

Yes, they were trying days for her too. Our support came
very irregularly into her hands because of the severe
restrictions of the German banks, making it extremely
difficult to get money through from America. That was a
constant worry and anxiety. But she was brave and I was
proud of my companion in suffering.

Now we again had the blessing of home life and
fellowship, and I prayed fervently that nothing should again
rob me of those privileges.

Part III: Into the Haven of Safety

38. THE GESTAPO'S INTEREST IN ME

Through the open window came the excited chatter of a sparrow whose peace seemed to be disturbed. It died down to give place to the pleading note of another bird, but I had no time or interest to analyze its character or source. Unique problems of my own were seriously oppressing me just then.

Voices from another entirely different world where little feathery birds need not be troubled by a Hitler and by a Nazi Gestapo, was the fleeting thought that faintly crossed my mind like a diminutive snowy white speck of down bathed in sunshine flits past in the skies above.

"What did that policeman bring you?"

The voice startled me and I gave a sudden involuntary jerk. My wife had come into the study, and for a moment had halted behind me, glancing over my shoulders before speaking. I was deeply engrossed over the contents of a slip of paper and bitterness was battling within me for the mastery. Just a few weeks ago I had been able to leave that terrible cell behind me, where I had spent weary months in agony—agony by desperate battles in suffering and trials. It had left my whole physical being depleted and in an acutely depressed condition. Since then it was a constant struggle to regain strength. To adjust myself to normal living and acquire equilibrium and poise after that ugly ordeal called *Schutzhaft* ('protective arrest') was certainly not an easy task. Yes, they had "protected" me from the enjoyment of life.

167

They had deprived me of even the least life's essentials. To shake off such an imprisonment experience entirely is easier said than done; it lingers and lingers deep down in one's consciousness and only inch by inch can one be lifted out of its hideous clutches.

"That man of 'Law and Order' seemingly did not say much, but evidently without uttering many words he succeeded in administering a blow which stunned you," my wife continued. She had become very sensitive to my moods since I returned from the cell and sensed my inner battle in a vain attempt to dismiss that terrible prison atmosphere.

"Yes indeed," I answered. "He dealt me a new blow. I receive a shock every time I see those uniformed creatures. They are the embodiment of ill-omened developments." Here,—read this. I handed her a legal-sized sheet of cheap paper, its grayness symbolizing to me the future it offered. In her characteristic quick movements she reached for the paper.

"You are to appear at this office on Monday, June 14th, in the case of your application to find employment," Margaret read, emphasizing every word.

"They perhaps have forgiven you, and even desire to atone for the wrong they inflicted upon you in keeping you such a long time for investigation," my wife ventured in an uncertain tone, visibly trying to comfort me.

"Forgive *me!* For mental tortures, sapping out my very life's energy! Arresting me for 'unlawful' religious activity, but in secret suspecting me of spying for America? Forgive me, do you say? If my great and wonderful God had not miraculously preserved me I would not be alive today and they would have to find another object for their insults," I retorted impatiently.

"Perhaps they desire to manifest their good faith. Why should they bother at all about you? If I were you, I would go to them and see what they offer me, then you still would have time to refuse the offer on some ground," my wife suggested. She was gravely concerned, not only about me but about our children who would have to share suffering if the Gestapo became enraged.

"You know, Margaret, there is that well known true saying, 'Give the devil your little finger and soon he will take your hand and the whole being.' That is what I feel in this case. If the Gestapo gets me into their hands, there is no limit to the things they will force me into. The Gestapo agent was quite enthusiastic when he saw my passport with those scores of visas of the many countries, and he remarked, 'You have seen much of the world and would be very valuable to us.' They only want me to give them my little finger, then I would forfeit my American citizenship and they could do with me as they please." These words were spoken in answer to my wife's remark and came out of my deeply troubled heart as I clearly felt the sword hanging over my head. But what could I do? I felt something like a man locked in the den of lions, helplessly exposed to the whim of their rage. One move, further enraging them could cause them to pounce upon me and crush me into oblivion.

It might seem to some as very simple just to say an emphatic "No!" But that would surely have had the effect of further spurring their ire and speeding their new attack to dispose of me. I had to handle the case in a way which would enable me to win time. Here, carefulness was extremely necessary; I had to match wit against strength and brutality. God surely would find a way of escape, I hoped, for he had said to me repeatedly, "I will lead you to victory through the enemy's camp." Until then, I did not understand the term, "through the enemy's camp." In these moments I recalled again the conversation I had had a few days ago with one of the Gestapo functionaries.

"Is internment in a foreigners camp a likelihood for my family and me?" I asked him, who was all too persistently interested in me. He was the one to whom I had to report every few days, besides registering in the next police station ever so often.

"In-tern-ment!" he repeated the word, drawing out the syllables elastically and giving me a piercing look which was not at all camouflaged. "We have another place for you in case you misunderstood our good intentions. Do not forget that your wife is a German citizen. So are the children, even though you have had their birth registered in the American Consulate. We have no German blood available for other countries." He spoke those last words with reverence and devotion.

"What are then your intentions with me, an American citizen whom you suspect of secret religious activity, equal to espionage for my country, for which you kept me imprisoned six and a half months, until you had to admit yourself, that you could find no substantiation for your suspicion? It is evident that if you had found any tangible proof you would not have released me at all. Still, you sentenced me for that period of time and held me for investigation. Why don't you expel my family and me from your country as soon as possible, in order to get rid of such dangerous persons?"

"It is quite evident that you make full use of your American citizenship, thinking that we do not dare to employ our methods of making you willing to do your duty toward your own Germanic race. It is true that to a certain extent we are compelled to respect your citizenship, because unfortunately we have many more of our citizens in your country, than America has in *Gross-Deutschland*. ('Great Germany'). But do not make the mistake of your life, of banking on America. Remember, I would not sit here and lose one minute conversing with you if we did not value your services highly enough to try to obtain them. If I were you, however, I would not emphasize America too much; it is a hollow shell and an anachronism—it is bound to fall to pieces."

"And still that 'anachronism' as you choose to call it, has seriously checked your First Reich and can cause still worse trouble for you than ever before. America is very keen on protecting human rights, not only within her boundaries, but wherever they are violated."

"Human rights will be interpreted and also protected by the Third Reich in the future." There was a nervous twitch on his right cheek and his eyes flashed with hate. He ended the conversation abruptly. I was dismissed with the admonition: "do not let the only opportunity slip to prevent a turn, which could be very unpleasant, even more unpleasant than experiences you have had in the past." What that hint meant was quite plain to me. I had had a little over half a year's time to assimilate the methods of the Gestapo, their procedure and treatment, in milder form, of such poor mortals in whom they had become interested.

From the next room I heard the innocent, childish and silver-clear voices of my two children as they were merrily playing hide-and-seek. A new "hide-and-seek" play had also begun in earnest between the greatly to be feared Gestapo and myself.

"O God, you who have so marvelously disentangled me from the meshes of imprisonment, can also point out a way which will lead me past this new mortal danger, threatening from these spiders who are so subtly spinning around me a web of entanglement," I sighed to my God out of the deep valley of anxiety.

That was the background of events which began to shape themselves now. The visible token of my new troubles was that ominous slip of paper, requiring me to appear at police headquarters the following Monday, to give them my reaction to their "benevolent gesture" of proffered employment.

39. SORE DISAPPOINTMENT

My children made an end to these contemplations as they stormed into the room. Ruth was then nearly six years of age and little Karin was one, and still taking her painful lessons in the art of walking erect. Her trouble was that she was often too slow in discovering that she violated the law of equilibrium, and paid in hard experience by painful bumps. She came swayingly into the room seeking consolation from one of these unlearned lessons which now demanded my attention.

The day passed and in the evening my wife and I committed our serious problems anew into the hands of the one who said, "Lo, I am with you always, even unto the end of the world." Many, many times during the previous months had I come, weary and heavy-laden to my compassionate and loving Savior for solace and help, and he always had divine comfort and renewed strength for me. Oh, how I love him!

My main burning concern and problem now was our return to the United States. Right after my release from prison I had taken the necessary steps in the American consular office, but because of wartime conditions, developments matured very slowly. At this juncture, I was most anxiously awaiting word from the Missions Headquarters in Chicago, and I wondered what could possibly happen to bring about a turn in this dangerous and distressing situation now confronting me. On Saturday, late in the afternoon a cablegram was delivered to me which had been released from Chicago on the 19th of July, at 1:12P.M. or 7:12P.M. Central European Time, exactly the hour when we, in our home in Danzig, were earnestly praying for the Lord to help us out of our predicament. That means that when the policeman brought the notice, and we were very much concerned about the future, there,

172

in the Chicago office, the finishing touches were being placed on the preparations to inform us about our return passage. The cablegram read as follows:

PASSAGE YOU FAMILY PREPAID LISBON NEW YORK STATE DEPARTMENT CABLING 600 AMERICAN EMBASSY BERLIN FOR AIR JOURNEY TO LISBON AND LIVING EXPENSES IN LISBON.

God had stepped in and taken hold of the situation as he had done so often before in my life when I found myself in a very difficult position, not knowing which way to turn, and at times not even being aware of the importance of my decisions. God then acted in a most marvelous manner, watching over me every step and turn of the way. This was again such a moment. The Nazis had been very anxious to get me into their service. Most of all because of my extensive travels and experiences during many years in many countries. They also were well aware of the fact that the American law prescribes that if one does any service to an unfriendly or an enemy nation, it means forfeiture of citizenship in the United States of America. That was just what they desired, because I would then become a person without a country, at their mercy and they could do with me as they pleased. It was indeed a dangerous situation, for an application had been filled out without my consent. Had I dared to refuse abruptly, it would have signified defiance, and I knew that would immediately send me to a concentration camp from which there would be no more hope of escape. But God, in his wondrous and divine wisdom had found a way in the form of this cablegram from Chicago.

On the following Monday I went to police headquarters, to the Department for Foreigners. The man recognized me and immediately went to the files to take out a folder in which they had papers accumulated concerning my case. Quite casually and in a friendly tone he said, "I suppose you are now ready to go ahead with our plans? I have a good position for you and you will be well taken care of."

"I'm afraid that it will not go as smoothly and quickly as you anticipated since I have received a cablegram from my organization in Chicago, ordering my family and me back to the States. Here is the summons," I replied, offering him the message. With an impatient jerk he took the cablegram and read it.

"Do you intend to return?" he asked.

"Yes, there is no other choice for me. I am duty-bound to obey and desire to return to the United States."

"And that means that you will not consider our kind offer?" he demanded.

"That's right. Under the present circumstances, it is impossible for me."

Angrily he took the papers, including the application, tore them up and threw them into the waste basket. His great disappointment released within me a wave of joy and I gave silent praise and thanksgiving to my Jesus because he had released me from a threatening danger in such a masterly way, and that without me appearing too abrupt to the Nazi official. Having said goodbye to him, I walked to the door.

"There is more than one way to spoil your pleasure even in your own land of unlimited opportunities. We have taken care of that eventuality," he finally called after me.

That remark puzzled me greatly but I took it as just a peevish remark and went home.

Preparations for our return to the United States were immediately begun, with a new and lively hope that soon we would depart from the scene of extreme sufferings. As we were informed later, our voyage over the Atlantic was booked on the steamer *Excalibur*, to sail October 10th from Lisbon. My wife somehow could not overcome the fear of undertaking that long trip as we had to travel from Danzig all the way to Lisbon under very poor facilities. To her,

Danzig appeared as a quiet and comfortable corner where she was surrounded by many friends.

As soon as I was informed about the date of sailing, I made application for a German exit visa. Every foreigner had to have such permission before crossing the border from Germany. Here I was once more at the mercy of the Nazis.

"How long will it take to get that exit visa?" I asked the officer who took my application.

"As soon as we will have news from Berlin, we shall notify you," he answered with an air of finality which allowed not another word.

Several weeks passed without having heard anything from that police office. Then I went over to ask whether any reply had arrived.

"Have I not told you that we shall inform you when any news arrives?"

"I came to the office to make it easier for you," I replied.

"We do not need your assistance. Neither are we sure whether a reply will arrive at all for your convenience," he ventured to say.

"Judging from the suspicion which meets me here, I should think that you would be very glad to get rid of me," I threw in sarcastically.

"Perhaps there is more than one way to Rome, but I am wasting time. Do not come again, you will be promptly informed as soon as action is taken on your application."

There was nothing more to do but to go home and wait. Trunks were standing in the rooms, ready packed and we were anxiously waiting day by day. Once more I ventured to make inquiry. When he saw me he had a real fit of rage and ordered me out of the office.

In the meantime, I had to make my calls at the police station to register day by day, and I also had to show myself once a week in the Nazi office of the Gestapo. The latter were often anxious walks, as I never knew whether I would return. I always had to be ready to disappear and not return to my home again. The Lord, however, protected me very graciously so that they could not put their hands on me, as he had other plans for me, and who can withstand him? It will always be a sweet mystery to me that I always returned to my home instead of being sent away to the concentration camp as had happened to so many thousands of others.

Another very serious situation developed for us in the form of lack of means for our livelihood. Our support from Missionary Headquarters in Chicago came very irregularly and when it arrived, the German banks, on the pretext of some technicalities, held back the money. As the Nazis had created a law which forbade not only their citizens to give any support to foreigners, but also foreigners to receive any gifts from German citizens, we were thrown into severe tests and had great struggles to go through. In most marvelous ways the Lord stepped in every time, sending us help and supplying our needs. To him be the glory forever and ever!

The Nazis knew our financial condition only too well, and that our funds many times must have been exhausted. I had to fear therefore, that they might come and question me about the source of our aid, which would have greatly embarrassed me and my friends as they insisted on helping us in some way. The Lord, however, who is a "discerner of the thoughts and intents of the heart" shielded us from any new complications.

The deadline for our departure came nearer and nearer and we were still without our exit visa. Needless to say, my tension and anxiety increased. Those days of waiting were far more strenuous than even the time when I was shut in that terrible cell. Mine was a double task and a dual heartache; namely, waiting for the exit visa, and also praying for my wife that the Lord might bolster up her traveling courage. All kinds of weird stories were coursing about journeying and passing through those different countries. Robberies, murders, holdups and long delays would meet one on the way because of war conditions. Furthermore, some friends of mine warned me, saying that somebody had a strong desire to keep my wife and children in Danzig. Several indications seemed to verify to me that such a suspicion was in order.

"Do you have a special enemy here in this city?" an officer asked me one day. He was kindly inclined toward me and was puzzled about certain conditions and developments.

"I have no enemies as far as I know. None except the Nazis who certainly do hate me," I answered.

"The attitude and the behavior of some of the officials point to the fact that your family is to be held here at any cost. That must be the reason why there is no answer to your application for the issuance of an exit visa," he remarked. I felt that he knew more about it than he dared to tell me. Later I learned the facts and had to admit that I did have an enemy who posed as a friend of mine and frequented my house. He was a Nazi agent who called himself a child of God. As is usual in different sections of the old world, when Christian friends meet, they kiss each other. That fellow gave me the brotherly kiss to put me off guard and all the while, he was my bitterest enemy and influenced the Nazis against me. What a terrible degradation of a human being to pose as a child of God and at the same time work mischief against him whom he apparently befriends. That was the case here.

"Has any messenger been to your home?" the official asked me when I entered the Foreigners' Department at the police headquarters once more, in order to inquire about the exit visa.

"No one called in my home from your department."

"That tallies with my record," he interrupted me, "and that means first, that we have no news, and secondly, your five senses must tell you that there is nothing to report," he snapped at me in sarcasm.

"There are only six days left until the time of our departure, so it will be reasonably clear to you that I am anxious to get my papers ready."

"It is incomprehensible to me that you should insist on stealing my time. What I told you a number of times, I tell you again. I shall notify you immediately when news reaches my office. I hope this ends our conversation!"

With a heavy heart I went home and continued waiting and waiting, until finally the deadline for our departure had passed, so that we could not have reached the ship before sailing time. Then, on the next day, a police official came and brought us the answer to my application for an exit. It was a negative answer. That was plain mockery as any answer would have been futile. We were left behind. My disappointment was boundless. A deep melancholy gripped me and it was all the more bitter because my poor wife was rather relieved, now that it was unnecessary for her to go on such a perilous trip under war conditions. There were the trunks, all packed, ready to be transported on a moments notice, yet, we were left behind. Hopes for ever reaching our homeland had faded and vanished away. On the other hand, that little gospel activity which I ventured to carry on in secret was not satisfying, but kept us in constant tension and perilous danger. To remain entirely inactive was impossible in the face of such a great need among the saints, many pastors having been drafted into the armies.

How often in those days I lingered in solitary wordless prayer, just looking up to Jesus, questioning what should become of me and my family. I would have been content to remain there if I could only have carried on for the Lord and work for him. But it was extremely dangerous for me to preach, even in our local assembly in Danzig as I was watched very closely. However, the Lord did not let me remain entirely unfruitful. God's people came to me and often while taking a walk in a nearby forest the Word of God was discussed and on our knees we met the Lord and some souls who were in great distress were led to Jesus. Most of such secret activities I could not even disclose to my wife for the sake of shielding her in case she should be questioned about my movements.

40. HE CARETH

The grim winter of 1941–1942 set in while I was waiting for the Lord to open up the way somehow and move on our behalf to get out of Germany. After much prayer, God helped me to find an official who had an understanding for my troubles and he helped me to get a permit to make short trips into Poland where I could preach the gospel in some of the assemblies.

A wonderful token of God's faithfulness was manifested in how he supplied our needs continually. The war conditions and the antagonism of the Nazis had made it almost impossible to draw the money from the bank that had come to us from America. Again I experienced the special mercy and love of my Savior, Jesus Christ—who removed denominational lines and allowed me kindness and consideration from the brethren of the Baptist Union. At times when funds were entirely exhausted, I suddenly would find money in my coat pocket or in the mail box. Some of God's people who knew of my reluctance to accept of their means, were responsible for these "secret finds." Thus the Lord in marvelous ways took care of our needs. Food in Germany became more and more scarce. While the sending of food to foreigners by German citizens was unlawful, yet it often happened that food packages were sent or brought by children of God secretly. Thus, providentially, we hardly ever were without some extra supplies, in addition to the scanty rations for foreigners. Praise the Lord forever!

The time came when our support from America was entirely cut off for a period, and we faced a very aggravating situation. As the Nazis did not recognize our claim of trusting the Lord, but were only interested in the question of where the money for our livelihood came from, I knew that I jeopardized the safety of my assisting friends when I was obliged to accept gifts from them. On the other hand, if I took employment, I endangered myself, for in so doing, I automatically slipped into membership of the labor-organization, which was a government agency. In process of time I felt I could no longer endanger others at the expense of my own safety; so I threw myself upon the mercy of God and was ready to accept suitable employment. Soon I was offered a position in the office of a concern and was assured a good salary. I was certain that the Lord would guide me aright and protect me.

After being thus employed for three weeks, instructions came from the Military Intelligence Office in Berlin to dismiss me immediately because of the danger of espionage. First, I was greatly disappointed as I again faced the problem of taking care of my family.

I soon realized however, that it was divine intervention freeing me from entanglement with Germany, and from being unfair to my own country in a time of national emergency. Had I continued to work in the German Employee's Organization it would have made it extremely hard for me to leave that country, being subject to their rules. Yet, I was desperately praying and hoping that a repatriation would be arranged between the government as is usual, thus giving us a chance to return to the homeland. As numberless times before, I observed the guiding hand of my God in a sweet and marvelous way, giving me new confidence that he would ultimately find a way and lead my family and me out of that country into safety.

When diplomatic relations were severed between America and Germany, Switzerland took over the interests of the United States in Germany. In the spring of 1942 I received notice through the Swiss Legation that citizens of the United States of America were to be repatriated and that we should register for that purpose at once. Immediately I visited the next Swiss Consulate and undertook the preliminary steps for making preparations for our return to America. Prospects were bright again and my heart was very full of gladness and rejoicing. My poor wife, who felt too deeply rooted in her own hometown, Danzig, still looked with horror upon the great dangers of a trip during that perilous time of war. She could not decide joyfully to take any initiative in the preparations for our repatriation. This case always reminded me of Peter who was able to walk on the surface of the water until he saw a big wave coming. Because he looked too squarely on the obstacle instead of on Jesus, he lost faith. The hesitating attitude of my beloved wife left the whole burden of initiative on me and it required desperate, endless prayer and encouragement and admonition to get her from time to time, at least, to partially consent to the preparations.

Those were anxious days for me as things did not look very favorable by reason of that hesitancy. Life in Danzig at that time seemed tranquil enough, the battle line being thousands of miles away. True, there was not much to eat, but there was no actual starvation. Deep down in my heart I had a conviction which I could not strictly define, urging me with an almost supernatural power to get away with my family, out of Germany at any cost. Thus, week by week, month by month passed by. One repatriation transport after the other was moving out of Germany. I was told by the Swiss Consul that the call to the eastern part of Germany in which Danzig was located, had not been given as yet. We were to wait until our turn would come and an order issued to join the repatriation train in Berlin. We had been notified to hold ourselves ready for immediate departure from Danzig, should the call come. Accordingly, our trunks were packed and ready.

It was extremely tragic when finally a letter reached us from the Swiss Consulate which I thought contained final orders and instructions for our departure, but which read as follows:

A halt has occurred in the repatriation of the German citizens residing in the United States and the citizens of America who are still under the jurisdiction of Germany. The possibility of their return has become fully uncertain. If and when new deliberations between the interested governments will be renewed, is unknown. If such occurs and when they are successful, repatriation will be resumed. In such case you will be informed in time.

Stucki
The Swiss Consulate

It cannot be easily understood how deeply I was shocked. I took this as my veritable death sentence, realizing the enmity the Nazis manifested toward me. I did not, however, at that time realize that my poor wife had lost her last opportunity for escape. Only after the last development months later, did I understand the reason for the great depression and sadness which gripped me, following the receipt of that letter.

We waited until August without unpacking our trunks. Repatriation had suddenly broken off because of some disagreements and we were left behind. No more hope was given by the consulate for our return. I was left to cope with the momentary dangers of possible arrest. This time it would have been the concentration camp from which there would be no escape. I must say that during the following weeks and months I lived through greater agonies than those I had experienced in that awful cell. The waiting now was with even less hope than when I was imprisoned. That there was special trouble brewing for me was quite evident from utterances of Nazi officials with whom I had to deal.

Knowing the dangers I was facing, I would have welcomed internment as then I would have been together with foreigners, removed from the jurisdiction of the petty little provincial Nazi officials who were usually striving to outdo their bosses. Then we also could have had the possibility of further repatriation.

"Are there any prospects of my family and I being interned?" I asked an officer again one day.

"Interned!"—he repeated the word thoughtfully. "Not internment is waiting for you, but another camp stands ready to receive you very soon if you will not comply to certain conditions which will once more be placed before you."

One day my wife was called to the block unit office of the Nazi party and the Chief Nazi Officer said to her, "Your husband will be taken away into a camp, and, unless you separate from him, you and the children will be sent there as well. We have refrained until now from taking those steps to spare you the heartache. I desire to save you and the children from that suffering. The conditions are that your husband leaves you at once and departs from this city." So I was to be forced by threatenings, to abandon my family. My distress grew and conditions pressed me to decide. There was no law that could have restricted the Nazis: they were a law unto themselves. Neither was there any appeal possible to consulates as the Nazi government was not impressed by any protests of other governments. My only recourse was God, as I faced the absolute certainty that they would carry out their threat, and I would be absolutely helpless.

My poor wife feared the consequences and was very deeply distressed and fully convinced that the threats would be carried out if we remained together. It was a time of greatest anxiety for both of us and the burden increased. I had to decide, but how? There was no other alternative except to leave my family submissively, or be forced to a concentration camp which would have meant a sure and early death. In this, my great plight, I fled to the Lord and told him my sorrow and distress. It seemed impossible to leave my family behind, realizing that I would not see them again, as the Nazis were not satisfied with mere separation. I knew they meant to do away with me in their way.

I racked my brain and cried to God to show me a solution which would avert the worst and spare my wife and children greater sorrow and pain. The Lord made it possible for me to speak to a friend of mine who had influence in circles of authority. Through his help some way evil threatenings were counterbalanced, action against me was postponed, and I had a little more time to make a decision.

"Have you heard anything from the authorities lately concerning your case?" one official asked when he contacted me while off duty.

"No! Since they showed their great concern about my family's safety, I have not had any further news," I answered.

"I fear that no news in this case is bad news. It is rather the calm before the storm. If I may make a suggestion, I would recommend that you contact a private councillor and describe to him your whole trouble. I shall contact him about your coming."

The information given to my wife by the local Nazi chief, I now revealed to this officer. He very likely felt that his jurisdiction was encroached upon.

"That gentleman from the block office has nothing whatsoever to do with the sending of anyone to the concentration camp. That is the business of another resort." He went and looked through some records in another part of the building, then returned and said in a subdued tone: "To send someone to the concentration camp, more than personal reasons are necessary. Records show that in your case no final decision has been made as yet."

While a regular police official was, in effect, powerless against Gestapo plans, it is probable that this conversation was the reason for the delay of the contemplated concentration camp development. That cloud, however, continued to hang over my head like a formidable danger, for I knew I was earmarked definitely to be torn away from my family for the sake of separating us permanently.

How long the good influences could counterbalance the evil plans was dependent on conditions and moods prevailing in the Nazi offices, and on the jurisdictional rivalry among those officials concerning me. From other sources I learned that they dealt with my case at length, and there was usually disagreement as to the mode of procedure regarding me. The regular police officials were in favor of dealing with me correctly as an American citizen, while the Nazis were determined to eliminate me in their own way and manner.

41. MY ESCAPE

A few weeks later the officer who had kept me informed, notified me that the danger was increasing and that they would take action. "It is imperative that you go into hiding somewhere, otherwise you are not safe from arrest," he advised me earnestly.

In my distress, I fled to the Lord in prayer and, as I pondered over the officials' advice it seemed to me that to hide from the Gestapo within Germany would be ultimately unsuccessful. I desperately cried to God to show me his way out of that dilemma and direct not only my steps but also my thoughts and actions.

As I was waiting on the Lord and calling upon him, I heard his voice speaking to me saying, "I will lead you *through* the enemy's camp to *victory.*" Pondering over these words and my case of trouble as to what I should do, it became more and more clear to me that instead of waiting until my enemies would take action; I rather should throw myself upon the Lord alone and let him arrange his way of escape. He had promised he would lead me to victory even if it be *through* the enemy's camp. What that meant exactly, I could not then determine nor understand. Moreover, the conviction crystallized within me that I would have to flee from Germany in order to get away from the Gestapo's grip. Very casually I then made allusions of such a plan but soon had to abandon the thought as my wife objected, considering such a venture utterly unfeasible. I had to admit the impracticability of taking her and the children along because of the threatening dangers. It then became clear to me that I could not tell her my secret plans as she would have to face the whole brunt of investigation after my departure. It would be easier for her if she could say with good conscience that she did not know about my flight, and had no hand in the preparations thereof. I did however, tell her that I would go on an extensive trip somewhere in Germany. Knowing about the great pressure that was upon me, this intention of mine was not strange to her.

I then frequented some restaurants in the harbor district where many sailors spend their time, and there I gained information about the possibilities of such an undertaking. Finally, I came in touch with a gentleman from the Polish port of Gdynia, whose confidence I won. He had been robbed of everything he owned after the Germans occupied that section of Poland. He told me that for a long time he had been busy helping Poles and others in their flight from Germany. He had secret contacts with sailors.

After he was sure about my identity and my intentions, convincing himself that I was not a secret agent of the Nazis, we began to make definite plans for my getaway and I kept in close contact with him so I could act as soon as an opportunity presented itself. However, while these preparations were going on, I still hoped that somehow the Lord might turn the situation which would make a separation from my family unnecessary.

New warnings which came from friends made action imperative. To be arrested again and to be sent to a concentration camp would have meant sorrow and trouble without end for my wife and children. In such camps it was only a minor formality to put a human being out of existence. Should a flight to Sweden be successful, then I would be safe and could perhaps also do something to get my family out of Germany in a legal way at an opportune time. So the balance of the scales for me finally swung over in favor of my fleeing and with a heavy heart I made actual preparations for the flight to Sweden.

How hard it was for me I can never explain, to contemplate leaving my family behind in a strange and wicked country, and expose myself to a perilous flight in which I had hardly one chance in a thousand to be successful. However, I was convinced that it was the one way out of a situation which had only tragedy in view for me. My friend from Poland agreed to find a possibility to get me over to Sweden on a ship. Time and again the Word that the Lord had spoken to me, "I will bring you to victory *through* the enemy's camp," rang within me.

Such a flight from Germany to Sweden was not as unattainable as it appeared at first glance. There were quite a few ships plying between Gdynia and the Swedish Ports, both German and Swedish steamers. My adviser explained to me that in some respects a German boat would be preferable, inasmuch as such boats were not watched as rigidly as foreign ships and also they were manned not only by sailors of German nationality, but also by Poles, Lithuanians and others. Most of these other nationalities, in their hearts, were really enemies of the Nazis and easily accessible for such deeds of assisting someone to flee.

We finally agreed on the actual preparation of the flight and I promised to pay that gentleman three hundred marks the moment he lodged me on a steamer. He then gave me definite instructions as to what I could take along and warned me to hold myself ready for departure on a moment's notice, whereupon I was to follow a certain procedure. Time passed in suspense—then—shortly before Christmas he told me again to be sure to hold myself ready for an immediate call. Fleeing meant to me, leaving all my belongings behind. Among them were valuable manuscripts and books which had escaped the vigils of the Gestapo, and all of my clothes.

As I could not hope to return to Germany for claiming my effects, I obtained the agreement of my guide to fill a suitcase and a burlap sack with some of my most cherished and needed belongings. He also advised me to take along a little satchel with food supplies.

Without telling my guide, I further decided to take along my portable typewriter. All was packed and held ready, keeping myself on the alert for departure on a moment's notice. Christmas passed and New Year's Day approached. It was my last Christmas with my family. Finally the signal was given. During the night I carried my luggage down and concealed it behind the stairway, and at four o'clock in the morning of January 2nd, I was down on the street. It was Saturday. The luggage was already loaded when I came down. To my wife I had properly explained that it was to be a secret departure during the night as I was to go on this trip without receiving a travel permit.[7]

Once more it was my lot to go through the heartbreaking ordeal of saying goodbye to my loved ones. The uncertainty of the outcome, predisposed a final goodbye. I knew that when I reached Sweden I could not come to my family for a long time. There I stood again at the bed of my little Karin, then two years and ten months old. She had been my sunshine and comfort in her innocent behavior, especially since I had returned from my imprisonment. In her childish happy mood she often succeeded in making me forget sorrows and heartaches. Would I ever see my girls again? Would I again enjoy their beautiful smiles and hear their voices? I could give no answer to those questions. God has permitted our future to be veiled, and how good this is at times when calamity threatens. I did not know whether I would once more feel the little arms around my neck. Tears dropped on the face of little Karin as I bent over her sleeping form. She stirred. I kissed her. She opened her eyes for a moment, looked into mine and I saw the blue of divine purity in the depth of her soul. I heard her whispered utterance, "Papa," then she slipped off into that pure, sweet, innocent sleep of a healthy child. "Goodbye, my little sunshine, goodbye! It shall be my constant prayer from now on to be near you again."

---

[7] In *Songs in the Night* (1947, 1st Eng. ed.), the author wrote, "To my wife I could only disclose that I would go on a journey, without telling her about my intention of flight as it could have put her into greater danger." However, in his second book (*The Journey Home*, 1948), he clarified that she knew he would travel, but not by what way. It must have been gut-wrenching not to share his whole plan, but he chose to do this for plausible deniability, since he expected his family to be interrogated on his behalf, and they were all already under threat of concentration camp.

I went to the bed of my older daughter who was then seven years and five months of age. I aroused her and told her that I would have to go on a long trip. I stroked her cheeks and her forehead, my hand stroked over her blond, slightly wavy abundance of hair. It was an unspeakably hard task for me to say goodbye to my little Ruth. "Will I hear your beautiful and happy singing anew?" "O God, Father of widows and orphans, take my loving children under your wings and protect them. Take my poor, sorrowful wife into your loving care, comfort and keep my loved ones and grant that I may see them again in happier days."

I could not show the depth of my emotions when saying goodbye to my precious wife. Had I known then that I would not see her again, it would have been unbearable. "Goodbye, Margaret! Goodbye my little daughters, 'till we meet again. Goodbye, my cozy little home. From now on I shall roam homelessly; perhaps will have to be a burden to other people where I shall remain a stranger without a home." Quickly I tore away from that heartbreaking scene and went downstairs. My wife insisted upon following me into the street. I climbed into a small covered business truck. There was my guide, and there a chauffeur. In my last glance toward the house entrance while the car was set in motion, I caught one more fleeting glimpse of a precious, lone form in the doorway, my wife. I could see faintly the last wave of her uplifted hand. Then I was off and she was left behind. I was not to see her again in this life.

I sighed as I speeded away. "My God, why must this be? Why that diabolical hatred of the state police which compels me to do such an awful thing? Why could not human beings live together as brothers without vicious methods of hatred and cruelty?"

Mercilessly that truck tore me away mile by mile, farther away from my home, from my loved ones. I was driven away through the night, away from my home, away from my wife and children. Hidden in a business truck—a fugitive, escaping, not from the law, but from a vicious, inhuman, cruel and murderous system of hate. It was just a miniature picture, a detailed act in a world distorted by hate, wickedness, lawlessness and a wild lust to destroy, logical consequences of a world which had dethroned Christ and put up other Gods who are not gods but miserable little wretches who think they are great, but live under a satanic delusion, a diabolical lie, whereby the masses became intoxicated and insane with hate. Propaganda of evil masterminds who succeeded in injecting hatred into hundreds of millions of human beings who would otherwise have no interest to hate, but who would gladly live together in peace with their neighbors. Yet, because of vicious political leaders who are ambitious to rob their neighbors of property, goods and peace, the whole world is put into flames and is being destroyed. Centuries old civilization and attainment sinks into ashes and ruins as a result of that satanic lust to destroy in the name of "justice," a lust that has gripped the world of our days.

Twenty-two years ago I had come into this very city of Danzig, then called the "Free City of Danzig." I was on my way to Poland in the will of God. With flying colors and pent-up energy, I came, determined to work for God under the call which he, the Lord of the Harvest, had given me. I knew no other interest than that of the gospel. Throughout all those years I braved many storms, I escaped from many threatening snares of Satan; I made numberless trips into the far distant and wildest corners of eastern and southeastern Europe. The best years of my life and the energy of my robust body were spent for my blessed Master until my health diminished, finally to be knocked out almost completely by that ordeal of Nazi imprisonment when they took me into their jaws and almost snuffed out my life.

Here in this city I had laid to rest my first wife in 1929, after she had used up her life's vitality in eastern Europe in an unselfish and energetic work for the Lord who filled her with blessing and overflowing joy. Two weeks after her burial I had broken down with typhoid fever. Only by the direct intervention of God in answer to the desperate prayers of the deacons of my church in Danzig, was I brought back into life's activities once more, and was working all those years since then until World War II terminated my blessed ministry which had resulted in so many thousands of souls having been brought to the Cross of Jesus.

All that passed through my mind as I was being whisked away from Danzig to the Port of Gdynia, a distance of 18 miles. Now I was a fugitive, fleeing in the dead of night to escape the dread danger of the Nazis' wrath, who were determined to destroy and tear me away from my family.

So here I was, fleeing, choosing the least of two perilous dangers which threatened.

I was reminded of the Apostle Paul who also fled at times to slip out of the hands of evil men who would have liked to bring his usefulness to a premature end, but the Lord was in his life and kept him, because it was not his time to be offered up. I was also reminded of Paul as he, against sincere warnings of his friends, insisted on traveling to Jerusalem with a passionate desire to preach that wonderful gospel, which his Master had revealed to him. And then, after hardly a week in that city, he was in the hands of his enemies and left that beloved city as a prisoner and remained such for years, until he finally laid down his life for his Christ in Rome. Then I was reminded of the host of followers of Christ who went into hiding, or undertook perilous flights to avoid prison, sword, torture, or death.

What will my lot be? I had entered the greatest danger of my life, the future was dark. My heart was very heavy.

As I looked up beyond the stars, I sighed, "O Lord, I am not the first of your servants to be on such a secret flight; I am not the first one to be compelled to leave wife and children behind." As I scrutinized my conscience, I was sure that no selfish motives had brought me to this course, but by this act I was trying to shield my family and also myself from greater dangers and from possible destruction. "You, O God, who dwell beyond the stars, guide me and mine own that we shall be reunited soon in happier days, and grant that we then may continue for you in the work which has been so sadly interrupted."

Strong premonition of impending dangers which weighed down and filled me with an undefinable urge to leave was not without reason, when viewed in the light of the tragedies which were enacted since, in Europe. It was the Holy Spirit's warning of that coming disaster which struck that whole region in the path of the Bolshevik hordes. Unspeakable crimes were committed also in Danzig when the Bolsheviks struck there. Among thousands of others, a number of girls of our own assembly lost their lives through murder and rape. The Bolsheviks left in their path, murder, shame and destruction. As they had me on their black list, there would have been no escape for me, even if I would have been spared by the Nazis. Either the Nazis or the Bolsheviks would have ended my career, and from that fate the Lord was urging me. If I would have overlooked the Lord's warning and would not have undertaken that flight, I would be buried today and very likely my two girls would have perished as well, because there was no one else who could have been able to extricate them from that chaos in Germany.

So it was God and God alone who took me out of that danger. He preserved my life by bringing me to that haven of safety, Sweden. It can hardly be doubted that if my wife could have taken the initiative and followed me from Germany, perhaps she would be with us today, and my girls would still have their mother. That trend of reasoning is unfruitful and extremely painful. It proves, however, how important it is to get the mind of the Lord, even though some developments in our life are not to our liking. We must be willing at all times to say: "Thy will be done, and Thy will is best, O God."

Many centuries ago pioneers of the gospel ventured into Europe. They came into enemy country. Many of them laid down their lives because of the savagery of the primitive tribes of Europe. The gospel was victorious. Europe became a torch-bearer of civilization. The ingredients of that civilization came entirely from the Bible and the gospel of Jesus Christ. Europe headed the march of light, wisdom, and science and was at the helm of humanity as a whole. Cities sprang up, tremendous monuments in stone, arose as visible proof of the power of the gospel of Jesus Christ. Churches and cathedrals arose, towering above every other edifice in those splendid cities of Europe. Wisdom, knowledge, art and science towered above that of any other peoples on this earth. But that wisdom became a snare to the Europeans. When they reached the top of prosperity and influence, they began to criticize God and pluck apart the Bible; they became independent, rebelling against God's leadership, and that spelled ruin and calamity for them. Had they adhered to the teachings of Jesus Christ, they would have lived together in peace and tolerance which would have made wars unnecessary. But no, they rather submitted to higher criticism, heading for atheism. The culmination of that rebellion against God and Christian civilization was the springing up of a system which grew in strength rapidly. The name of that system is "Communism."

Communism and atheism always march hand in hand. One is the result of the other. A vicious plan of aggression took the place of the teachings of the humble Nazarene to love their neighbors. They believed in robbing, stealing and cheating each other until it culminated in that first great World War. Deceit increased afterward by leaps and bounds. Systematically, atheism spread until it became a system of government. "Away with God! Away with Christ!" the cry was heard everywhere. "We do not want heaven, we want the earth!" the Bolsheviks clamored. The Nazis shouted, "WE have created God, not he us!" Hitler thought he was strong enough to take the place of the living God. The result was the Second World War. Slaughter and deceit increased in the whole world. "He who is the greatest master of lies will win the war," Goebbels screamed and others applauded. But their applause froze on their lips when calamity struck them. Christianity and Christ's teachings had been pushed into the background. Europe has her atheism in abundance, but groaning, sighing and hunger are their steady companions under the system created by themselves under satanic influence.

There was I, fleeing for my life from the wrath of the atheists. What a difference! What a tremendous change in Europe, which plunged from Christianity into hatred! The representatives of God had to flee for their lives in the dead of night! It was an ominous sign, a sign that spelled utter calamity for Europe. The Spirit of God, the love and mercy of Jesus wanted to keep me alive so they prompted me to flee, hiding in a little truck, from Danzig to Gdynia. God's mercy abounded and I was kept alive. How wonderful God's grace is! How great a God have we! How wonderful is his counsel! How marvelously he is able to help! Even unknown to us, he directs our very thoughts and decisions. He plans for us and carries out his designs, injecting into our thoughts certain impressions which cause us to decide and follow on a path to bring results planned by him. How fortunate it is that we have a living God who plans for us. Should we not rely on him more? How sad it is that we often resort to our own understanding which is so limited.

God has the ability to guide us one-hundred percent if we only give ourselves into his keeping.

42. A STOWAWAY FOR CHRIST

Ever since my activity in the gospel work had been curtailed by the Nazis, I had an irresistible longing lo get back to my homeland. In numberless agonizing prayers I pleaded for the privilege of taking my family to America. Here I was, alone, in effect, fleeing from Danzig on my first phase of the journey home. How strange circumstances were under which I had to leave my field. Instead of departing openly under farewell functions as I usually journeyed, I had to resume my departure secretly in the dead of night. Like an irrepressible sting it pained my heart because I was even compelled to leave my beloved wife and my two daughters behind, while trying to reach Sweden, the haven of safety from the wrath of the Nazis.

That little truck was speeding on while these thoughts surged through my mind. I was sitting on a straw pillow on the floor of that truck. We reached the entrance of the harbor of Gdynia, where a guard at the entrance intercepted us. My guide must have supplied that sentry with an abundance of alcohol which was very scarce in Germany, for he came staggering out to the car, swaying to and fro, hardly able to stand, as he asked for the papers of identification. He glanced at the one handed to him but positively could not read because of his extreme drunkenness. He handed it back and then swayed as he made his way back to his stand while we proceeded. The guard had not looked anywhere in that truck which was covered. It would have been easy for him to detect me.

Some distance from the ship, perhaps two blocks, our truck stopped and all three of us took the luggage and went into hiding near the steamer. My guide went on board to see whether everything was safe. The complete blackout and a dark night made our task as easy as was possible under such circumstances.

After about ten minutes my guide came rushing back and said, "Now quick, follow me." With my luggage we rushed on deck noiselessly. He opened the door to a shack, shoved me inside with my luggage and, taking the money I had promised him, he was gone as lightning. I quickly closed the door, bolting it from the inside. Thus, I was alone on a German steamer which was filled with a load of coal for Stockholm. The shack in which I found myself had been the quarters of an air defense crew in the beginning of the war. As the Baltic Sea was cleared of the opposing war craft, the air defense crew was taken off the ship months before and these shacks simply served as a depository for discarded and worthless objects. The room was, of course, pitch dark. My guide had given me a tiny little candle and said, "you cannot make more light than that, and then only for moments." In the flickering light of that candle I saw old boards, broken tables, parts of chairs, and all kinds of old implements covering the whole place. There were big tin cans, baskets and drawers. That certainly was not a fit place to receive a passenger; no abiding place for a world traveler.

January is a very cold month in the Baltic. I had a fur coat on, but there was no place to sit or lie down to sleep. As well as was possible and without making a noise, I carefully began to clear the place of debris and all the things laying around. Then I found an old door which I laid down on the grimy floor to make a sleeping place ready for me.

My guide had instructed me that until five-thirty in the morning there would be complete quietness, everybody being asleep but one Latvian watchman who, he said, spends much of his time below in the machine room. At half-past five the crew would begin to appear and then I would have to be extremely careful to avoid detection.

As I learned later from the steward of that ship after my surrender, the watchman was drunk that night and actually spent more than his allowed time below deck, because he could not walk. He, too, must have received more than his share of whiskey to make the way clear just for me. Never in my life had I worked so carefully and noiselessly as when I cleared a section of that floor and prepared a place to lie down. Before I lifted any object, I felt around it to make sure that nothing would fall down while in the process of lifting it. I was well aware what a detection would mean. Any charges whatever could have been made against me, even that of an attempt to blow up the ship. At any rate, it would have meant my execution by the Nazis. As nothing more could be done but wait, I stretched out on that floor, but could not trust myself to sleep as I feared I might be restless in my sleep or snore. Therefore, I forced myself to keep awake. I was determined not to do anything which might bring a calamity over myself. Freezing weather made it anything but comfortable for me in that place.

My guide who had brought me onto the steamer assured me that in the morning the loading of coal would last another hour or two and that the ship would be filled and start on the voyage to Sweden. It was my sole hope that the ship would move out of the harbor very soon. At seven o'clock I noticed that the cranes began their work. I heard the tramping of footsteps back and forth right behind the board partition. I heard voices and commands. All that made me feel as if I had been placed in a loose, feeble box within a cage of lions who, just by pushing with their nose against the box would expose me to their view and attack. The cranes kept on groaning, rattling, and hissing without end. I ate a sandwich and took a cup of coffee out of my thermos bottle. My watch had moved forward to eleven, then twelve; one, two passed and still the cranes were plying. Then at last, after two o'clock the noise ceased. Presently I heard the characteristic manipulations and commands which accompany the last preparations for the ship to move from the pier. Then further orders and commands, and presently the machines began working and finally, at three o'clock, the steamer slipped away from the pier and out of the harbor as I could faintly observe while looking through a narrow crevice in my "prison."

Truly I was on my way to Sweden. Under the thudding noises of the machines, and the gurgling of the water, accompanied by a stiff wind that blew, I was more free to move about unobserved and make myself acquainted with my "cabin." The tiny little windows had been closed with cardboard, very likely by the freezing crew. These were steeped in semi-darkness even during the day, but there was just enough light to observe some details and I proceeded to close every crevice with paper, to hinder any light from possibly being seen on deck from my hideout. Then I carefully moved things aside to make space to allow me to walk back and forth in that room. I also placed a box under one missing leg of a chair. A larger box served as a table. Then I took my Bible, but found that it was too dark to read. Because of the darkness inside and the light of the day outside, I could judge pretty well that my room was a perfect counter-blackout. That meant that I could use the light on the inside without being easily detected by the crew on deck, which gave me comparative safety and made things easier for me.

My feeble little candle had been used up by this time and I was in a quandary. The prospect of sitting so many hours in utter darkness was everything but pleasant. I looked around the room, saw these scores of objects as drawers, wooden boxes and baskets, everything laying around. What kind of resourcefulness would be necessary to get me out of that dilemma of being without light? A wishful thought struck me—perhaps I could find some pieces of candles among the contents of the boxes or drawers. I had plenty of time at my disposal and began to search the whole room. Systematically, I went from one object to the other, looking for the much desired candles. After a long, futile and weary search, I actually found, in a drawer, some old twisted and curved candles of a heavy size. Don't tell me that God cannot direct our thoughts and actions! Evidently they had been discarded because they had lost their fitness in happier days.

Once more in the afternoon I carefully searched every part of that board partition for some undiscovered crevices and closed every place where a little speck of light might penetrate. On the "table" I piled up some boards and other objects between which I put my candle in order to prevent the light from being thrown directly against the partition, possibly to shine through to the outside in the evening. Now I could sit down and read my precious Bible. When it became really dark I extinguished the light for fear that after all something might be seen from the deck.

My greatest concern which made me uncomfortable during that strange journey was the fear of being detected by some daring or carelessness of my own. Later in the evening when everything was quiet on deck and the ship covered in darkness on the surface of the Baltic Sea, I made ready for going "to bed" on those hard boards. In vain did I look for an old cot or a mattress or a pillow somewhere. There was nothing of that sort in the room. I buttoned my fur coat, put up the fur collar, slipped over my head the fur cap tightly, as it was miserably cold. The wind was blowing through the room as I lay down on that floor. I actually fell asleep, but after a few minutes was awake again and turned on the other side, which action had to be repeated every few minutes, the hard board hurting my bones quite keenly. I said to myself, finally in my exasperation, "It would be interesting to know how many new sides you found during that night to turn over to."

Every night, even the darkest, comes to an end—however dreary and sorrow-filled it may be. So it was now. Another day broke. It was Sunday. A gray and dismal day it was as is only possible on the sea. There on that dilapidated "table" reposed my Bible. I reflected in my mind that it was the same grand old book, the same truth, even here as when it was in my own home. The promises of the Word were the same. They were the same here as when the book lay in the palace of a king amidst splendor and tranquility. I kissed it in deep affection as so often before, then I read its message, beginning at the first chapter of John.

"In the beginning was the Word, and the Word was with God, and the Word was God." I read through the first chapter, then meditated in that miserable shack, God's vehicle carrying me in safety. My thoughts went back to my home, my wife and children. I tried to follow them in what they might be doing at that time. I thought of the brothers and sisters who would gather for worship on that Sunday morning at nine o'clock. Leisurely steps behind my shack partition on deck aroused me and brought me back to the gruesome reality. This shack meant either death, or life and liberty for me.

Over twenty-four hours had passed, and they had not discovered me. It spelled hope, hope by speeding away from my loved ones, putting mile after mile between them and me. How strange is life, how strange the developments on our pathway. Results of the world conflict, of satanic forces ruling this world, driving it into misery, heartache, tears and sorrow.

For a while I stood leaning against the boards, my face pressed against the partition, looking through a slit in the thin wall. I watched the water as it lazily seemed to flow toward the rear. Fog was lifting a little, clouds were speeding on. I saw nothing but water, mist and clouds laden with snow. My stomach reminded me that it was time for a meal, but it did not bother me greatly. I was used to going without meals for twenty-four hours at a time, even forty-eight hours sometimes with only a few dry sandwiches. I had been in that cell where I learned to submit to the tortures of hunger. Yes, a human being can stand a lot when it is necessary. My hope was riveted on Sweden. I tried, as it were, to shove time ahead, to get on speedily. Thus I waited and waited, walking silently back and forth in that shack, like a ghost.

Late in the afternoon when dusk began to spread over the weary day, the steamer stopped. I peered through a little hole again, trying to locate our point, to get my bearings. Very likely we were in Swedish waters and could not continue in the darkness of the night. Straining myself to look through the narrow slit, I faintly saw a shoreline in the distance and decided that it must be Sweden. A warm feeling of longing and hope surged through me anew. My Polish friend had told me that if life became intolerable I could come out of hiding after reaching Swedish waters, surrendering to the captain, because then, he said, "There would be no more danger of being taken back to Germany." He was, however, too confident as to international laws. I had to learn later on, that my hope regarding international laws, inspired by my guide, almost took a turn which could have had fatal results for me. Who respected international laws in this last war? It was a fight unto death. That Sunday afternoon, however, I had hopes that international law would keep me in a comparative safety.

After fervent prayer I had received new confidence from the Lord, and decided not to spend another night in this hideout no matter what happened. Sooner or later I thought, they would discover me, and then no doubt I would have to go through ordeals not of my own choosing. I fell on my knees to wait on the Lord for sometime, after which I asked him to give me strength for whatever might be awaiting me. Then I arose, pulled my fur coat around me, buttoned it firmly, as if undertaking a trip on a stormy night in subzero weather. I pressed my big fur cap over my face, lifted my fur collar so that only part of my face was visible, nose and eyes to be sure. I unbolted the door, opened it slightly, and when I heard footsteps on deck, I put my head out and looked.

That must have been a strange sight, to see a head protruding from a shack in which no one was known to be, and I must have been terrifying with just my head visible; very strange to a sailor especially. I perceived that the man who was coming toward me stopped short, as I stepped out slowly from my shack to show myself. He evidently received a terrible scare, thinking that he was confronted with a spook, a hobgoblin, a terrible apparition or a sea-ghost, one of those who dwell on abandoned ships which drift into the Sargasso sea, according to sailor lore. The scene was terrifying enough to cause the sailor to turn on his heel and run away. For the time being I almost appeared to myself as a hero, and amidst all the tragedy, I had an urge to laugh out loud, but I realized it was only a lull in the battle. He had turned and run away, but returned with reinforcements in the person of the first officer. They focussed very strong flashlights on my face, which blinded me so completely that all around me seemed afire. Perhaps they feared that their "sea-ghost" might make use of a modern weapon, and desiring to keep on the safe side, each one roughly grabbed one of my arms, holding me with an iron grip. The officer shouted, "Who are you and what are you doing here?"

"I am an American citizen, fleeing from Germany to reach Sweden. Please take me to the captain," I begged.

Grumbling and cursing, as well as handling me roughly, they led me into the captain's room.

"Here is another one of those stowaway pests. We just caught him on deck in the moment when we came out of the 'air-crew shack,'" the officer reported to his captain nervously. The eyes of the captain, I shall never forget. Like piercing arrows they shot at me, an outburst of rage and curses sweeping over me and for moments I thought he would strike me with his fist.

"Two Frenchmen who sneaked on my ship, we managed to discover before we started. We delivered them to the police, and here is another one—this time an American," he shouted through clenched teeth and clenched fists.

"Do you know what that would mean for me if I were not to bring you back to Germany? It would mean concentration camp for me. You might be a dangerous spy, taking with you secrets which could be very harmful to my country," he said more composed and purposeful.

"I am not a spy, and am taking no secrets with me except the secret of having Jesus Christ, my Savior within me—He who gave me eternal life. I was imprisoned in Danzig six and a half months because of being a preacher of the gospel, and that is enough, as you will admit. When they began to trouble me again and I could not preach the gospel any more, I tried to leave Germany in a legal way, but the Gestapo refused to give me the necessary permission to leave. When no way remained open for me to get back to my country, and when they threatened me with concentration camp, I had to find a way of escape, although I had to leave my family behind. By rules of international law I claim a haven in Sweden as a political refugee." That was a long speech but the captain listened to me.

"Ha! But there is an 'if' involved. 'If' the Swedish police will not know nor hear your story, then what? As for me, there is only one thing to do. This ship is German ground and you are still under German jurisdiction, therefore I will keep you locked up in isolation so that the Swedish police will not see or know about you at all. I MUST bring you back again and deliver you to the German authorities."

That was the end of the interview. He did not permit me to say another word. He called his officer aside and whispered instructions to him. Then my papers and luggage were all taken into custody of the captain and I was locked into a tiny cell on deck, which was heated, however, and I had a cot to sleep on. I even received a little portion of food and was taken out for a half-hour walk during the next day. But I had to walk right before the eyes of the captain in front of his bridge. There I walked back and forth, breathing the fresh and free air of my Father in heaven.

As I learned soon enough, the man to whom I had given such a keen scare when coming out of my shack, was the steward, and now he received orders from the captain to take care of me. He received the key to my door and had to vouch with his neck for my safe-keeping. He was curious enough about my venture to ask all kinds of questions. First, I thought that he was just out for some spying, but I became convinced that it was pure curiosity of his to pry into my experiences. When I told him some details he laughed heartily, as it seemed funny to him, even after the way I scared him. In my whole life, when I was in extreme danger, I appeared the calmest, and so it was here.

"There is absolutely no hope for you to get away from the captain or to reach Sweden. You are going to be returned to Germany. The captain will get you back to save his own skin. Truly, I am sorry for you," he would say repeatedly, attempting to arouse fear within me, but my calmness fascinated him. Usually I did not argue with him.

"It all depends upon what God wants to do with me. If he has planned to get me through into Sweden he can lift me up from this cabin by an angel and put me down right into the Swedish king's palace, because I have a mighty God who has helped me out of many troubles in my life," I would counter his remarks.

"God! God!" he would exclaim exasperatedly. "I have never seen God. I wish there was one. But if there would be a God I would not be here on this ship. I just came on this ship to take this job because I wanted to get away from the heart-breaking scenes that one must witness every day in this terrible war."

"You have never seen God! I am sorry for you. Even if you have never seen God, it is no argument, weakening God's position. I suppose you have never seen your own heart, but that has not caused you to doubt that there is such a little machine which makes, normally, 70 beats a minute, and expands enough energy in twenty-four hours to lift a two-pound weight twelve miles into the sky," I answered. He stared at me for a while, doubtfully, then switched over to something else, not saying another word on the subject.

43. LANDING IN STOCKHOLM

On Wednesday afternoon, on January 6, 1943, the steamer finally reached the dock near the gas works in Stockholm and the ship made fast to unload the coal which was on board. My heart was calm. I somehow had the assurance within me, that the Lord would not permit me to be taken back to Germany to fall again in the hands of blood-thirsty Nazis, but would make a way for my escape— out of the hands of the Gestapo. Dusk enshrouded this sorrowful and groaning earth once more. Tension within me arose.

In my tiny cabin there was one circular window, or "bull's-eye," equipped with that brass blind which is screwed down tightly by strong wing-nuts to withstand pressure by the battering waves. The steward had very likely received orders to keep that blind tightened over the window. I had tried several times to unscrew and open it, but it proved impossible. I had calculated that in order to overcome my imprisonment and seclusion, I would have to make myself known to the Swedish police or custom officers. If I only could open the window and have the light on in the evening, they would notice me in my cell. And I further reckoned that as a freighter is not permitted to have any unregistered passengers, but only the crew on board, the Swedish officials would search the ship to find any concealed persons. When the darkness of the early evening came on, I once more tried to unscrew the wing-nuts, but it was impossible. Then I prayed and cried to God, and as I tried the screws once more, lo and behold! The nut suddenly loosened and I unscrewed it and opened the blinds of the "bull's-eye." As my electric light was on, the ray of it was visible from the outside. So as not to arouse attention too early, I immediately put out the electric light.

I had guessed right, that the customs formalities would be handled quite stringently, and presently I heard voices and talking which I concluded was Swedish. I knew the Swedes were on deck. Now I reopened the blind, turning on the light so that a customs officer would have to see that someone was in that room. Presently the door rattled slightly as someone tried to open it. He knocked and said something in the Swedish language which I guessed meant that I should open the door.

"The door is locked from the outside, and I am kept a prisoner here. I came as a stowaway on this boat, fleeing to Sweden," I called out, then repeated it in German and also tried to say something in Swedish but did not succeed. However, he seemed to have understood me and I heard receding steps as he went away. After a while the ship officer came and led me to the captain's quarters. There I met a Swedish policeman.

"Quickly, get yourself ready, you are coming with me off this ship," he said sternly,—as if I needed persuasion to follow him! He seemed to be in a great hurry and several minutes later we were off that steamer. Some of the crewmen carried my suitcase and a sack from the ship. I was brought to a police car and whisked away to the city, a final get-away from the Gestapo's grip.

The moment I was on Swedish soil, I had a thrill surging through my being which I cannot describe; a thrill of liberation, the thrill of being free. It was a feeling which I did not even have when I walked out of that prison cell in Danzig. I always had similar thrills when returning from my missionary work in Europe, stepping off of the ship in New York. A feeling of real liberty, of not being watched by police anymore! Nobody being interested in where I would go or how I would do things! A feeling of being complete master over myself! That feeling I had only in America. In Europe it always seemed that a policeman or a secret service man was following and observing me. I had so much trouble with police throughout the years and had to report for cross-questioning so many times. A certain fear or concern was ingrafted within me, but it usually left me when I stepped on America's soil in New York. Now, here in Stockholm when I had Swedish soil under my feet, I had a similar feeling, a feeling of being safe and being free— unobserved by police or detectives.

The police car carried me speedily into the city. A policeman sat beside me, which I felt was strange. It was late in the evening and I wondered while sitting in the car where they would let me off and how I could contact my friends so late in the evening to find a night's lodging. As we drove through the center of Stockholm's streets the gay street lights and electric display of advertisements fascinated me. For years I had walked through dark, black-out cities, and here I faced the flood of light.

Then I began to wonder more anxiously where they would let me off, as I longed to plunge into the mass of humanity on these streets; longed to get off right here in the midst of this flood of light. But the car did not stop. I was driven over a bridge, and then into quieter streets, into a section called Kungsholmen, as I later learned. Suddenly we drove through a gate onto a driveway, then merged into a courtyard, bounded by high buildings. Before a door, the car stopped. I was asked to step out of the car. I took my luggage while one of the police officers helped me. We walked through the door into a corridor, stopped before a door which opened. I stood before an elevator. I was asked to step in. The luggage was put in as well, then I was whisked up some several stories. The elevator stopped again, the door was opened and I was asked to step out of the elevator. Now I found myself in a very long corridor. The first thing I observed was a long row of doors rather close together, and I noticed the little "bull's-eye" in the center of the door, so familiar to me from the Danzig prison. I was led to a desk behind which a police officer was seated.

"Put all the things you have in your pockets into that little box," he said in a casual voice, not unfriendly at all, as he shoved a box about ten inches by six inches by six inches in size toward me.

"This kind of routine, I am used to. The Nazis in Danzig taught me this art when they took me into their 'protective arrest,'" I said rather sarcastically. I was dazed, as I could not be mistaken! The row of doors were cells.

The contents of my pockets were carefully tucked away into the bin of a shelf. My luggage was taken into storage. A door right beside the desk opened and I was asked to enter. "Bedding will be brought soon. You will sleep on the cot," said the officer who followed me into the room, pointing to a cot which was equipped with a mattress. I found myself in a dimly lighted room of average size as we find in private homes. It contained three cots, two of them already occupied. This part of the building was not a prison but the receiving office of such persons who were brought in for questioning without being arrested. In utter bewilderment I realized that I was once again to be placed in a cell, only this time in the custody of the Swedish Police in Stockholm. For such a turn of events I was unprepared. It stunned me.

44. THE HAND OF GOD OVER ME

On the way over from the ship I had pondered over the question of how I would be able to notify Pastor Pethrus so late in the evening, and I had rejoiced over the lovely prospect of seeing some of my friends that very night, and now, this cell!

"Where are you coming from and why are you here?" one of the men in my new 'lodging' asked me in Swedish.

"I am an American citizen and cannot speak Swedish, although I understand a little," I answered.

"I speak English too," he replied in my language. As I learned later he was a Swedish sailor and proved to be an interested listener when I told him of my whereabouts and the manner in which I had reached Stockholm.

Next day came the usual routine of questioning, but I was treated respectfully. The procedure brought back to my mind very vividly the agony I went through in the Danzig Prison. Again most of my life's history was recorded, as I related every important event of my life. And again I dwelt on my salvation with intended thoroughness. Telling the story of how the Lord found me and how I started out on my way of life; how the Lord called me into his service; how I reached Europe with a determination to work for him; then of the ordeal of the Nazis' treatment in my imprisonment and my release and the anxious weeks, months, and years, after which came the flight as a stowaway, and finally arriving in Stockholm. All this was very interesting to my curious questioner.

Food was brought into our cell by a waitress. I especially noticed that snowy white apron she wore. This type of service bore a sharp contrast to that practiced by the Nazis in my Danzig Prison. The food here, compared with my prison diet in Danzig, was no prison food at all.

A snag developed when I asked to be put in touch with my American Legation and with Pastor Lewi Pethrus.[8] They were kind enough and promised that it would be arranged. I did not notice any sign of refusal but they evidently forgot about it. Although I made the request several times, it always met the same fate. Again I was dependent on an attendant to put me in touch with the outside world. No explanation was given me as to why I was not to have contact with my legation. When I was released, I learned that they suspected every newcomer as a possible spy. As I had come from Germany they were especially suspicious of me. Usually the Swedish Government Commission for Foreigners handles such cases and decides about the course of procedure, therefore they did not desire to be interferred with by a legation nor by friends. Very likely they planned to send me to an internment camp where thousands of other foreigners already had been placed. There, such persons were under reasonable observation and were hindered from making any mischief.

The greatest and most urgent factor of my flight from Germany was not only that I wanted to get away from restrictions, but also that again I could preach the gospel and serve my Lord. I thought that anticipation would be realized when I reached Sweden, but here I was in this cell; although comfortable enough, I was shut away from the

---

[8] Lewi Pethrus (1884–1974) pastored Philadelphia Church in Stockholm from 1911 to 1958. Pethrus had a monumental influence in the formation of Swedish Pentecostalism. He supported numerous ventures and edited a daily newspaper, *Dagen*, for 29 years. Eventually, he even founded a political party. His autobiography, *Ett sagolikt liv* (1976), has been translated into English under the title *Lewi's Journey* (2005).

world and could not act on my own volition. An unspeakable sadness came over me as I realized that I was so near my loving friends in Stockholm where I had experienced so much brotherly love before, and yet I was so far removed from them, not being permitted to be with them nor inform them of my arrival.

"Do you know Pastor Lewi Pethrus?" I asked the Swedish sailor who was with me in the cell and with whom I had lengthy conversations.

"Oh yes," he answered. "I was at his meeting once in the Philadelphia Church and heard him preach."[9]

"Did you not say that you are only here for questioning and that you expect to be released within a day or two?" I ventured.

"Oh yes, I am only here for questioning and I shall be released tomorrow, or the day after," he answered.

"Would you then be kind enough to inform Pastor Lewi Pethrus about my arrival? You just need to mention my name and where I am from, and he will know who I am."

"Oh sure, I will gladly do that as soon as I get out of here," he promised.

The Lord knew well how obstinate the Swedish authorities would be and that they would not permit me to come in touch with the legation or with my friends in that city, so he had prearranged circumstances and had a Swedish sailor ready for me who could speak English, a man who was to be released soon and would take the

---

[9] Philadelphia Church (in Swedish, *Filadelfiakyrkan*) in Stockholm was consecrated on November 2, 1930 under the leadership of Lewi Pethrus. This church originally seated 3,500 people and was involved in innumerable projects, some of which were already mentioned: a Bible college, a high school, a rescue mission, a publishing house, a weekly magazine (*Dagen*, still in publication), and a radio station in Morocco. In 1958, the church had a membership of 7,000 and helped support 400 missionaries.

message with him out of that prison and thus thwart the plans of the enemy. What a wonderful God we have! Should we ever doubt him? How justified Jesus was when he said, "O ye of little faith."

It was Wednesday evening, January 6, 1943, when I was brought into the Police Headquarters of Stockholm. The sailor was taken out of my room on Thursday and I did not see him again. On Friday evening he was released. Around twelve o'clock on that Friday night the phone rang in the home of Pastor Pethrus. It was the sailor keeping his word, informing Pastor Pethrus about the prisoner at Police Headquarters whom he had met. Next morning the sailor appeared in Pastor Pethrus' office and told the strange story of my flight from Danzig as far as he knew it. What a strange development! I had visited that city in the winter of 1919 and 1920, preached in his assembly, as well as in the Methodist and Baptist churches, and had attended the autumn conference in the Philadelphia Church in 1937. Now the news reached him that I was held at Police Headquarters. On that day, Saturday, he could not do much in my case. Of course, as yet, I was unaware of the fact that Pastor Pethrus had been informed about me. Day by day I had frantically but unsuccessfully tried to be put in touch with the American Legation.

During my imprisonment in Danzig I had come in touch with very strange characters, and here at the Police Headquarters in Stockholm, I met these two in my cell. The Swedish sailor and another, an elderly man who was there because of his habitual drunkenness. Having been caught repeatedly, he was to be sent to a drunkard's sanatorium, and he openly confessed that he wanted to get there. He remarked that somehow when he is in a cell he feels much more at ease and quiet than outside.

"When I am in a cell I receive my food and there's someone who always tells me exactly what to do, and I do it without having any worries whatever."

"I cannot entirely agree with you, my man. I'd rather not have anybody tell me exactly what to do. I want to do just as I please, and as God leads," I answered him.

"Well, perhaps you have not received enough bumps in this world yet. But you will learn when you get older," he said ruefully.

That man, too, was taken out of the cell and transported somewhere into one of the government institutions where they try to cure drunkards from their bondage. But I was not alone very long. On Friday and Saturday I received several transient companions of like fate in my room. There were two young Poles who also had fled from Gdynia, having reached Sweden as stowaways and having been offered free passage to England without any delay if they would volunteer to be incorporated into the Polish Army. They did so and were brought to Stockholm to be flown over to England. These two Poles were, of course, full of hatred against the Nazis and desired to oppose them.

Saturday, late in the afternoon a police officer, the same who had questioned me, came and called me out of the cell.

"I am taking you out of here," he began, "but I am sorry not to be able to release you! I must bring you into another building." He did not tell me what kind of a building that would be. I was despondent and did not care to talk or ask questions.

Presently I resumed my march into another building through long corridors, stairways up and down, until I finally was ushered into a receiving office of the Stockholm Jail, as I soon recognized. Painfully did I realize that I was very well acquainted with this kind of place.

Before I started to this office my belongings had been returned to me. Now I had to repeat that ugly ordeal of emptying my pockets again. It was shocking to me that the office furniture and also the procedure was very similar to that of Danzig, with the exception that it looked cleaner and the officials were less forbidding and heartless. After the customary registration and after a "ceremonial" bath, I was sent up a stairway. Those characteristic, plain, iron stairways, which are almost transparent and which give a hollow sound when one walks on them, still make me shudder.

On top of the stairs on the second floor, I was received by an attendant who invited me to walk forward past a number of cell doors. At cell 247 he stopped, unlocked it, invited me to step inside, locked the door behind me, and I was alone, a prisoner. There was the little shelf about two feet in width on which I saw the inevitable three-piece eating utensils, soup bowl, plate and mug. There in the center of the door, the "bull's-eye"—I fell on my knees at the edge of the cot, hands crossed over my face. I lingered to seek the presence of my Savior, the Friend and Helper of the sorrow-stricken and the helpless.

This was nothing new to me. Many times I had struggled to find the face of Jesus and to be conscious of his presence. Here again after silent and mute waiting before the Lord, I felt his nearness. But I could only sigh and groan. I knew that he who said, "Lo, I am with you alway" would hear and understand even a prayer without words; A prayer beyond words. Yes, he was with me also in that new cell. I felt a distinct chill creeping over my body. Climbing up on my cot, I knelt where it was a little warmer and tried to catch a sound from the Infinite, the Invisible One.

While I thus knelt on the cot, seemingly forgotten by everybody, hardly a dozen blocks away there were several hundred children of God on their knees, surrounding the throne of God and, praying for that servant of God who was kneeling on the cot and sighing in that desolate cell. Pastor Pethrus had informed the saints of the Philadelphia Church in their Sunday evening prayer meeting, asking them to pray for me. Around 500 people had gathered as on every Saturday, and this night they were praying and interceding especially for me. Although that was unknown to me, the invisible hand of God was moving and soothing me. My spiritual ear was tuned up and focused upon my God, as he spoke to me comfortingly, saying: "My hand is over you, fear not. I will lead you and care for your needs."

Again my wonderful Savior was faithful. In these moments of distress I heard Jesus speaking plainly to me as many times before. It seemed nothing sensational to me, but it was as if a good and kind friend in great compassion tried to comfort me. I took these words and absorbed them within my heart. The awful crushing heaviness which had pressed me down, vanished and deep peace took possession instead. For a long time I tenderly repeated the words, "Thy loving hand is over me" while tears were flowing, tears of thankfulness and love for my Savior. His hand is over me, the loving, soothing hand of God. I began to worship him, Who had stepped in again, easing the weight of care and sorrow which had been so heavy on my heart; he came to me, one of his own helpless children. I sang Psalms unto the Lord in other tongues, in tongues of praise—psalms in the Spirit. During the same evening, words flowed out of the recesses of my heart and I was prompted to write them down. They are as follows:

> Thy loving hand is over me;
> It soothes and calms me in my misery.
> Thy precious hand is on my brow;
> It stills my fears just now, just now.
>
> Thy loving hand is over me;
> It turns my gloom to joy and victory.
> Thy precious hand is so divine,
> I hear thee say, "My peace is thine."
>
> If but thine hand is over me,
> Then it is well, whate'er my lot may be;
> In prison cell, in darkest night,
> As thou dost lead, 'tis *always* right.

INTO THE HAVEN OF SAFETY

My precious Savior, wondrous Friend,
I will be true to thee unto the end;
I know I'll never be alone,
Thou leadest me up to thy throne.

My spiritual equilibrium was established again. I did not care what would happen. I was reconciled to the condition. Fullest trust in my precious Savior made me carefree and I was praising the Lord for being completely in his loving hands, a hand that is strong enough and also would be protectingly held over me.

It is marvelous to have Jesus, to have a Savior in such moments of trial and perplexity. My heart was more and more filled with praises and thanksgiving to God for leading me safely through that perilous, adventurous voyage when fleeing from Danzig, and for being now under the protection of Sweden, a nation friendly to my country, a people who respected human rights. That made all the difference. Whatever will happen now, it is right and it will be bearable. Fears and misgivings had vanished. I knew, yes I was completely confident that the Lord would make the Swedish authorities deal with me justly. They would treat me kindly. Even now, in the cell of this prison in Stockholm I felt the difference. The prison guards somehow had another atmosphere among them. They were not so heartless and did not have such a forbidding look. True enough, they were stern. Can one retain a smiling face if he sees nothing but tragedy and wrecks of human existence? But they were kind, they answered questions and gave information. Their hearts apparently were not petrified. One had courage to confide in them.

Sunday morning, after the regular breakfast had been served, an attendant came and opened the door of the tell. I saw in his hand that proverbial round-faced coffee can. "Do you want a cup of coffee?" he asked. At first it seemed a strange question as I had already received coffee at breakfast, but it was substitute coffee.

It was on my tongue to answer, "No, I have had coffee already," but then that pleasing characteristic whiff of good coffee made me say, "Yes, I will have a cup of coffee."

It proved to be a real Swedish cup of coffee, the first one I had had in a long, long time. I often smiled when thinking about that experience. Among many other things I hoped to have in Sweden, it was the bright prospect of getting a real cup of coffee, but I did not guess that the first taste of such a desired liquid would be offered me in the jail of the city of Stockholm. That was indeed a new thing under the sun in my life. That good-hearted attendant even came and offered me a second cup of that fine drink.

"You seem to be very liberal in this country with your good coffee," I remarked.

"I am glad you like it," was his curt reply.

On that same Sunday morning, mine and all the other cell doors were opened wide. A state-church service was conducted in that long prison corridor. The prisoners were free either to come out or stay in their cells, to hear the singing, the praying, and also the sermon. I stayed in my cell and listened to that service with mixed feelings as my thoughts lingered there in the Philadelphia Church service where at that very time several thousands of saints were gathered for Sunday morning worship. As I was privileged to attend those meetings in bygone days, I could fairly hear the swelling, mighty organ music and the singing of that vast congregation. I could see, in thought, the choir consisting of five hundred voices, as they arose to sing those wonderful songs of Zion; I could picture the long row of deacons on the platform in the center of which the pastors of the Philadelphia Church were seated. One of them then would preach the message of the cross. But I was separated from them. New loneliness and longing gripped me, a strong desire to be with God's saints.

There in the corridor I heard the monotonous and doleful chanting in the prison, and then that formal sermon which I could not understand. What strange freaks of human justice. Here I was lodged with all kinds of criminals. My only offense was that I fled from the Nazi terror and sought a haven of safety in Sweden; still, I was among criminals of all shades, treated in the same way. God's justice works differently. Even in its severity, it is just. God has the ability, the power, and the wisdom to mete out graded punishment for actual violation of eternal laws in every individual offense and never collectively, nor arbitrarily. How wonderful it will be when his just judgment and righteousness shall cover the earth as water the ocean floor. God has a way to counteract the unjust and clumsy methods of human justice. God has proven it in my own case sufficiently.

The demon-inspired Nazis had held me in their fangs. Humanly speaking, there had been no escape for me. Others perished who had no God in their life in whom to trust. But God helped me to get away from the power of the Nazis, bringing me into a friendly country. In him I trusted now regarding the outcome of my case. I knew that he would find a way for me to get out of that trouble in the Stockholm prison.

45. LED INTO LIBERTY

Early in the afternoon on that Sunday, a visitor came into my cell. He was the commissioner of the prison, one of the high officials in that penal institution. He addressed me in English, manifesting kindness and understanding.

"You are an American citizen, I understand. I am sorry to see you here in this prison. You need not be alarmed however, for you will suffer no injustice. You will be here until your case has been considered by the Government Commission of Refugees. You might not know that our country is flooded with many thousands of refugees from all over Europe, coming over our borders from the neighboring countries, seeking refuge in our land. We do not know who they are. They might be spies or agents of other countries whom we do not care to have running about in our land, misusing our hospitality," he explained rather embarrassingly.

"Thank God that I was able to escape from the grip of the Nazis, and no matter how my state is at present, it is better than to be in the fangs of the Gestapo. However, I can hardly understand the necessity of being confined in this prison. There are Swedish citizens who have known me for many years, and they will gladly vouch for me. All of my friends know that I have never been a member of any political party. My sole interest was the propagation of the gospel of Jesus Christ. Since I am held here at Police Headquarters I have tried in vain to get in touch with the American Legation. I am not permitted to communicate with Pastor Lewi Pethrus. Would you help me contact them?" I asked the commissioner.

"Ask the attendant for some writing paper and write to your legation and to Pastor Lewi Pethrus. Hand the two letters to the same attendant. These letters will be mailed immediately," he said.

"But now, I must attend to that for which I really came. Do you have any special wishes? If you are able to pay, you can have some fruit, candies or chocolate brought into your cell," he suggested.

"That sounds wonderful! It is different from the Nazi system. I shall be very glad to make use of the opportunity and ask you to send me some apples and some chocolate, because I have not tasted such things for several years."

"You shall have your wish realized during the afternoon," he concluded and departed. That same day the attendant came and brought me assorted candies, explaining that it was impossible to get fruit that afternoon.

In response to my request, writing paper and pen was brought and I wrote the two letters. I was confident that if I could notify these two sources of my whereabouts that soon something would be done for my release. When I handed these letters to the attendant he assured me that they would be promptly sent out of the prison and placed in the mail. There was nothing special to worry me now as everything that was possible, seemed to have been arranged. A human being is not created for imprisonment but for liberty, and especially is that the case regarding children of God. Reasoning thus, my bonds were a sore trial to me. I had seen so much of the narrow walls of a cell previously that it was a horror to me, staring again at those empty, bleak, and monotonous walls. Confined within such a place, it is even extremely hard to concentrate in prayer before the Lord. I tried to praise and worship the Lord, then tried to read his word and sing songs, yet peace and quiet would not come. However, time never halts; time marches on in sovereign equality and independence for the one on the bed of pain, for the other in his palace, and the third in the cell. To one, the time creeps; to the other it gallops swiftly, but it is the same sovereign time. Only our condition makes a difference as we look at time and watch it from different angles. When we are happy, we would like at times to stop the race of that eternal march; while at other times, when we are in pain and suffering, we would like to push it along faster, but time's answer is a grim smile.

Sunday passed into eternity. Monday crept on in its grey monotony, and Tuesday uttered defiance as it slowly moved on in its leaden hopelessness, as it seemed to me. In reality there was feverish activity in progress on my behalf, as my case came even to the attention of a government minister

221

whom Pastor Pethrus contacted and thereby the Lord worked out his own plans and moved in a mysterious way for me.

Wednesday, January 13, 1943, a new day dawned. My life in the cell was exactly the same in every detail as the day before. The same little duties as I had performed them the previous day and every day, were before me. I cleaned the cell, dusted the few objects and then resumed waiting and pondering over the situation and gazed at those painful, monotonous, grey walls of my little world. Through prayer, waiting on the Lord and reading the Bible, I tried frantically to keep above the waters of despair. The cell was opened at noon-time. The same commissioner of the prison entered.

"Here in Sweden we connect our good-morning greetings with the question: 'How are things today?' But I realize it would be a little out of place to ask you such a question this morning," the Commissioner ventured.

"I suppose you can guess very well how things are and how I feel about it," I remarked.

"Perhaps my visit will have some effect on your feelings and outlook. Do you know that you are getting out of this jail today?" he asked in a sympathetic vein, like someone coming to a good friend with a gift of reconciliation.

"I must confess that I have not heard such good news in this isolated little cell, although I have waited hourly to be released. What I hear you say causes me to rejoice," I replied, while my whole being was thrilled.

"It surely pleases me to be the first one to tell you the news. Pastor Lewi Pethrus is coming at three o'clock this afternoon to take you out with him," he said, watching me very closely to see what reaction it would cause.

Listening to these words, it seemed as if they emanated from afar, out of another world, bidding me to open the door and observe the bliss and the joy which awaited me there. Hour by hour I had been pondering over the situation, had wondered whether he knew about me being in this prison. I wondered whether my legation had received the letter in which I informed them about my predicament. I was sure that if they received my letter they would surely have tried to get in touch with me ere this. Now it didn't matter so very much, as news of getting out of this prison lighted up the situation. In fact, it is hard for me to explain the reaction that swept over me. To be out of this prison, to move about on my own volition was almost too much to grasp. Hour by hour I had been thinking about Pastor Lewi Pethrus, and now we were to meet at last, and under such dramatic circumstances, after the great storms which had swept over my life. In 1937 I had seen him the last time. Now he was to be the instrument in the Lord's hand to free me from that cell. My heart was full of praises and thanksgiving to him whose hand was lovingly over me and who was doing all things well.

At a quarter of three in the afternoon of that day I was led into the booking office of the prison. They brought that ominous box which contained my articles from my pockets, placed it before me and invited me to take charge of everything. The officer looked at me scrutinizingly as if to discover something.

"Haven't we met before, somewhere here in Stockholm? Have you been here before?" he asked with unmistaking curiosity.

"Yes, when I first followed the call of God in 1919 I came to Stockholm and was privileged to stay here until March 1920, when my betrothed and I left for Poland.[10] I preached a number of times in the Philadelphia Church,

---

[10] According to Roman Soloviy, Schmidt was the first American Pentecostal missionary to arrive in Poland. See "Pentecostalism in Western Ukraine: Historical Development and Current Theological Challenges," *Occasional Papers on Religion in Eastern Europe*, vol. 40, no. 7, p.92.

there in the original hall, at Uppsalagatan 11; and I also preached in a number of other churches of this city," I replied.

"Then I have met you, and if I am not mistaken, you are the one who brought the message before my water baptism. I also recall that a certain young lady who later became your wife, was baptized at the same time." This news startled me, in fact, it was amazing to meet again under such strange circumstances.

While I waited in that office of the prison for Pastor Lewi Pethrus to arrive, in my thoughts I recalled those months of blessing in Stockholm in the winter of 1919 and 1920, at the very beginning of my missionary career twenty-three years ago. Now my work in eastern Europe had terminated and I was here in Stockholm again as a fugitive. How strange the ways of life develop! Instinctively I remembered the Apostle Paul when he was on his way to Jerusalem in a deep desire to preach the message of the cross which filled his whole being. How it must have pained him to be in the hands of his relentless enemies, the Jews, before two weeks were ended after his arrival in Jerusalem.

When I left Stockholm in March 1920, the fire of zeal burned in my heart. I was called of God to be his servant. With great expectancy, full of vigor and determination, I entered the work. Now my service for him in the field of my call was done, and he led me back into Sweden again, but as a prisoner of the Lord. Many storms had swept over my life. Marvelous blessings have often been overwhelmingly glorious even in their memory. Those years of sorrow had left me physically depleted. Yes, I had spent my life's best energy, but how wonderful the thought that it was spent for the Lord and not in vain because eternal values were created. So I can say, although my natural life was weakened and spent to a dangerous degree with my health impaired, still, I am glad and have nothing to regret except where I fell short of the expectancy of my Lord and Master, Jesus Christ.

Pastor Lewi Pethrus finally appeared a little later than announced. The meeting was dramatic, in the office of the Stockholm prison. After a hearty embrace in real Swedish fashion, which calls for repeated strokes with embraced hand on the other's back, we walked out of the prison building to a taxi which had been ordered special, because of my luggage, consisting of my suitcase and sack.

While pacing over the courtyard of the prison, together with my liberator, I was very vividly reminded of that marvelous incident when an angel led the Apostle Peter out of the prison in Jerusalem.

"In Jerusalem an angel led Peter out of the prison," I remarked while turning to my esteemed companion.

"And after nearly two thousand years, Pethrus comes and takes out an angel from the prison in Stockholm." Pastor Pethrus had taken the words out of my mouth and completed the sentence.

We both smiled heartily, praising the Lord for his wonderful ways. Although things happen differently .it times from what we would expect, still it is a blessing, triumphant victory and glory to walk with him, our Savior. Hallelujah!

To me it was self-evident now that Pastor Lewi Pethrus had received my letter, and subsequently had taken action which resulted in him coming for me now to lead me out of that prison. But while I was waiting in that booking office of the prison for Pastor Pethrus to come, the officer handed me the two letters, addressed in my own writing, to the legation and the other to Pastor Lewi Pethrus. So it was also evident that the censor of the prison refused to release the letters to get me in touch with the outside world. For a little while it looked like a Chinese puzzle—to me—but I concluded that God had outwitted them.

I learned later that the Government Commission weigh every case brought before them and then they reach a decision and send these certain refugees whom they consider dangerous, into internment camps where they confine them and they are made to do some kind of work. The Lord did not agree with such a procedure in my case, so he had that Swedish sailor ready for release in our cell—to become the messenger to Pastor Lewi Pethrus, informing him on that eventful Saturday. The Philadelphia Church began to pray on Saturday, continuing Sunday. On Monday morning, Pastor Lewi Pethrus approached the government's highest personages and received the permission to take me out on the condition that he would be responsible for my safety and good behaviour. The commission stipulated that Pastor Pethrus would take me to their vacation colony high in the woods of Sweden's Småland Province. The agreement further stated that I was not to leave that place without government permission. The next town was sixteen miles away—not even a barber was near. So when I needed a haircut I had to petition the government in Stockholm for permission to visit that town. Such an arrangement took about two weeks. When I walked out of that prison yard, I did not know anything about such details. Pastor Lewi Pethrus took me to the Philadelphia Church office and then into his own home where I was very lovingly received.

46. A REFUGEE IN SWEDEN

My arrival as a refugee in Sweden was sufficiently stormy and disappointing. Never had I dreamed that I should make acquaintance with a Stockholm prison cell. By the time I walked out of that prison I was illumined enough to realize that my lot as a refugee during the heat of a world war would not be very pleasant. Even the Swedish police officials in their unbending attitude made me realize that they did not trust me. The questioning at Police Headquarters was severe enough for me to realize that they wanted to get behind certain imagined facts which they wanted proven into existence and taken into calculations.

The agreement between Pastor Lewi Pethrus and the Government Commission stipulated that I was to be taken to my place of exile immediately. My demand, as an American citizen, to visit my own Legation, could not be denied me, but had not been anticipated by them. When I arrived in the American Legation, I soon learned that nothing had been reported to them about my arrival, which in itself, was a breach of good neighborliness by the Swedish police authorities. That which embarrassed me the most was that even my own legation officials harbored suspicions about my coming to Sweden, but must be excused as it happened during a terrible world calamity. They wanted to know the ins and outs of my experiences and the reason for my sojourn in Danzig.

Never having been a politician nor ever belonging to a political party, but knowing Europe in almost every corner, I was able to form my own opinions as to politics. Not adhering to any political school of bought, I was able to weigh things according to their inherent values—good sides and bad sides of every country, including the Bolsheviks and Nazis. I knew the Bolsheviks very intimately regarding their bloody and utterly brutal record since the Bolshevik Revolution in 1917. Their brutality disposed of my two brothers, after having forced them into slave-work because they were not Bolsheviks. They had to perish by the Bolshevik's hands. I also knew the Nazis who had adopted similar methods from the Bolsheviks. It was feared that perhaps I was a Nazi spy. Of all things, to be a spy for those who had treated me so cruelly that I was only kept in life by the mercy and performance of miracles, by God! "I am no

227

more fit to be a spy than a cow is to play the piano!" I told one of the Swedish questioners quite emphatically in exasperation. War twists the brain and logic of many people, so I had to suffer that suspicion and be satisfied in making the best of it as I did the Nazi suspicions. Thank God that he had helped me to get away from the Nazis and brought me to a country where the authorities treated even those whom they suspected, justly and in kindness.

I was now in a country that was friendly to my homeland, so all this did not matter very much. The officials of the American Legation also treated me kindly. Reminiscences in times like these were quite in order. Many years ago I had come from Russia where human life never was worth much and where personal liberty was not even thought of. So it was under the Tsar regime, and it was more so under the Bolsheviks. The only safety in Russia was the vastness of that country and the teeming millions of her subjects, where there was a possibility to hide for a time if anyone earned the displeasure of the police. There man could not expect any leniency.

After roaming about in Europe I had finally reached the United States. I immediately had loved my new country and adopted it as my homeland. In due time I had the joy of becoming a citizen of the United States in 1919, and gave the oath of allegiance to this country without any mental reservations. It was and is my country. There was never any question in my mind as to the limits of that allegiance. When the Nazi State Police began to be interested in me and finally put me into prison, offers were made to me—first, under cover, and later openly. And I had realized during my time in the cell that I could get out of prison any time I desired if I would have consented to step into the service of the Nazis. They needed men with a knowledge of several languages and such who had traveled much and knew many countries. That possibility of terminating my imprisonment was never a temptation to me, because I knew that the American laws forbade stepping into the service of other governments. Even after I had come out of prison I had my opportunities, as already described in these pages. Perhaps the Nazis treated me more leniently for some time after my release from prison because they still hoped to win me over to enter service for them, but the Lord had helped me to avoid all entanglements. The discovery of being suspected in Sweden caused a pathetic feeling within.

My expectation when fleeing, to be finally free again to preach the gospel, had been shattered through these developments. I was forced to spend my time in the back woods of a Swedish province, far away from modern life. But I soon had to realize that it was God who made all these arrangements, because he wanted me to have a special ministry. God works in manifold ways. If he has a special task for us he can get us there somehow, if not in one way, then in roundabout ways. That lesson I had to learn in a special way during my life as a refugee in Sweden. The Lord had a special assignment, a particular errand for me, and it was not easy for me to grasp it and get into his will. But step by step he showed me his will, prying me loose from my preconceptions.

My plan was to preach and testify, but God's plan was different. He had to change my mind which blocked my sight in that direction. Pastor Lewi Pethrus in great kindness had taken me into his home outside the city limits of Stockholm. Thereby, unknowingly, he violated the agreement which he had entered into with the authorities and was reprimanded. The American Legation had requested the Swedish government to permit me to stay several days in Stockholm instead of making me proceed immediately to my place of banishment. With mixed feelings I registered this situation within me, realizing that I was the object of such diligence by the Swedish authorities.

The developments tend to show that the beginning of my life as a refugee in Sweden in January 1943, was not on smooth waters. Perhaps the Lord had planned it more pleasantly, but the enemy succeeded in complicating the situation so that sorrow was added.

Through the intervention of our American Legation I was permitted to stay in Stockholm a few days and during that short period I enjoyed the kindness and consideration of Pastor and Mrs. Pethrus, as well as other spiritual leaders. All seemed to be only a pleasant dream after the fateful events of the past days, weeks, and years, which had held me under such extreme tension and pressure. My status as a refugee made it impossible for me to appear as a speaker in public, but I testified in the membership meeting of the Philadelphia Church. A private meeting was also arranged by Pastor Lewi Pethrus in the home of an assistant pastor of his Philadelphia Church where I spoke nearly the whole evening, giving a detailed account of the experiences during my imprisonment in Danzig, and my dramatic escape to Sweden. Pastor Pethrus interpreted for me.

Having been forced to leave my family in Danzig and fearing that publicity might possibly cause them harm, I requested that my testimonies should not be made use of in any way. However, my extraordinary experiences proved too great a temptation to a certain literary minded listener and lead to a break of brotherly tact. My story was novelized, as I learned much later, and was published and commercialized without my permission, causing much sorrow and embarrassment to all concerned, reminding me of Solomon's utterance: "There is a way that seemeth right —but the end thereof are the ways of death" (read: *sin*), Prov. 16:25.

When Pastor Lewi Pethrus received me from the Stockholm prison he assured me that I could consider myself to be a guest of the children of God in Sweden and that I should feel at home in their land. This assurance was made good by the Christian people in Sweden. The few days which I was permitted to spend in Stockholm were most touching and the kindness and love lavished upon me most Christ-like. One of the secretaries at Philadelphia Headquarters was delegated to accompany me to the stores to help me to replenish my personal needs. Suit, winter shoes and other clothes, even a new suitcase were selected and paid for. Thereby, I was properly clad and prepared for the severe winter of Sweden. When fleeing from Danzig I had to leave everything behind, but the Lord caused the saints in Sweden to take care of me. I shall never cease to thank God and deeply appreciate that which the children of God in Sweden did for me and the love they manifested.

The time came when I had to proceed to my new place of banishment. For years I had travelled on those primitive and often dilapidated trains of continental Europe. When I was seated in the clean and extremely comfortable train in the Stockholm Terminal, it was quite a sensation. That third-class in which I travelled was much better than even second-class in Poland. It took me several hours on that overland, limited train, southward from Stockholm, to reach the Province, Småland. There I changed trains and after a few more stations, was awaited by Brother Israelsson, the manager of the colony, who took me another half an hour's trip in a car until we arrived at that little vacation establishment called Sjöarp, owned by the Philadelphia Church in Stockholm. It is located in one of the most beautiful backwoods in Sweden, which was to be my home for the time being.

A nice room was given me which overlooked a picturesque lake which at that time was frozen by a thick layer of ice and covered with deep snow. The house was located on a hill within a wooded, rolling region. This beautiful white winter landscape appeared like a fairyland.

47. My New Assignment

The reception in my new home was very, very warm and I was surrounded with all available comfort and treated as a guest of honor.

In Sweden a cup of coffee is very essential and greatly appreciated. It could happen that if one would make ten calls in one afternoon, he would have occasion to drink coffee and eat pastry as many times. Although coffee was rationed during the war, a good cup of it was offered to me every morning. During the evening hours several of us gathered in the private living room of the manager, Brother Israelsson and his good wife. As both of them spoke English, we had a most pleasant time together while drinking coffee. We would sing songs of Zion and relate instances of God's leading in our lives. As there were only widely scattered farmhouses in the neighborhood, and everything in a rather primitive state, not even a main highway passing through anywhere in the vicinity, I realized that a monotonous life began for me there. The snow being very deep, it was impossible to take promenades over the field. The only chance to take a walk was on the little country road which was quite narrow and troublesome when vehicles had to pass, usually horse-drawn wagons.

It was during one evening, and the next day when I was in prayer, that within me one word rang out very clearly. Again and again I could hear it spoken, "write," "write," "write," "write." For quite a while I wondered over that word. First I tried to explain it as mere imagination and didn't pay much attention to it, but I meditated over those words during the night and came to the conclusion that the Lord wanted me to do a certain thing—to write! What to write about was not clear to me as yet. I waited on the Lord until it became very clear to me that I was to write about my life's experiences.

On the very next day I sat before my portable typewriter and began to write about my parents, my childhood and boyhood days. As later I meditated, I fully realized that the Lord managed every detail of my life. He even made the selection as to what I should take along when fleeing from Danzig. It had been a mystery to me on my trip to Sweden why I should have grabbed the typewriter, insisting on taking it along on such a perilous flight. Now, it began to dawn on me that God was in it. When I looked over the whole situation and the developments, I recalled that I had lost everything which I left behind in Danzig—books, writings, notes and manuscripts—but I had taken just those notes and the day-book of the time during my imprisonment. I knew and realized that God indeed manages every detail of our lives. Without my faithful typewriter and the notes, I could not have written the books which since have appeared.

Lost were all the things which the Gestapo had taken away. That which I still owned at home was left behind, except those things which the Lord prompted me to take along in order to fill the assignment with which he entrusted me. Everything I left in Danzig was lost, but that which was absolutely essential in his eyes, he let me keep. Indeed it is marvelous how God plans and executes the details of our lives. Even though we may be ignorant of the import of certain actions which we take, if the Lord does not visibly come and tell us what to do, he works through our faculties, prompting our decisions in view of future requirements.

Here I sat in this little room, hidden away in a corner of God's great realm; away from everybody, not in touch with the great world at all, here before my typewriter and beginning to write. First I elaborated on extensive notes of my life's experiences and happenings, still groping in uncertainty as to the form, the material and subject I should record, but I felt the urge within me to write. It seemed logical to me that if I write, it should be about my life from the beginning. Only much later when I had noted down many things out of my early life, the Lord was able to focus my attention on writing down the experiences of my imprisonment.

Looking back on the past, upon those days and the arrangements, it all indicates that a Mastermind engineered every detail. There could not have been a more suitable place chosen than Sjöarp for the task of writing memoirs. On the other hand, such an isolated little vacation home would have become unbearable in monotony and loneliness for one as I, used to a most active and shifting life, except for writing. It allowed complete and undisturbed concentration on my subject. The Lord had arranged for me to stay there shut away from every contact with the outside world; shut in with those magnificent trees, the ice-covered lake, and the surrounding wooded slopes. It was as if the Lord said, "This isolation would be monotonous, but you are to write, and that will remove the danger of monotony, and you can live in your experiences and developments of your early life."

Until then I had never written a book, neither did I ever plan to write one. My life was too busy with other duties in my position as Field Superintendent of the Mission. There was no time for settling down to write an extensive manuscript which would be suitable for a book. Now the time to write had come; so he had arranged it that way, precluding the possibility of deviating from that duty. Under other circumstances I should have easily used my time for traveling from place to place, holding meetings, but that was made impossible by God fencing me in here in Sjöarp. So here I lived in this place with all the concentration and leisure to focus my whole thought and attention on that one subject which was to be written.

Several little groups of children of God in the vicinity invited me to speak. Naturally I had to deliver my messages through an interpreter, as I did not know the Swedish language. Usually the wife of the manager interpreted for me.

Another arrangement by the Lord in that home, proved to be a great help to me for breaking the monotony; namely, there were twenty-one little boys and girls, children who had been brought from Finland for recuperation. One little girl of about four years of age always had a wonderful smile and showed much interest in me. But whenever I drew near she called out, "Inte!" as a warning,—the Swedish word for "don't!" She meant to say, "do not come near." She just wanted to admire me from a safe distance. She reminded me so much of my little Karin and I would have loved to have taken her in my arms but I did not succeed. From this incident we can draw a valuable lesson regarding our attitude toward the world. We should act like the little girl did, when lured by the world and worldly pleasures. Although some things might be desirable, still there should be within us the solemn warning not to be caught in the meshes of worldly things because they prove bitter afterwards.

Devastating storms broke the monotony of life at Sjöarp at times when trees were uprooted and electric lines crossed. One evening we sat together peacefully, when all of a sudden the electric lights went out and we were plunged into Stygian darkness. Next day we learned that many thousands of trees had been blown down in the extensive forests of Sweden. Several more such storms occurred during my stay in that place. One time we were without electric lights for three days as trees had blocked the current lines and it took such a long time before proper repairs could be made.

During these weeks of seclusion the Lord wonderfully enabled me to continue writing and to make good headway. Often showers of blessing flooded me as I lived through in the Spirit the trials and victories experienced in the past.

Part IV: The Journey Home

48. PANGS OF SEPARATION

Since I landed in Sweden, I wrote to my wife regularly and hoped that the letters would reach her, but I remained absolutely without news from my family. Realizing that after my departure the Gestapo would have striven to know as much as possible concerning my movements and whereabouts, questioning my wife, I was deeply concerned. Day and night I pondered over the possible safety of my family. I had been absent from home for months at a time in previous years during my gospel activity in eastern Europe, and I thought I had learned to suffer, being separated from my dear ones, for Christ's sake. But this kind of an absence proved to be different. Now I had to realize that there was an insurmountable barrier which could not be bridged. I realized again, as so many times in recent years, how helpless a human being is. Even though there was a possibility of writing to every corner of the earth, I found that I was completely helpless, not knowing whether my letters reached my family; neither did I know whether they had received knowledge of my whereabouts.

Slowly the situation began to pry and eat into my very soul. I was surrounded with all the comforts that an average person could wish for; I had ample good food to eat, but every time I sat down to a meal there stood before me, my slender, worn-down wife and my two children. They had only that coarse and black bread to eat, and not enough butter. Milk I knew was very scarce. All this knowledge resulted in making it impossible for me at times to swallow my food. I had to bear that gnawing and hammering sorrow within me, carried it into my dreams and lived through distressing scenes. In one dream I heard my wife say, "Yes, if I would have gone with you to the United States, then this would not have happened." It all made me ponder over the question of what might have happened in Danzig since I left that city and my family behind. New tortures came upon me from day to day as all seemed so hopeless. Prayer often did not bring relief but made my feeling of distress and lonesomeness stronger. These battles usually ended for me when I succeeded in forcing myself into the line of my former experiences of victory, so that I could continue to write, forgetting for hours that which oppressed my mind so terribly.

They claimed that this was a mild winter. In my estimation there was an abundance of snow, but they told me that the snow had been twice and even three times higher than it was that first winter I spent in Sweden. Day by day I gazed at that lake which, during the winter, could hardly be recognized as being different from the adjoining landscape except that it was so very even and smooth. Nothing was seen, not even the ice—just snow—and snow covering everything upon the earth. When a fresh snow fell and the weather wasn't too cold, even the trees were laden with snow and nothing but a white world was visible as far as the eye could reach. Warmer days came on February 26. The snow began to melt, and in one afternoon a great change took place on the lake. It all happened in an incredibly short time, as suddenly the ice cover broke up and was swallowed up by the water. The lake in its beauty and natural appearance was before me without any ice being visible. How strange nature works. I began to realize how beautiful nature must be in this section during the summer months.

In the course of time the snow melted away and I was again able to be out in God's nature. There was a little hill about 300 yards away from the house. It sloped down abruptly into the water. Giant rocks protruded in bizarre shapes. One of these rocks especially fascinated me and I found it a desirable place to sit down and read my Bible, and there I also knelt in prayer quite often. It became to me a hallowed spot, as I always loved to pray and worship my God in his nature, where I was not surrounded by the walls of a house. Trees often talked to me, their gnarled, bent or wounded appearance, healed over, contained messages of truth which I absorbed while walking about in God's wonderful outdoors. I had to seek such meditations to occupy my mind in spiritual contemplation, in order to overcome the danger of melancholy.

My birthday came. My wife had always had loving and thoughtful surprises for me on that day. What would it be like today, shut away amongst strangers who could not be expected to have special interest for my personal red-letter days? Melancholy seized me with an iron grip and I felt despondent and forsaken. I could not even flee into writing about my life. This continued a few days until a wonderful relief came when I received a letter from my wife, and also a birthday card. The Lord was mindful of me, and the spell was broken. It was not a long letter and did not contain much news, but the very fact that my wife had written, telling me that my girls were in fairly good health was in itself wonderful news. I was also informed that they had received a food package, the first of several which I had sent—food that was so desperately needed there. It made me rejoice; I was greatly relieved, and I worshipped the Lord for his wonderful help.

As the weeks dragged on and my sojourn in that place of banishment in the back woods added up into two months and more, I had a terrific battle against loneliness and despondency. I could not speak Swedish, even though I could understand a great deal when I heard it spoken carefully. Conversation with the manager and his wife in English was the only possibility for me to interrupt my solitary life of quietude. By the wise planning of my Jesus, I had something to flee into. It was the writing about my life's experiences. I became so engrossed in my subject that I lived through again those scenes in my life during the time of my imprisonment; felt that agony and distress, and also the blessings again which swept over me in those periods. At such times the hours passed by without any special notice. When finally I received an answer to a petition obtaining a permit to visit the next town nearly twenty miles away, it assumed the proportions of a sensation. Together with the manager of the home, we started out to visit the town called Vetlanda. My main object of the trip was to get a haircut after over two month's time.

That day also gave me the opportunity to spend a few hours in a Swedish private home and I enjoyed the hospitality of Swedish children of God. Conversation was impossible, but we somehow made ourselves understood. Those dear folks were greatly elated to have a real prisoner of the Lord in their home. I was an object of curiosity. It was sensational to the Swedish saints to see a brother in the Lord who had actually escaped from the Nazi grip and from their prison.

The American Legation required my presence in Stockholm to have my passport and my status in Sweden as a refugee examined. So I received a summons to come to Stockholm, which was a very pleasant call for me and a very welcome change. On April 7, 1943, I started out from Sjöarp and arrived in the capital city of Sweden on the next morning. In a Christian hostelry I made my abode.

The "vacation home" in the backwoods of Sweden which had been my home for three months was offered for sale. New property had been purchased by the Philadelphia Church some twenty-two (English) miles from Stockholm.

This meant that I was not to return to Sjöarp, but would stay in the new place which was to become a private Christian high school of the Philadelphia Church in Stockholm.

The weeks following my return from the vacation home were spent in Stockholm, but did not rescue me from loneliness. There, while moving about in the midst of thousands of people I experienced extreme and utter loneliness. The constant gnawing worry about my family from whom I had no detailed news kept me in a state of agitation and nervousness. I remained a stranger mainly because I did not speak the Swedish language. I was well taken care of by the missionary-secretary of the Philadelphia Church who had orders to pay my bills in the hostelry. I received pocket money and even clothes were purchased for me, which I shall always consider and esteem as acts of kindness and love, but what I needed most was fellowship with the saints, which meant not only fellowship in church meetings but the friendship of individual Christians.

It was hard for me to remain in the hotel room for any length of time. Restlessness drove me out into the parks and streets. For hours I would walk about, thus at least being diverted from my own worry by observing city life with its kaleidoscopic variations. How wonderfully relieving it was when the Lord lifted me up into his presence in times of prayer; when I could forget the world of sadness and bask in the sunshine of his love. Those were times when I could repose without feeling the weight of great and almost overwhelming concern over the welfare of my absent loved ones. In my deepest troubles I realized that although friends may be concerned about us in our sorrows, they cannot share our burdens unless they too, have a special sorrow upon their heart. Sorrow must usually be borne alone. A mother perhaps is the only one who will not grow weary, but will really try to bear at least a part of her child's burden because love teaches her how.

The Easter season of 1943 I shall never forget. As the Saturday before Easter dragged on, I was gripped by a deadly loneliness and despondency. I went out and walked about on the streets and in the park to get some relief and distraction. On the eve of such an approaching feast everybody is busy with himself and with the immediate members of his family. I missed my loved ones, or at least a cozy family circle. I was desperately longing for the fellowship of a Christian family. At dusk I walked over once more to the Philadelphia Church office to ask whether some mail had arrived. The janitor said when I encountered him, "Oh, I am glad that you came once more. I have something for you." He walked away and presently came with a little package and handed it to me as an Easter greeting. Upon reaching my room I opened the package and found it contained a box in the shape of an Easter egg, very nicely decorated and filled with chocolates. This was the only Easter greeting I received. Nothing had reached me from my family.

I went down on my knees praising God that someone had remembered me. I was not without an Easter greeting after all. One of God's people had shown me kindness and love. How it is possible that such a little token of friendship from another child of God tan cause tears of thankfulness and appreciation to flow, can ordinarily not be understood, but so it is. I still have that Easter egg which contained those timely candies and chocolates, and I have often refilled the box in memory of that brother and sister—a souvenir, a visible token of kindness bestowed upon a lonely servant of God by saints there in Stockholm who, in their Easter happiness, were mindful of one deprived of his family.

As I was a refugee, it was not possible for me to be active and speak in the churches. Whenever I had an invitation to speak, I was obliged to submit such invitations—or if it was more than a speaking engagement, the whole itinerary—to the Foreign Department, then a traveling permit was issued. These formalities made traveling in gospel work quite annoying so that it seemed most advisable for me to remain at home. That was exactly what the Lord desired, but such life was monotonous in the extreme.

Another event contributed more disappointment and disheartening; namely, the American Legation had received orders to take away the American passports from American refugees who happened to flee to Sweden illegally. In my case, things were aggravated because, when I arrived in Stockholm, I was ordered to return to the United States, which I had to refuse because my family was in Danzig. "How can I return and move into safety while my family is in mortal danger? I have to stand by and try to get my wife and children out of Germany," I said emphatically.

"Then we are obliged to take your passport away from you in order to keep you from the temptation of making further illegal use of it while away from home."

"But then, I am practically a man without a country. Does it mean that I am liable to lose my citizenship?" I asked anxiously.

"That all depends upon your attitude. Whenever you come to this office and prove that you are returning to the United States, your passport will be returned to you," he assured me.

"Can you give me that statement in writing?" I ventured to ask.

"Yes, if you desire I will give you a written statement," the consul stated.

"Thank you, that satisfies me."

I left the legation with a statement in letter-form reading as follows:

Mr. Gustaf Schmidt: The Legation wishes to inform you that acting on instructions from the Department of State,

Washington, D.C., it has been necessary to take up your American passport. As an American citizen, however, you are entitled to receive a validation of your American passport at such a time as you declare your intention and present proof thereof to return to the United States to reside.

DAVID H. MCKILLOP
American Vice-Consul

That letter satisfied me. I knew that I would not lose my American citizenship and that as soon as I could return to America, my passport would again be handed to me. But it was an unbearable thought that I should even contemplate returning to America in safety while my wife and children were in Danzig under the power and domination of the Nazis. When I came to Sweden, I was confident that I would be able to do something to get them out of the clutches of the Nazis, but I soon was compelled to realize that I could do but very little. No one was able to give me any hope as the Nazis did not consider international laws and rules to be binding. I could not even get in vital touch with my family. The few letters which came to me in my anxious condition were so meaningless. Neither did I have any assurance they received my letters. Wherever there seemed to be the possibility or a ray of hope to help my loved ones, I tried to avail myself of such opportunity, but all was in vain. The only satisfaction that I had was in sending food packages to them, although I seldom received any acknowledgment since letter-writing was very much restricted.

49. NEW HOMES AND NEW PROBLEMS

During the summer I spent several months in the new vacation home which the Philadelphia Church had purchased. It was an ancient castle, built by a Swedish nobleman.[11] Later it changed hands until finally it came into the ownership of the church. There I finished the manuscript, *Songs in the Night,* and also started my other writings, *Faithful Unto Death,* dealing with the sufferings of the saints in Russia during the time of the last Tsar.

The castle Kaggeholm was surrounded by beautiful parks and forests. I loved outdoor work and so I became greatly engrossed in working in the garden and park surrounding the castle and also in the nearby woods. However, it was not God's will that I should spend too much time in other occupations, as he had delegated me to write. So, in order to give me a reminder, the Lord permitted it to happen that I hurt my knee quite severely, from which water developed in the knee-joint, making it difficult for me to walk. I could walk up the stairway only under severe pain. For a year and a half I could only go about with the help of a cane. My work in the park was thereby ended, but I could write and did make ample use of the time recording my experiences.

Kaggeholm was twenty-two (English) miles distance from Stockholm, located on a little island in the beautiful and picturesque lake-region called Mälaren, which is connected with the Baltic Sea from the Scheeres, forming hundreds of small and greater islands extending far inland. I often had occasion to visit the city of Stockholm, calling on the legation or seeking contact with authorities in my endless, yet fruitless attempt to do something which would help my family or bring them out of Germany to Sweden.

It was always a problem to find a night's lodging. I dreaded hotels and the loneliness which I was always

---

[11] Kaggeholm Castle (Swedish, *Kaggeholms Slott*) was built in the 1720s on the island of Helgö by Count Lars Kagg (1595–1661). The castle was purchased by Philadelphia Church to house a Bible training center.

battling. As I believed that the Lord could find a way, I earnestly prayed to God for a solution. One day I renewed my acquaintance with a faithful brother whom I had first met in 1919, when I came to Europe for the first time on my way into my missionary activity. During the years this brother had become a very successful businessman, now being the head of a wholesale firm. When he learned that I had difficulty in finding lodgings on my visits to Stockholm, he very cordially invited me to stay with him, saying; "Just make this your home. Come and go whenever you please. We will be glad to have you stay with us on such occasions." This development came directly as an answer to my prayers. Our Savior and Elder Brother, Jesus Christ, had opened to me a wonderful place to stay. That precious family extended their hospitality to one of God's homeless elect, who through tragic events had lost home and family. He planted that Christ-love into the hearts of these true saints for which I praise God and give honor and glory to him for his wonderful help. Hallelujah!

That home was a wonderful place of prayer where I spent many lovely hours in fellowship and with the precious Word of God. I shall always cherish the memory of the kindness and hospitality received in that cozy home. How wonderful it is for a child of God when the Lord is permitted to impart the secret and love of hospitality to God's saints! The Word of God states that such have unawares accommodated angels (Heb. 13:2). I am sure the reward of that family in Stockholm will be great on that day when we shall stand before Christ our Savior and Judge and hear his, "Well done, thou good and faithful servants."

As time passed on, restrictions were not applied to me so rigidly, making it possible for me to accept invitations more freely, and it was always a very pleasant change when I was permitted to speak in different assemblies and make gospel trips through Swedish provinces. In the fall of 1943, the Lord opened a new home for me in the village of Möklinta, about one hundred (English) miles northwest of Stockholm. There in Möklinta I settled down. The Lord had especially appointed that lovely place of rest and refuge for me, where I had complete liberty and the feeling of being at home. The hostess, Sister Hildur, as she was called, was a "Martha" and "Mary" combined in one person. She managed a telephone exchange for many years and was beset with many duties which at times were almost crushing; but I never saw her upset or impatient, but always willing to serve and ready to please. In my memory I class her with those precious members within Christ's body who belong to the nobility in God's realm. In her unassuming attitude, it is easy to classify her in the category of those who will say to Jesus:

"Then shall the righteous answer him, saying, Lord, when saw we thee a hungered, and fed thee? or thirsty, and gave thee drink? When saw we thee a stranger, and took thee in? or naked, and clothed thee? Or when saw we thee sick, or in prison, and came unto thee? And the King shall answer and say unto them, Verily I say unto you, Inasmuch as ye have done it unto one of the least of these my brethren, ye have done it unto me."

Matt. 25:37-40.

Often, very often I said to God in my prayers in Sweden: "Lord, how great is your love to me, that you have opened this precious and quiet home of the two sisters for me, where I can really feel at home, can relax and am treated with such kindness."

In that noble home I finished my manuscript, *Faithful unto Death*. There I also wrote my other manuscript, *God in My Life*, dealing with my life's experiences in early years. I further wrote, *God Finds Ways*, dealing with the trials of a young girl whose parents opposed her very bitterly after she was saved. God had delegated me to write and he, in his compassionate love, led me to a home where I had the right background and surroundings to give me the quiet and proper relaxation. Praise his holy and wonderful name forever!

My first book, *Songs in the Night*, was published by the Evangeliipress in Örebro, Sweden, in October 1943. Dear Brother Florantius Hällzon and his son, Ingemar, acted very kindly and brotherly and the book had a very warm reception among the children of God in Sweden. Soon new editions were necessary, and in the winter of 1945, the fifth edition appeared. My other books followed, one each year in succession.[12] All of them were very kindly received. Many letters of thanks were sent to me and a number of cases came to my knowledge of people getting saved, others receiving healing in their body, and backsliders were reclaimed through the reading of these books. That was positively God's work alone. He helped, yea, inspired me in a wonderful way, bridging my inability and lack of experience in writing, proving also in my case that he can do whatever he decrees. I positively could not claim to be a special writer. I ascribe all that which is commendable to my loving heavenly Father who enabled me to write, and paved the way for my books into the hearts of God's people in Sweden, and later, in Norway and here in our United States.

Möklinta meant complete isolation from the outside world, lovingly arranged by the Lord. Although the folks in

---

[12] G. Herbert Schmidt wrote at least five books; however, they were all first published in Swedish, and English translations have never appeared for *Faithful unto Death*, *God in My Life*, or *God Finds Ways*. *Faithful unto Death* appeared in Swedish, Norwegian, and Finnish. He also translated into German a book of hymns, which was never published.

whose home I dwelt had a telephone exchange which gave them very much to do, peace and tranquility dwelt there and I was much strengthened and could concentrate on my writings fully without disturbance. God had done all things well and I experienced and thoroughly enjoyed the wonderful winters which turned the countryside on every hand into a real fairyland.

The Swedish autumn is very beautiful. Trees take on a fiery hue until night frosts come and the leaves fall to the ground. When I arrived in Möklinta and made my home there, winds often rattled the windows. In November, snow began to fall and nature was utterly changed—being transformed and blanketed in immaculate white. My room faced the north and I could see the beauty of the sunsets and the lingering lights in the evenings which keep darkness away until ten and even eleven o'clock—after which partial darkness comes gradually. I would walk up the narrow stairway to the second floor of that nearly one-hundred-year-old house where there was quite a spacious landing around the stairway. From there I entered my room through another door. The great stove made of white Dutch tile was very conspicuous, almost reaching to the ceiling. Wood is available in great abundance in Sweden and so my room was heated with wood. Through two medium-sized windows I could observe the northern sky in the evening. The frequent appearance of northern lights in the skies caused me to meditate upon God's mysteries of nature; also displayed through the majestic sweep of light coming from his hidden source of electric storehouses with indescribable beauty of coloring and kaleidoscopic changes.

The Lord had very lovingly arranged a place of quietness and blessing for me where I could relax while accomplishing the work which he had bidden me to do. Yet, anxiety followed me with depressive onslaughts, even to that peaceful place of abode.

During the summer I had received a short note from my wife, saying that she intended to visit friends in Lodz during Whitsuntide. After this message had reached me, everything remained silent for a long time. Only early in the fall did I receive another note from her in which she wrote as follows:

> Since a few days before Whitsun, I have been very ill, suffering from a nerve paralysis which has also affected my heart. My fever was up to and above 104° for several weeks, but now I am a little better—enough so that I can write this letter. I manage to walk to the physicians, although it is very hard for me. My illness is aggravated by the fact that there are intestinal disturbances. My weight has come down to one-hundred and fifteen pounds, however, I believe an improvement must come.

That letter was a great shock to me. The following months I remained without further news of my wife's illness. Then on September 5th, I received another short note in which she wrote:

> Although I am out of bed, it is very hard for me to get around as I am so weak. Through my long illness and high fever I have lost nearly all of my hair. I have been down much, but recently have gained in weight and am now on the upgrade, weighing 112 pounds. God has helped until now and he will continue to help.

Comparing this letter with the former one of some months ago, I had to realize that my wife was losing in the battle, although she tried very hard to make it appear as if there was no danger. The above quoted note proved to be the last letter that I received from her. I was left without news until I received that tragic message from my friend, Brother Jung, the pastor of my Danzig Assembly. The only indirect contact I had with my family during those months were the receipts from the food packages. I knew they received them because they were guaranteed. Usually, after a number of weeks, the receipt card from the firm was returned with the signature from a member of my family. That card usually bore the signature of my wife. There in the bank of Stockholm I also was shown the last note from my wife, directed to the firm in which she requested information about a certain food package which had not arrived.

The terrible uncertainty regarding my wife's condition for long months, aggravated by the fact that I knew that she was seriously ill, and remaining without news was a serious drain on my depleted vitality, and most of the time I was under a similar tension during the time I lingered in that lonely cell of the prison in Danzig. It seemed to me at times that I was again in the prison and all the news about my family was being kept away from me. This endless anxiety for my loved ones, especially my wife, brought about a serious decline in my physical condition which finally culminated in a serious breakdown at Christmas in 1943, when my heart action became so feeble that I actually felt my call from this life would come at any moment. Plunged into that melancholy mood during the summer and the autumn, I seemed to have the premonition within that this would actually be the last year of my life. That mood was also expressed in my letters to my wife, and in one of them I wrote from Kaggeholm under date of October 6, 1943.

During the day I look out into the Castle Park, an oblong lawn bounded by giant lime trees which give it the shape of a giant and magnificent amphitheatre. The trees are clothed with fiery hues, reminding me of marvelous multi-colored sunsets. It is the last display of the beauty of nature before it sinks into the death of winter. Soon the bare trees will stretch forth their branches as accusing arms toward heaven, then comes death also to Kaggeholm. From my window I look out and see just a little part of the Mälaren Lake, with its many islands and straits; and it always gives me a creepy, gruesome feeling because it is quite cold here already. We can expect snow to fall any time now. Sadness enshrouds me day by day. If I would only know at least why I do not receive any news, perhaps it would be easier to remain without a word from you, but I know nothing. All kinds of fears are working within my soul, not only because of you but also because of our children.

50. THE ENEMY HARASSING ME

The deep anxiety for my family was not the only burden which weighed me down. The enemy always will take advantage and aggravate a difficult situation by working into our life other problems which will keep us under tension. As I had no passport, my status was very uncertain. It puzzled the Swedish officials. They began to consider me as a man without a country. To give me a status they issued a Foreigner's Passport of their own, but when I examined that document I found that they had classed me as a Russian national because I was born in that country, which made me vulnerable to their claims.[13] The Bolsheviks could demand of the Swedish government that I be repatriated to Russia. That would have meant execution for me, as they had me on their black list. Needless to say, I was deeply shocked and sent that paper to the issuing office demanding correction of that error. It took three months until the passport was returned to me corrected, for which I praised the Lord sincerely.

The tension in Sweden during the war was terrific, because it was there all the political interests converged from all the countries of the world and clashed. Tragedies were enacted as conflicting and opposing elements intrigued against each other. One suspected the other. Positive indications proved that not only did the Swedish detectives desire to know details about my movements and my activity, but there were other forces which were

---

[13] The author was born in Volhynia. See footnote on page 37.

interested in me. I had come from Nazi-dominated Danzig. I am sure that some of these secret service men of different countries had occasion to hear my testimony in religious meetings which they attended. Praise the Lord!

One day as I walked through the streets of Stockholm, a tall, black-haired young man, elegantly dressed, accosted me, walking a little while beside me. "You think that you are smart and that you can go along without being discovered. We know exactly what you are doing. If I can give you any advice, I'd say you had better stay away from Stockholm. If you don't, then something will happen to you which will make you very miserable," he said, uttering real threats.

"Who are you and what do you know about my smartness? The way you talk I am positive that you know more about me than I do myself," I replied. While I was saying that, I glanced around for a policeman. He noticed that.

"Remember what I told you, because I desire your good," he answered quickly and then disappeared.

I was greatly puzzled at the thought that somebody suspected me of something and knew about a certain activity which did not exist in my life, as I was not interested in any politics, much less in secret manipulations. They must have had me confused with somebody else and that could have serious consequences for me, although the suspicions did not apply to me. Someone's blundering could be repeated and cause me great embarrassment. I, of course, had no reason to heed that warning, but it made me uneasy. I went to Stockholm whenever I found it necessary, and nothing further happened, nor did I ever again encounter that young man. However, I received a new warning when I walked through a business street in Stockholm. A gentleman in Swedish police uniform joined me while I walked along the sidewalk. He, too gave me a very earnest urgent warning that I should stay away from Stockholm or something serious would happen to me.

When I talked about the incident to a real Swedish policeman, he questioned very much the official identity of the one who had accosted me. He admonished me sternly that if such a thing happened again I should immediately notify the authorities. But nothing further happened which gave an occasion for such a step.

Considerably embarrassing to me also was the publication of the book which had novelized and distorted my prison experiences. Like most novels, the story told in that book had a happy ending, climaxing my experience in the flight to Stockholm where I supposedly received an invitation by the Finnish Consul and was confronted by my wife who, according to that book, had been brought to Stockholm by kindly friends. Also, according to that story, I was told there in the Finnish Legation that my two daughters had been secretly brought to Finland and were in the care of other friends of mine in that country.

I had nothing to do with the writing or publication of that book; neither could I prevent its distribution. In the meantime, my own book, *Songs in the Night*, describing my actual experiences and sufferings during my imprisonment and flight to Sweden, was published. Its sensational contents brought about a rather extensive circulation. The two books did not, of course, tally in their details. So the Nazis, who did not like the exposure of their methods in Sweden, took advantage of these discrepancies. In their Nazi newspaper, published in Stockholm, a cynical article appeared with a heading, "The Smart Gentleman from Danzig." They wrote that I was exploiting war conditions, inventing certain things which were supposed to have happened in Danzig, for financial gains.

"One book is not enough," they went on in their tirade, ridiculing Christianity, "but two books are telling the 'true' story, whereby nice profits are being made." They, of course, described the whole story in both books as having been manipulated and published for the sake of piling up profits.

It was the plan of Satan to bring about my destruction in one way or another, with the result that my anxiety and worry was increased and multiplied. God, however, still kept and led me on step by step, protecting me from the snare of the enemy. Praise and thanksgiving, and honor and glory be to my wonderful Savior forever and forever!

51. In Bereavement

As time progressed, I tried every avenue of possibility to contact my family, but in vain. I had appealed to the Swiss Legation which took care of the interests of America since the United States and Germany were at war. They gave me no hope of receiving a quick answer, but I was assured that they would do their best and very likely they did—yet I waited weeks and even months until finally a negative answer was the result. Food packages had gone forward and indirectly I learned that the packages were delivered in Danzig. Until the beginning of May 1944, I had waited daily to receive some kind of news about my wife's condition. Many of the saints in Sweden prayed for my family and especially for my wife. I had also contacted my friends in America and they published calls for prayer, so thousands of children of God were praying as well, but no news came from my family.

The night of April 30th was very restless for me. A nervous and sleepless night had passed. I looked at my watch which registered 7:30A.M., then I fell asleep for a short time and dreamed that I was with my wife and our two children in their room in Danzig. We conversed as usual, but I could not remember the subject of our talk.

After a while my wife took Ruth in her arms, pressed her to her bosom and kissed her goodbye. Then she took Karin, lifted her to her heart and pressed the child's face to her cheeks. "Now, I must go. Goodbye, until we meet again," she said while she continued to press the child to herself, kissing her goodbye. Finally she put the child down, embraced me, also saying "goodbye" once more, then she walked out of the room and closed the door. As I had often dreamed about her and the children, I did not put special importance in this dream. In reality, my wife came to say goodbye to the children and me, while she actually died. I awoke at ten minutes to eight o'clock and when I received the news of her passing later, and as her death certificate shows, she actually passed away at 7:45 in the morning of May 1, 1944.

On May 5, while I was still waiting and hoping for more cheerful news, I had been invited to have a cup of coffee in the home of friends in the afternoon. About two o'clock I left the house to cycle over to that home. As I walked out of our yard leading my bicycle, the neighbors dog began to whine and howl pitifully. I never had heard this dog do that before or afterward. On that May 5 at two o'clock in the afternoon was the time when the earthly remains of my wife was carried and laid to rest in Danzig. When later the short notice of my beloved wife's home-call was handed to me, it was doubly sad and bitter, realizing that while my wife's funeral was being held and ignorant of what had happened, I was on a visit in the home of some friends.

It was on May 10 when a letter was handed me from Danzig. In nervous haste I opened the envelope and took out a little bereavement card written by my friend, Pastor Jung, and I read the tragic news of my wife's home-going and the date when her funeral was held. It was unspeakably sad and cruel news. No details were given. Considering the short time since that message was written and mailed to me, it was next to a miracle that the news reached me in barely ten days; whereas in a period of war it usually takes several weeks for a letter to get through—if at all. God's mercy had been active to bring that sad news to me in such a short time. The suspense was finally terminated. I had definite information now that my wife had passed away. I never learned more details, but I realized then that my two little daughters were left without a mother, in the care of a feeble and sickly old grandmother, during a time when greatest distress and tragedy were nearing.

Now my heart was burning with a longing to clasp my little Ruth, then nine years old, into my arms; to comfort that child who loved her Mama so deeply. It was impossible. As if bound by a thousand chains, I was held in the distance. I could not even know whether my letter to my girls would reach them.

From day to day I waited for some crumbs of additional news, but in vain. In those days of bereavement something had snapped within me. Ever since then, bereavement, even that of strangers, overwhelms me—tears will come. A funeral will invariably break me up. I must avoid funerals.

Month after month I waited—all in vain. Ruth was ailing, Mama had gone—it was too deep a shock to her—as I learned a year later. She grew melancholy. I did not know whether any of my letters reached my little Ruth—they did not. In a letter many months later, Ruth wrote me chidingly, "Papa, why don't you write to us?" The child could not grasp the fact that I was unable to reach them. To my bereavement and grief, anxiety was added as news about my daughters' well-being failed to come. I realized how terribly sad Ruth would be and I realized the helplessness of little Karin.

As during the war it was permissible for enemy countries to confiscate property and belongings of belligerent nationals, I feared that the Nazis would forthwith liquidate the home and rob us of all our belongings, leaving my daughters destitute. It all became an utterly unbearable burden which weighed down upon me. In my helplessness I often exclaimed: "I am as helpless as a worm."

I made renewed and desperate efforts to get some news through the legations, but every effort was in vain. I remained in the dark. During those weeks and months I learned to know the love and concern of the children of God in a special way. A number of saints tried to help me and did all they could in some way to get news regarding the whereabouts of my children—but to no avail. It was also in that period when I gained contact with my dear friend, Brother Pfeifer, who took a special interest in my girls as if they were his own. Through his personal influence he gained access into the highest circles of Sweden and appealed even to the Crown Prince and to other very influential personalities. All of them showed warm concern and sympathy—but none were able actually to do anything.

Some clothes were given me to be sent to my children and I hoped a way could be found—but that also proved impossible. Not even the Red Cross could do anything, to which I, in desperation appealed. The whole world appeared to me as a cauldron of calamity and helplessness. The war was raging, giant battles were being fought, tens of thousands of men were disappearing in graves there in Europe and other parts of the world. My vitality was so spent that I could not hope to carry on much longer under that great burden of sorrow and anxiety. Every way was blocked. How often in those days it touched my heart very deeply when I received letters of sympathy and concern, and their assurance that prayer was going up to Jesus from the children of God. That was of great comfort to me, but my grief and perplexity in general was beyond description.

52. CLIMAX OF TRAGEDY

The fateful year 1945 began. The Russian Armies resumed their westward march from the great Vistula Bend with lightning speed. The hope of the Danzig people faded and the terrible fear of Bolshevism gripped the inhabitants, but everybody was helpless.

Among the many thousands of other terror-stricken people, there was also Mrs. Staehler, who knew my wife from childhood and was a cherished friend of my family, as well. When my wife had reached her dying hours she exacted from Mrs. Staehler the promise to take care of Karin and deliver her safely to me at any cost. She did not rest until Mrs. Staehler had given her solemn word that she would take care of the child, come what may. As I learned later, my wife, for some reason, was very anxious that the little girl would be in Mrs. Staehler's keeping, who promised that she would do all in her power to look out for the welfare of Karin and give her back to me safely, if at all possible.

As the Russian Armies moved nearer Danzig, Mrs. Staehler's anxiety for the child increased and she re-membered her promise to the mother. Her uppermost thought now was to take the little one away from Danzig and go westward—but my mother-in-law refused to let the child go. The time of emergency however, had arrived, and Mrs. Staehler contemplated fleeing Danzig before the Bolsheviks would arrive. The increase of the Red Army's pressure finally caused her to take Karin away without the consent of the grandmother. Secretly she arranged passage on a little freighter to take them over the Baltic and then make their way to her brother in central Germany. This took place early in January 1945, when they boarded that little ship on their hazardous journey.

The voyage was very perilous as thousands of people in their flight over the Baltic perished in the bombings of refugee ships—but Karin was safer here than she would have been in Danzig. In fact, if she would have remained with her grandmother, there would not have been one chance in a thousand for her to have survived. God had arranged this for the safety of my helpless little daughter.

All these developments were, of course, unknown to me. Surely it was God who worked in answer to prayer and rescued my child, dove-tailing the events as Mrs. Staehler received word from her sister urging her to board the diminutive boat that took them over the Baltic in that frosty January weather, under the awful onslaught of the enemy air force which cost the lives of thousands of refugees. The Russians were coming with their airplanes and sinking the refugee ships. Thousands of corpses later drifted to the shores of the Baltic. Through that awful danger the Lord directed my child's flight from Danzig without having a chance to take provisions along with them and just escaping with their bare lives. To have a conception of how terribly perilous it was, it might be said here that one great German excursion steamer on which there were 9,000 people, crowded to the very limit, was bombed and sunk by enemy aircraft. All were drowned and thousands of corpses drifted to the different shores for months afterwards.

Mrs. Staehler and my little Karin, however, came through under the protection of God, borne by the prayers of thousands of saints, until they finally reached Suhl in Thuringia. The Lord in a miraculous way had protected them on that trip; they landed safely in Flensburg, from which place it took them three more weeks to make their way to Mrs. Staehler's brother in Suhl, Thuringia, in central Germany. All that took place without my knowledge, being absolutely without any news whatsoever from my daughters.

THE JOURNEY HOME

After Mrs. Staehler and my Karin had arrived, she wrote a letter at the end of February informing me of what had happened, and that they had arrived safely in Suhl. As chaos began to grip the whole of Germany, there was hardly any hope that a message should find a way through Germany and to Sweden. Strange to say, however, in the month of May of the same year, that communication came into my hands, giving me the welcome news that my child was still alive at the time of writing and that they were in a safe place, far removed from the Bolsheviks, praise God forever!

Danzig was occupied and destroyed by the Red Armies on March 30. An utterly hopeless chaos gripped the city which spread westward to central Europe.

Ruth and my mother-in-law had remained in Danzig. As the Russians drew nearer and the battles became more intense, Ruth and her grandmother had to spend most of their time in the cellar, and during the last week of their stay, they could not come out at all. Day and night they had to remain in that damp and dark hole where there was no place to sleep; neither did they have anything to eat but some bread that was brought in by other kindly friends.

Finally they were warned that if they did not immediately leave the place, they would be surrounded on all sides by fire and would have to perish. Out of that cellar they fled, leaving behind them home and everything that it held. So my old mother-in-law and Ruth had left the cherished home, taking hardly anything along, as they could carry very little with them, having no remaining strength. The Russians were already in some parts of the city when Ruth and her grandmother made their way out into a nearby forest, westward of the city. Tens of thousands of people, consisting mainly of women and children were milling about in the nearby forests and in the fields. They were without food; most of them exhausted from wandering hither and thither in their fright and distress.

My mother-in-law and Ruth also joined that great mass of humanity; fires had been kindled at the edge of the forest where they could warm themselves. They intended to spend the night there with thousands of other women and children.

Only recently I received a letter from Sister Blumenstein, a member of my Assembly in Danzig, who disclosed some details of that afternoon and the following night. She was also fleeing from the city, wandering about, when in the afternoon she stumbled, as it were, upon my mother-in-law and Ruth, my daughter, so she joined them. That sister did not desire to spend the night outside and therefore urged my mother-in-law to try and find shelter, even though they were deadly tired and hungry. My mother-in-law had an affliction on her knee and could hardly walk further. Then her ailing heart made it seemingly impossible to wander about anymore. She simply desired to stay where she was and await the night. Sister Blumenstein finally insisted that they go and find a house in which to spend the night. That perhaps is the reason they did not lose their lives—or that something even more terrible did not happen to them during the darkness in that night of satanic origin.

After some hours of searching they finally found shelter in a house in one of the suburbs of Danzig. There were many people in that house already, but a little corner on a sofa in one of the rooms was still available. Sister Blumenstein took charge of my daughter. They sat down and awaited the evening. There was hardly anything to eat and nobody could prepare a meal. During the night two Russian soldiers with lanterns, entered the room. They aroused every woman and girl, looking into, and examining their faces. A number of younger women were taken out. Then they came to Sister Blumenstein. A soldier roughly grabbed her by the arm and pulled her out of the room.

Ruth remained alone on the sofa, for the time being, unmolested.

"Are you a Jewess? You look like one!" the Russian roughly asked.

"Yes, I am a Jewess," she answered. An urge within her had caused her to give that answer, and there was a slight reason for that since through her ancestry, there was some Jewish blood in her veins.

"Are you really telling the truth?" the soldier insisted, scrutinizing her.

"Yes, I am telling the truth," she answered.

"Then, I will not molest you—and when other Russian soldiers come to trouble you, just tell them that you are a Jewess, then you and your daughter will be safe." He left her, giving his attention to other women.

The fact that the Russian soldier thought her to be a Jewess and taking it for granted that Ruth was her daughter, saved her and my child from a terrible fate. Sister Blumenstein writes that while she was conversing with that Bolshevik soldier outside, she heard the cries and screams of thousands of women in the nearby forest. Thousands of the Red Army soldiers were carrying through unspeakable orgies of wickedness. On the next day Sister Blumenstein was again separated from my mother-in-law and Ruth. The Lord had sent her for the purpose of rescuing my child from brutalities of the bloodthirsty and bestial Bolsheviks during that terrible night.

The next day Ruth and her grandmother were again roaming about to find a room where they could stay permanently. They finally reached a street intersection, not knowing where to turn or what to do. My mother-in-law, who is an experienced child of God, did some very earnest praying. Presently an elderly woman came along.

"What are you waiting for?" she asked my mother- in-law.

"We are homeless and do not know which way to turn or where to go," she answered.

"Then you come along with me. I have some people already in my home but I must make room also for you," the stranger said after some hesitation.

They went along and were given a room which they occupied during the next few weeks. With thousands of others my mother-in-law and daughter faced actual starvation, as there was absolutely no distribution of food. When the Russians occupied the city of Danzig they burned it to the ground, including the house in which we had our home. Ruth and her grandmother had fled and finally found shelter in a Danzig suburb. From there, late in May, she wrote a letter to me, in a seemingly hopeless attempt to get it through to Sweden. It was written by her just before Ruth was taken to the hospital with typhoid. The letter was dated May 29, and after many weeks in the mail, actually arrived at my place of refuge in Sweden. It reads as follows:

> For a long time you have not heard from us. Now I shall send you our address. Ruth and I live at present in Oliwa, near Danzig. Since last week, our dear Ruth is severely sick and I ask you urgently to send her nourishing food, such as butter, milk, and flour. That would be a great help to her. In her high fever, Ruth speaks constantly about the lovely cake Papa used to send her. In the next letter I will write more.

That promised "next" letter never arrived. This message disclosed indirectly that our home was lost and that they were living with other people in a suburb of Danzig. It also showed that my child was very ill, doubtless from undernourishment.

There certainly seemed to be no possibility for a letter to get out from within that chaos. Yet again, God did direct the letter which finally came through and reached me late in the summer in Möklinta, Sweden.

Only after the children had been restored to me again, and through letters they brought along with them, I learned that Ruth had utterly broken down in health and had been taken to the hospital with typhoid fever. I also learned that the child was lingering between life and death for three long weeks, during which time she was unconscious. There was very little food to be had in the hospitals, and terrible disorder prevailed as medicine was gone and but little service from doctors and nurses was available. In that chaos, my child was down with typhoid, that deadly disease.

Although humanly speaking, no hope for her recovery remained; still, our wonderful and merciful God let her come out of the coma and she rallied again, and finally, after long weeks of suffering in the hospital, she came out, free from typhoid, but with only skin and bones remaining. The Lord had preserved the life of my precious child because thousands of faithful saints were praying and interceding, and the Lord did answer these prayers. Hallelujah! Ruth was again under the care of my mother-in-law, but sorry to say, there was hardly anything to give the child to eat. The little food they did find here and there was devoid of nourishment and utterly inadequate to help a convalescent. The Russians had charge of the city and had confiscated all the remaining food supplies, not giving the population anything to eat. Through that awful situation and the contamination of the water, the typhoid epidemic had struck the city and finally, also afflicted my daughter, but my Jesus preserved her, praise his holy and wonderful name forever!

Not having proper food, we can easily imagine in what condition the child must have been during the coming weeks. Then finally, in spite of my convalescing child's condition, only a few weeks later, two Polish policemen, one afternoon in July, came into the room and brutally ordered them out—forcing them to vacate their room within five minutes. My mother-in-law had to take my feeble child in her weakened condition and go down on the street. They were told they should go to the station and there would be a train waiting to take them to Germany. They went to the station, waited and waited the rest of the day—but no train came. They had to spend the night outside, and on the next day they again roamed about, still waiting for the train to arrive—but no train came on that day either. They had to spend another night under the clear sky. Finally, on the third day, a refugee train pulled in, consisting of freight box cars, already crowded. There were no seats or benches in these cars, but they had to crowd into one of those freight cars. My child and mother-in-law now found themselves in a car with over seventy people jammed into it. There was not even enough room to sit down on the floor— not to speak of lying down and sleeping.

It was a long train crowded with homeless people who had lost everything they possessed in life, and did not even have food along on which to subsist. Nobody cared for these refugees nor did they receive any meals. Thus, they were moving westward in a tragically slow manner. Whole days the train stopped somewhere and my child again took critically ill—there was not a spot for her to lie down. When the train stopped somewhere as it did at times for hours, or for a long day, Ruth was taken out and laid on the ground, thus enabling the sick child, at least to stretch out her weary body.

One day, the end seemed to have come for Ruth. My mother-in-law in her desperation ran into the nearby town trying to find a physician, but in the existing chaos such was impossible. She roamed aimlessly about the streets weeping. Suddenly an old man with snow-white hair stood before her.

"Why are you weeping?" he asked her.

"Near the station in that refugee train I have my grandchild, a girl ten years of age, and she is dying. Now I came rushing into this town in search of a physician—but it seems in vain," she sobbed.

"My good lady, there are many people in a dying condition in our days. Take this little bottle and give it to your grandchild, a few drops every few hours," he said kindly, while he took a little bottle without a label out of his pocket and gave it to her. My mother-in-law returned and began to administer the liquid potion divinely sent, and it actually revived the child and enabled her to pass the crisis, and thus her life was preserved.

53. HOMELESS AND SEPARATED

After seven days on that train they reached Mecklenburg, a province in northern Germany. From the station they were directed to walk to a little village four miles distance, consisting of merely a half dozen farmers. Their time of acute distress continued and hardly anything was given them to eat. They just had a little room about eight by eight feet which they had to share with another grandmother and her grandchild, a girl, one year older than Ruth. That room was just wide enough to give place for two three-quarter beds and there was about two feet of space between them. This was now their home. They had very little to cover themselves with, since they had not brought anything with them. Neither could the farmer supply anything for them. After five years of war almost everything was consumed.

Those farmers themselves being in a deep, poverty-stricken plight, and already swamped with a number of refugees, certainly were not enthusiastic about accommodating additional wanderers. Still, they were duty-bound to receive them. This situation did not create further harmony, but in most cases created severe tension between the refugees and the farmers, because to a great extent, they had to feed them all. But for my mother-in-law and Ruth, even this was a great improvement because now they had a room to themselves and a bed to sleep in and did not have to wander from place to place and ride in trains under unspeakable conditions. Hunger, however, remained their steady companion and was gnawing at the very vitals of their innermost being. The most distressing task was to find something for making a meal. There were certain quantities of food which a person was allowed to buy, but often there was no bread; potatoes were very scarce, fats and meats were seldom found to fill the rations; at times only a few ounces were allotted which did not help very perceptibly.

Ruth's grandmother, through extreme privations and hardship, had neglected her sore knee to such an extent that she could hardly walk out of the room. She also had severe and aggravated heart trouble, making it impossible for her to be out and try to find something to eat. The responsibility fell upon little Ruth, who was ten years of age and extremely weakened by the ordeals through which she had passed. Before sunrise and without any breakfast, she had to walk to the store every morning, four miles distant, to get there on time when the rations were distributed. When she was a little late, nothing was left for her. It must have been heart-breaking when she had to walk back empty-handed. Helga, the other little girl, grandchild of the other grandmother, who stayed in the same room, usually walked to the store with Ruth. It was tolerable enough to walk these four miles over and back again—that is eight (English) miles each day as long as the weather was warm in the summer, but when the chilly autumn winds came, and the damp cold which is so very penetrating in that part of the world, it made that trip a torture for the child. She says that at times they were so chilled they could walk no further. Then they would go into a nearby barracks at the wayside and cower there in a corner, and Ruth claims that it helped them, at least they were out of that terrible penetrating wind for a while. As poorly dressed as she was, my child must have suffered agonies in trying to get something into the house to eat for herself and her grandmother.

After returning home she received a little slice of dry bread without anything on it and a cup of substitute coffee. That was her breakfast. After that there were other worries; she had to walk to neighboring villages in order to try and get something additional to sustain them. That child also had to go to the nearby forest and gather fire wood. At times she had to use the axe and cut down little trees or split pieces to make them ready for use. Being hungry all of the time and doing all that walking and working, we can easily imagine what a life it must have been for the unfortunate little one. Remembering that she had just passed through that terrible typhoid ordeal in Danzig which had almost cost her life, her strength was sapped out to such a dangerous degree that she had very little power of resistance and hardly had any remaining hair on her head. Thus the child had to face all these hardships from day to day. And I lingered there in Sweden waiting for news. Since the announcement of the home-going of my beloved wife in May 1944, when Brother Jung sent the message and then wrote a short letter afterward, I had heard nothing further. Up to the early summer of 1945, almost the whole year had passed without having any definite word from my little daughters.

After my girls arrived in Sweden, they brought with them a lengthy report from Miss Ellen Klatt who had taken them into her loving and efficient care. Miss Klatt was one of the chief instruments in God's hands through which these dear children were saved from actual starvation. It will be well if I quote parts of this report which describe the conditions and the circumstances prevailing at the time when my daughters were lost in Germany. The report is dated January 3, 1946, and reads in part, as follows:

Dear Mr. Schmidt,

It will be a great joy to you, finally to have your two daughters with you after years of separation and many months of anxious uncertainty when you had no news at all from them, and when it was impossible for you to help in any way. My folks and I, who have gone through similar sorrows, privations and dangers, know how much your girls have suffered. Now, however, all that is past and gone for your children.

You will notice that your girls are not in as bad condition as one might expect considering what they had to endure. My country is in a terrible time of sorrow, about which Ruth will be able to tell you many details, some of which will be hard for you to believe. As you already know, we are in the Russian Zone where sorrow and tragedy is the greatest. After our arrival in Dahlem, Berlin, your letter was handed to me by the Consul. Many thanks. Your letter authorizes me to place the children in charge of the American Consul for sending them to you in Sweden. In some respects, it is very painful for me to part from the children. I love them as if they were my own, I know that there will be no further possibility of seeing them again in this life. As you know, I have been acquainted with your precious children almost since their birth. Karin, I held in my arms a few days after she was born, and I took care of Ruth part of the time while you and your wife were in America, so you will understand that the children have grown deeply into my heart. This is all but a memory now. After you had gone away, I often visited your wife and the girls in your cozy little place of abode. I would not want to miss for one moment the memory of those times of precious fellowship and friendship in your home.

I am very sorry that I could not talk to you personally about the things which happened after you left. I may, however, tell you that the tie of friendship between your wife and me was strong and deep to the very last, and that she asked me to look after the children and not to forget them—when she realized that she would not be permitted to be with them much longer. Gladly would I have given my own life to preserve the life of your wife for the sake of her own two children. Often, when time permitted, I was with your children to give them a little fellowship and try to comfort them.

The time came when the Russians approached Danzig. Karin fortunately had been taken to Germany by Mrs. Staehler. Ruth stayed with her grandmother. My service in the Kindergarten compelled me to stay in Danzig. When the Russians entered, our beautiful ancient city went up in smoke. For two whole hours my mother, my sister and I rushed through fire and air raids and roamed about, not knowing where to go. Everything around us was afire and bombs were bursting. Our lovely home and everything in it remained behind—but our lives were spared. Three days later we had to bury our precious mother in a cold, cold grave without a coffin—she had died of exhaustion. How I felt, I can never tell. We knew absolutely nothing of our father who had been drafted into the army only the week before. My sister and I stood alone, with nobody to help or advise us; wherever we looked we saw suffering, distress, death and crime.

The first thing we did after covering my precious mother with earth in that lonely grave, was to make our way to your former place of abode. The shock which we felt when we came to the house, seeing it in ruins to the very foundation, we can never describe. Everything was burned and utterly destroyed. It looked as if the direct hit of a giant bomb had struck your home. Upon a nearby wall, still standing in the neighborhood, I wrote my name and the following words: "Grandma Neumann and Ruth Schmidt—where are you? Aunt Elly is searching for you. You can find me at——— [Here the address followed.] Well did I know the feebleness of your mother-in-law and I was very, very concerned about both. Only long and weary weeks afterward, on June 29th, did I finally succeed in finding Ruth and her Grandma. Mrs. Neumann looked very haggard, which we expected, but how awful Ruth looked, having been in the hospital for weeks with typhoid, is beyond description. She had passed the crisis and we brought her to her Grandma that very day. We all wept as we pressed the little darling to our hearts. The first words she said were: "Aunt Elly, I feel as if my Mommy would come to me soon."

We brought the children home into the lodging place now occupied by her grandma, but she had nothing to eat, as food was not distributed to the German population who did not work, so of course we could not leave Ruth there. Fortunately, I knew a Pole in Danzig to whom I appealed and through him we were allotted shelter and some work which helped us to receive those pitifully low rations. I took Ruth with me for a while and we had decided to leave Danzig together, but things happened differently. We had taken Ruth to your mother-in-law, where she had been now for two days, when suddenly the Polish police came into our place and within five minutes, on the 20th of July, we were thrown out, again leaving those pitifully few things behind which we had acquired. We were crowded into a freight train with a hundred and twenty others; infants, old and feeble, healthy and sick men and women; all were crowded into that little train and we were transported for six long days and nights. We had to get along as best we could without eating and without drinking. In the city of Küstrin, we were unloaded, and we stood there not knowing which way to turn. Wherever we looked there were only ruins. Russians and Poles were waiting for us as their victims. Usually, they grabbed people and tore some of their clothes off their bodies, after which they threw them into a camp. Some unspeakable crimes were committed against the women. By a miracle, my sister and I were able to sneak through these chains of bandits. For twenty long days we roamed about, walking barefoot, not knowing where we would spend the next day or night or where we would get something to eat.

On August 23, 1945, we finally arrived in Jerichow, where our distant relatives lived. We were haggard, distressed, and in a down-and-out condition. There we lived one month. Then we were given a little furnished home and could finally relax somewhat. By making toys for children, and wood-carving, I made my living. It was impossible for me in that little town to find a position as a kindergarten nurse. Immediately we wrote a letter to Mrs. Staehler, whom we knew took care of your Karin. Fortunately we had her address, and through her we hoped to gain contact with your mother-in-law and Ruth again.

At the end of October 1945, we did receive a letter from Mrs. Staehler in which she described the terrible distress of your mother-in-law and Ruth. We had a little extra room, so

I wrote to them immediately, inviting them to come to us. The day was set when we were to meet them in Berlin, on the way to our place, but events transpired contrary to our expectations. Mrs. Staehler had brought little Karin to your mother-in-law also, and thus, that little darling had to emerge into the hunger region where only misery and near-starvation prevailed. Your precious Ruth and her grandmother had been very low in health and spirits and in a far advanced state of undernourishment. Seldom did they know what they would find to eat the next morning. In this great misery and want, Karin joined them. While in Thuringia, Mrs. Staehler received some additional rations for the child, but this was impossible here. If little Karin could have stayed with Mrs. Staehler she would not have become so ill afterwards. Through this occurrence your mother-in-law and Ruth could not come to Berlin and it was impossible for me to meet them there, but she asked me to come and fetch the children as their condition had grown very serious.

In the meantime, an order was issued by occupational forces which prohibited anyone moving to another locality. It was only with greatest difficulty and through a special petition by your mother-in-law, that the two children could receive permission to move and stay with me—but the transfer of the children was delayed by the weakened condition of your mother-in-law, who was not at all able to travel. On December 3, 1945, I undertook the trip under the most terrible conditions. I made the journey in great discomfort but succeeded in reaching Gülitz and met your children. And how did I find them? Only your mother-in-law and Ruth were at home. Karin had been taken to the hospital with hunger-typhus.[14] The unfortunate child had been there for days and had been given up to die by the doctors. She was isolated because of having that contagious disease. Nobody was permitted to see her.

The only thing I could do was to take Ruth along—alone, to rescue her at least, from the threat of starvation, as I was able to give her better food and the greatest possible

---

[14] 'Hunger-typhus' is a historical term for murine typhus, which is typhus transmitted by fleas, rather than lice.

care. Karin had been taken into the hospital in November and remained all during December and until the 10th of January. When she had passed the crisis, we took her out of the hospital. It was most certainly the prayers of the saints that rescued the child from certain death.

Thus ends the first part of the detailed report from Miss Ellen Klatt, the young lady who saved my girls from actual starvation. It must be remembered that the above quoted report came into my hands only after my daughters had been reunited with me. From the early summer of 1944 until the spring of 1946, I had received only the two vague letters, through which I barely learned of their whereabouts. I knew nothing of their struggles, their serious illness and near-starvation; neither did I know anything about their movements which were arranged by the Lord for their preservation in answer to the fervent prayers of the saints.

Although I had no information, I sensed the crisis and dangers in the Spirit and had a never-ending burden of anxiety and apprehension for my girls—and so did several thousand saints; with the result that an uninterrupted flow of prayers arose to the throne of grace, and God was mindful, and worked in various ways, not only to preserve the life of my daughters, but also to shape circumstances in mysterious moves and ways in preparation for answering the prayers of the saints.

54. MYSTERIOUS MOVES OF GOD

In order to make me act entirely under the guidance of the Lord, he permitted the burden for my children to weigh me down and oppress me to such an extent that I was willing to do anything in my desperation, welcoming any opportunity whatsoever, which would tend to bring me nearer a solution.

During the many months, deepest anxiety for my daughters' whereabouts at times became a veritable torture, taking away my breath and making me gasp for air. The Lord had just permitted those two letters to reach me—the only avenue for my imagination which permitted me to have a reason for hope of tracing my girls. It would lead too far if I were to give an account of all the anxious efforts and actions I undertook in my efforts to help my children in some way. I shall now relate some of the essential steps taken which proved to be a help in making progress in the search for my little ones.

It was in mid-summer of 1945 when I learned that a Swedish ship, the M. S. *Princessan Ingrid* was plying between a Swedish port and Danzig, or Gdynia. The ship was returning displaced persons to Poland who had been brought to Sweden for recuperation. I came in contact with the nurse of that ship, so I wrote a letter asking her to visit my daughter Ruth, and my mother-in-law, who had found shelter in a Danzig suburb after our home was destroyed, when the Red Army entered the city.

The nurse agreed to do that and also to take along some food packages. After several weeks of anxious waiting, I received the following letter from her:

Dear Sir,

Referring to your letter in which you asked me to look up your daughter, I wish to inform you that I was told she and her grandmother had gone to Germany. I had great difficulty in finding the house as the Poles had changed the names of the streets. The Red Cross was not able to give any information regarding their address in Germany. Really, I do hope we shall find your child as I understand that you, as father, are very anxious about her. I hope that all will turn out for the best.

The explanation of the Poles was innocent enough, but since I learned the actual facts in the case, they evidenced a brutality which can hardly be surpassed. My mother-in-law and my daughter, Ruth, had not moved away. They would not have "moved" for an extended period of time as Ruth, after her severe spell of typhoid, and just beginning to convalesce, could hardly walk. But two Polish policemen came into the room and inhumanly gave them five minutes to get out of the house, literally throwing them out into the street. The details of this tragic action have already been described.

The Poles, in addition to their extreme brutality, told deliberate lies. I immediately guessed the truth. Realizing now through this news that my loved ones had been expelled and doubtless were on the march westward, my apprehension and fears were boundless. Not having heard anything about them, also knowing through other sources and through the newspapers how that tens of thousands of helpless women and children were left destitute and without care; and that without hindrance terrible diseases and starvation were raging among them, also knowing that the Bolsheviks took thousands of children into Soviet Russia and were there destroying their identity and giving them other names, I realized that the danger was very great and the hope very feeble that I would ever see my child again.

About my little Karin I had heard nothing since January 1945; neither did I know anything beyond the fact that she and Mrs. Staehler had arrived in Thuringia, a province in Germany, which had been within the American Occupation Zone, but later had been handed over to the Russians. All this made me realize that Karin was again in the Russian Zone, or perhaps they had been taken away to a new place unknown to me. I now feared anew that I may have lost both of my precious little ones.

Under such uncertainty I labored under an indescribable tension of hopes and fears. My heart was torn between perplexity and anxiety from day to day. Whenever I sat down to a meal with food so abundant in Sweden, I realized that if my children were still alive, they most certainly would be in a starving condition. This thought haunted and tormented me day and night. In my prayers when agonizing for my children, Satan would harass me by saying: "You are praying for your children! They are dead! They are buried! You are praying for the dead! There is no longer hope for them! You know how many thousands are perishing day by day. Your daughters are gone—you will never see them again!" Such were the diabolical and merciless whisperings of the enemy of souls.

While such disheartening interjections tormented me, I nevertheless, with God's help, lived through those days of greatest pain and terror, praise God! Once more, in the beginning of October 1945, I had been in Stockholm trying to do something which would bring me knowledge of my girls. The American Legation had warded me off many times. They simply could not do anything for my children. The American Consul told me, "If it were my own wife lost there within the Russian Zone in Germany, I could not do a thing for her." This made me poignantly realize and still more fully, how futile, hopeless, and in vain every attempt and every effort was that I tried to undertake in behalf of my sick and undernourished little ones.

From the legation I went to the Swedish Red Cross. I had also communicated with the International Red Cross in Geneva, Switzerland, appealing to them. Then I had contacted the government, and Brother Pfeifer, a close friend of mine had in turn contacted the Crown Prince of Sweden, who gave the assurance that when the Swedish children were evacuated from Germany these children would be included. Everywhere I sought to get some news or engage assistance in the great and soul-absorbing problem of contacting my daughters, but all, all, all— everything seemed to be utterly and absolutely fruitless.

When I stepped into the train in Stockholm, returning to my village, Möklinta, I fully realized and admitted within myself for the first time, that I was at the bitter and hopeless end of everything. I racked my brain for some way out.

Suddenly, like a flash, a brand new thought shot through my mind. I wondered later why I had never thought of it before. "Send a cablegram to President Truman immediately!" That thought quickly assumed stupendous proportions and appealed to me as an intensely practical one. In those exciting moments and in my depressed condition, however, I hardly realized the real and actual import of the thought. Only later I became aware that it was an inspiration from the Holy Spirit. It is evident to me today, however, that it became the key to the whole situation. When I arrived home, I wrote a cablegram, addressing it to President Truman, Washington, D. C. It read as follows:

> AS AMERICAN CITIZEN APPEAL TO YOU ON BEHALF MY TWO DAUGHTERS, ONE AGE 10 VERY ILL OF MALNUTRITION ACCORDING NEWS DATED MAY LIVING DANZIG—OLIVA, JAGOSTREET 10B, CARE KRETSCHMER, OTHER DAUGHTER, AGE 5, LAST NEWS MARCH THURINGEN, CARE MRS. STAEHLER, SUHL, LAUTERSTREET 12. ALL ATTEMPTS CONTACT OR BRING THEM SWEDEN FOR PURPOSE RETURNING HOME TOGETHER FUTILE. REASON MY SOJOURN EUROPE 20 YEARS FIELD LEADERSHIP, RUSSIAN AND EASTERN EUROPEAN NAZIS PREVENTED OUR RETURN IMPRISONING ME DURING WAR, FLED SWEDEN.

This cablegram was sent on October 7. Washington, of course, was busy with a thousand other things and could not pay much attention to such a solitary little case where one or two human beings were involved, while thousands of others were dying as a result of the chaos in Europe.

Disappointment and anguish began creeping over me when I did not hear anything more as the days slipped by.

Just to be doing something in the case and to find some relief from fears and anxieties striving within, I appealed to the Polish Legation. I was also advised by the American Consul to contact the Russian Embassy in Sweden. I was given the name of an official with whom I was to communicate. I wrote him as follows:

My daughters and I are citizens of the United States of America. In order to give you an insight into the situation, I am enclosing data of information about my daughters and myself on a separate sheet. In addition to that, permit me to say the following:

As a representative of an American Religious organization, I had been delegated to Europe for a number of years. In Danzig my family and I were overtaken by the war in 1939. When we were about to arrange for our return to America the Nazis incarcerated me in November 1940. Only by a miracle my life was spared and I was freed from prison. Daily in danger of being rearrested I frantically tried to get out of Germany with my family, but the Nazis refused to give permission. I finally decided to flee with the help of a Polish business man whom the Nazis had robbed of everything he possessed, and who was active in the only kind of vengeance possible at that time; namely, helping others to flee, thus, with the gracious help of God Almighty, leading men through the meshes of Nazi vigilance into safety.

In the night of January 1, 1943, I was led on deck of a coal steamer in Gdynia and hid in a little shack; leaving my wife and two daughters behind in Danzig. I arrived safely in Stockholm after an adventurous trip over the Baltic.

My wife died in Danzig on May 1, 1944, leaving my motherless children in the care of Mrs. Elise Neumann, my mother-in-law. They suffered much from undernourishment as the Nazis did not allow them sufficient food to keep normal health. After the defeat of Germany I hoped to get the children out of that region soon thereafter, but it proved impossible until today. Just a few days ago I finally succeeded in sending a food package to my eldest daughter, Ruth, which very likely went by your boat.

Now I appeal to you as representative of the USSR, asking you please to point out a way which will enable me to send food and clothes to both the children. I also ask you kindly to give permission and help that my children may be able to leave their present places and be brought to me here in Sweden, because they need special care and medical attention.

It must be said that the Russian Embassy did not show the slightest interest in my petition for I never received a single word in reply from them. On the enclosed list I had given them complete information as fully as I knew, about my girls and their addresses, so the Russians could have undertaken something as both of these cases were within their own zone.

A number of weeks had passed. I had informed the American Legation in Stockholm that I had cable-grammed to Washington and sent them a copy of that message. Finally the legation in Stockholm wrote, sending me a communication dated November 30, 1945, informing me that the President had received my cablegram. The communication was as follows:

Dear Mr. Schmidt,

The Legation has been requested by the Department of State, Washington, D.C., to inform you in reply to your cablegram of October 8, 1945, to the President; that inquiries have been made by the Department's appropriate representatives concerning the whereabouts and welfare of your daughters, Ruth and Karin Schmidt, and the possibility of their proceeding to Sweden to join you, and that upon the receipt of replies this Legation will be notified. This office will again communicate with you immediately upon the receipt of further information from the Department.

G. C. SIGMOND
American Vice-Consul.

I must confess that my hopes were not very high at the reception of these promises, realizing that all the departments of all governments were extremely busy with the welfare of millions of people who were helpless and that logically they could not pay much, if any, special attention to two little individuals. Thus, I faced another dreary and cold Swedish winter, living in that little village, day by day staring through the windows in my room, viewing that white and cheerlessly beautiful landscape as a veritable shroud of death. Unknown to me, my little Karin had been taken to the hospital in November and lay there sick with typhoid. In my dreams, my prayers, and in all my devotions the imagination and dread of calamity, disaster and death, held me in an iron merciless grip. The only time I could forget the awful heartache was when fully absorbed in my writings.

Even sleep was frequently broken and very restless as all kinds of troublesome and tormenting pictures shot through my mind. At times I had terrible dreams and premonitions about my children. One night I dreamed about Karin—it was just before Christmas. I entered her room at dusk; night was settling down, things were hardly visible in that long and narrow room. About five feet away from me I saw a little girl standing. Going nearer, I realized it was Karin. I picked her up and lifted her into my arms and as I did so I felt that there was very little flesh on her bones. I was dreadfully shocked and pressed her intensely to my heart. As I had my arms around her little body I felt every bone. The child shivered; she was as cold as stone. But it wasn't the coldness that arrested me especially, it was the condition of her body.

"Are you very hungry, my little sunshine?" I asked in deep pain.

"Yes, Papa, I am very hungry," she answered in a feeble, thin voice.

Even in the dream I was aware of my helplessness, feeling that I could not give her anything to eat. It seemed as if I was transplanted into the conditions within Germany where nothing could be found to eat. I was gripped by a distress that tore me out of my sleep. It was an agony and fear which seized me much greater than ever before. My starving child stood before me for days, but here I was, impotent and fearful in my utter helplessness. Just a few hundred miles away from my darling and yet I did not know where she was, or whether dead or alive. Afterward it seemed that I held in my arms—a corpse. Sleep would not come thereafter for nights and nights, and I was in greatest distress and tormented with apprehensions during the days. Yet I knew not that my child was at death's very door over there in that German province at just that time. She had been given up by doctors and by friends; but somehow I prayed more earnestly and fervently with many others, and I am sure that the thousands of dear saints who were praying for my children had been interceding for my little Karin, all unknown to me, and God was working, praise his holy and wonderful name forever and forever!

Over seven weeks the child spent in that hospital, isolated from everybody. What agonies she must have gone through in her loneliness, can never be told. There are times today when Karin is tired or when something sad has happened—then in her features appears that profound sadness and her eyes speak of tragedy and hours of lonesome waiting; suffering still lingers in her consciousness at times. But God has preserved her life. He did not permit sorrow and hunger to reach beyond his limits. To him be all the praise and thanksgiving!

The year 1945 came to an end—that tragic year which brought millions of innocent human beings to the verge of destruction and when hundreds of thousands fell prey to the diabolical passion and hate of depraved and debased creatures who found pleasure in their fiendish ability to

THE JOURNEY HOME

torture others. Christmas was inexpressibly sad for me, too, sadder than I could ever put what I felt into words. I was alone and in my spirit I sensed in some measure that crisis which involved the condition and very existence of my daughters. January 1946 came and went. February passed without having any news.

But now we must retrace our steps to the time when I had sent the cablegram to President Truman. After I had received acknowledgment by letter from the legation in Stockholm, late in November, nothing more was heard. Only after my children returned and I was in touch with the lady that took care of Karin did I learn the particular details of developments which took place as the result of sending that cablegram to Washington. The President gave orders to the Department of State to give attention to the matter, and they in turn, contacted the Russian Ambassador who reported the case to his government in Moscow. The Russian Government gave instructions to the Russian Military Headquarters in Germany.

It was only three weeks after I sent that cablegram when the Russian Commander of Suhl, in that little town of Thuringia, on October 27, 1945, called Mrs. Staehler to come to local headquarters. The officer ordered her to bring Karin to the office on October 29, ready to be delivered to the American Zone.

Mrs. Stachler was greatly frightened, fearing there was some kind of a trick hidden behind this demand. Many children had been forcibly taken into Russia. She was deeply perturbed and determined not to give the child into the hands of the Russians. She went over to the commander and told the officer that Karin's sister Ruth was in another province of Germany and asked for permission to take the child to rejoin her sister in order that they might be transported together to the American Zone.

Mrs. Stachler and also the local commander were of the opinion that it was a general order for the Americans to vacate the Russian Zone. This caused them to give consent to have Karin taken to join her sister. That meant also permission for Mrs. Stachler to travel that distance with the child from Thuringia to Mecklenburg.

Karin's living conditions in Suhl were more favorable as she had received special consideration by the authorities. It was in her grandmother's place where real starvation conditions prevailed as already described, and there it was where the child began ailing and was overtaken by typhoid, lingering between life and death for long weeks in the hospital. During that time, Miss Klatt came to fetch the children to her home, but Karin could not be taken because of her illness and weakened condition. Ruth, however, was moved to Jerichow, Miss Klatt's home, where she rallied wonderfully, receiving better care and nourishment. As soon as Karin was stronger and able to be moved, she joined her sister. How marvelously the Lord had directed the children's pathway; not only to bring them out of dire want and distressing circumstances, but moving them nearer to Berlin. Jerichow, namely, was only about sixty (English) miles away from Berlin where the American political office is located.

55. SUPREME SURRENDER

Days, weeks, and months had dragged and moved on well into 1946 without bringing any news of my children. Every attempt to get out of a deadlock failed. The hope aroused within me by my last tangible act—the cablegram to President Truman—had died. I was heading for a final climax in my anxiety. Despondency was gnawing at my faith's resistance. Friends tried to encourage me, but all was so hopeless. There was no avenue left to pursue in the attempt to help my children or bring them to me. Mine was a double sorrow. First, I did not know where they were, and secondly, I knew that wherever they were they were near starvation.

The night of March 8 was a sleepless one. My weakened heart troubled me severely and I expected momentarily that I would leave this world, fleeing from all worries to be with Jesus, my Lord. The morning dawned and wore on into early afternoon when I reached the climax. I came to a point where it seemed that control over myself would slip away. As I frantically paced back and forth in my room, I tried to pray but could not collect my thoughts sufficiently to form a prayer. Often before in such moments I resorted to worshipping and praising the Lord, even though my heart was in the clutches of despair. I called out the name of Jesus—that sweet and wonderful name—the name that strikes terror to the most desperate forces of the enemy. I called out that name now from the depths of my despair as I paced back and forth in the room. Often that act, continued long enough, gave me relief and caused me to lift my head above the din of hopelessness and despondency there in the prison cell.

This time it did not seem to work. I felt as if I were a hollow shell with nothing inside but misery. Then that noble and wonderful song, "Sweet Hour of Prayer," came to memory. I took my songbook and sang it through:

> Sweet hour of prayer! sweet hour of prayer!
> That calls me from a world of care,
> And bids me at my Father's throne,
> Make all my wants and wishes known:
> In seasons of distress and grief,
> My soul has often found relief;
> And oft escaped the tempter's snare,
> By thy return, sweet hour of prayer!

Sweet hour of prayer! sweet hour of prayer!
Thy wings shall my petition bear,
To him whose truth and faithfulness
Engage the waiting soul to bless
And since he bids me seek his face,
Believe his word, and trust his grace;
I'll cast on him my every care,
And wait for thee, sweet hour of prayer!

Sweet hour of prayer! sweet hour of prayer!
May I thy consolation share,
Till, from Mount Pisgah's lofty height,
I view my home and take my flight;
This robe of flesh I'll drop, and rise,
To seize the everlasting prize;
And shout, while passing through the air,
Farewell, farewell, sweet hour of prayer!

I took my guitar and sang it once more to the accompaniment of that instrument. While singing and playing I became oblivious of my surroundings. I was not even aware of pacing my room. A hallowed and sacred sense of his presence had seized me. One sentence of that song especially kept ringing within me. Finally, I uttered it before the Lord audibly: "I'll cast on him my every care, and wait for thee, sweet hour of prayer!" The song kept resounding and ringing within my heart. My thoughts lingered in sorrow upon my children's plight. There was a tremendous conflict as my heart and mind wanted to remain in the presence of the Lord, and yet, at the same time I desired to be in thought with my daughters.

"Where may my Ruth and Karin be at present?" rang out within me.

"O Lord, my little daughters may both be extremely hungry at this very hour. They may shiver and freeze," I sighed before the Lord, being greatly troubled.

Sadness swept over me anew. My eyes grew moist as I felt my complete helplessness; not even one morsel of food could I send to them, nor could I write to them. Separated from them both, my heart was pained unspeakably.

"I'll cast on him my every care," rang within me again and again.

"Lord, I have heavy cares which weigh me down day and night, but the greatest of all is the plight of my two innocent children who are stranded there in Germany. The burden is too heavy—it will crush me. I'll lay it down at your feet, my Jesus. I'll cast on you, my every care, O God."

I kept on pacing the floor while the battle within me raged.

"Where did you get your cares and burdens?" a voice suddenly resounded clearly within my troubled heart. I was startled. I stopped pacing—for a moment I remained silent. No words would come. I did not dare to speak.

"You have given me those burdens before. Where did you get them again?" the voice within me continued.

"My loving Jesus, how stupid I am. I picked up those cares and burdens and took them back with me again, every time after finishing my prayer and wearily I carried them along my pilgrim way. Forgive, forgive me, my precious Savior!"

Tears of regret flowed as I stood before my heavenly Savior. It was clearly a reprimand by Jesus himself, and I then realized how little the faith was which I had exercised. I realized also how deeply I had neglected to trust my Savior, and my precious and loving Jesus taught me in those moments a very valuable lesson which in reality I should have learned a hundred times before. As I meditated, I had to acknowledge that Jesus never refused to bear my burdens; neither was he ever tired of them. But we usually are too impatient, so we pick up our burdens again and continue to worry about them, thinking we can thereby hasten matters. That is why the Lord must permit troubles to come into our lives, in order to teach us the art of casting *all* our cares upon him and to lean on his strong shoulders. In this way he carries not only our burdens, but he bears us as well (Isa. 46:4). And that is why our burdens can become so easy and so light that we are able to rejoice even under the most trying circumstances. His yoke indeed is easy and his burden light (Matt. 11:30). We should let him carry our burdens and all that depresses or causes us discouragement. I had this lesson brought home to my heart very forcibly in those moments.

God was already working. The news was being framed already, unknown to me, under God's marvelous care for my children. Preparations were on the way far off to help my children. My Savior had already moved them into a better home and better care, glory to his holy name forever!

That afternoon I made a real transaction before the Lord. There in those afternoon hours of March 8, 1946, I finally laid my precious daughters into the tender and almighty hands of my Savior. Trustfully looking to him I finally made the supreme surrender; whether my girls were dead or alive, I laid them into his loving pierced hands, whatever might happen, or had happened to them. That afternoon my daughters really passed into the ownership of my precious Savior and Lord, and I said to Jesus: "Lord, if I never see my girls again, if my precious Ruth and Karin should be dead at this time, it is all right with me. The case is in *your* hands, they are *yours*, at whatever cost, be it life or death."

That afternoon I could fathom what may have transpired in the heart of Abraham before he walked up the slope of that sacred mountain to sacrifice his only begotten and beloved son. To Abraham, his only son Isaac was already sacrificed to God while they walked upon the mountainside. He could not have sacrificed him more if he actually would have plunged the knife into the body of his beloved son. Isaac had been surrendered. Isaac was dead to

288

his father Abraham, already. That is why the Lord did not require him to actually sacrifice his only begotten. He had made the supreme surrender. His heart was free, it was easy as he looked into the face of his loving Father in heaven and smilingly talked with him as he faced that supreme sacrifice.

And what a change takes place when we make such a surrender to God! From that afternoon on, I could not further agonize for the safety of my daughters. I *knew* God had taken the case—it was *His*. I had nothing more to do with it. In my prayers afterwards, I usually would say, "Lord, it is Thy case, whatever Thou doest or doest not, is all right. Thou knowest better than I what is good for me." Yet, actually I did not know anything more than before about my daughters.

While I was battling on the 8th of March before the Lord for my daughters, and made the supreme surrender to him, there in Berlin in the office of the United States Political Adviser for Germany, the door opened and a young lady came in. In each of her hands, right and left, she led one frail little girl; one, five and a half years old and the other ten years of age. The youngest girl especially, looked emaciated; the older one seemed in better physical condition. They had next to no hair on their heads. Hesitatingly, they walked to the desk behind which an American officer was seated. When the girl's names were mentioned, a flash of surprise, mingled with pity, showed in his features for a moment. Evidently the officer had some knowledge of the case. There had been a previous communication, not only with the young lady, but the case had been touched upon by the UNRA office. Inquiries had also come from Washington, D.C. So their case was on file and recorded. These two frail girls were none other than my daughters and the young lady with them was Miss Ellen Klatt who had them in her care.

Their status as American citizens was established and an American physician examined them. Afterward a report was dictated to a typist which reads as follows:

The office of the UNITED STATES POLITICAL ADVISER FOR GERMANY presents its compliments to the American Legation, Stockholm, and has the honor to refer to the case of Ruth and Karin Schmidt, 10 and 6 years old, respectively, the two children of Mr. G. Herbert Schmidt, an American citizen, presently residing at Möklinta, Sweden.

Until recently the two children were being cared for by their aged grandmother, and also partly by Mrs. Ella Straehler, but they are now residing at 2 Lindenstrasse, Jerichow, Über Genthin, c/o Miss Ellen Klatt, who has been appointed by the court as guardian for the children.

Miss Klatt called at this office on March 8th, together with Ruth and Karin, who only recently have recovered from an attack of typhus. Whereas Ruth has completely recovered, Karin is still weak but otherwise the children appear to be in a fairly good health condition.

The suggestion was made by this office to Miss Klatt to place the children in the Displaced Persons center at 87 Teltower Damm, Berlin, where it would be possible to feed them properly and also to give them medical treatment, if necessary. This suggestion was for the moment turned down by Miss Klatt who does not wish to be separated from the children and believes that it would be best for the children to remain at present under her supervision until at least such time as she would receive instructions from the children's father, Mr. G. Herbert Schmidt.

It would be appreciated if Mr. G. Herbert Schmidt would be informed of the contents of this note and requested to indicate either to this office or to Miss Klatt, his plans for the future of the children. In this connection, reference is made to Telegram No. 145 of November 16, 1945, received from the American Embassy, Moscow, indicating that the Swedish Alien Commission had informed the American Legation, Stockholm, that Swedish visa had been granted reportedly to American citizen, Karin Schmidt, born

Danzig, February 21, 1940, daughter of American citizen, Gustave Schmidt, residing in Stockholm.

There is enclosed a letter written by Ruth to her father, on the back of which there is contained a report from Miss Ellen Klatt. There is, furthermore, enclosed a sketch of Ruth. It would be appreciated if the letter and sketch be delivered to Mr. G. Herbert Schmidt, provided the Legation perceives no objection thereto.

When I struggled that memorable afternoon, I did not know what was transpiring there in Berlin. But God knew! That letter was mailed from Berlin. It had to go through Paris and it took considerable time for it to reach the American Legation in Stockholm. But I was worrying about my children. While I was agonizing there on that afternoon, the Lord could also see a letter bearing the date February 27, 1946, from Suhl, written by Mrs. Stachler who had taken care of my child. It had been sent to an English brother who served under the British Forces in Germany. This letter was sent to London to our mutual friend, Brother Greenstreet. It was on its way that afternoon of March 8. The Lord also saw a letter which had been written by my mother-in-law early in March which was on the way as well. And also a report was handed to the American officials in Berlin on March 8 and sent on to me in Sweden. From all these sources information had been sent and was on the way to me. A little letter written by Ruth's own hand was also on the way to me during the time when I agonized before the Lord that afternoon. No wonder that my precious Savior, seeing all that information and having already arranged everything to solve that great problem and anxiety for me, asked the question in the way he did, saying, "Where did you get your burdens?"

Two weeks after that eighth day of March, news that had been on the way began to arrive. When later surveying those developments, I saw myself in the role of an anxious little boy who bothers his father about problems which his parents had already taken care of and lovingly had worked out a solution. But the little boy, not knowing such, was still troubled. Seeing tears flowing from his boys' eyes, the father would say smilingly to his son, who was still uninformed: "My foolish little boy, where do you get your tears? Let your father shoulder your burdens permanently. He will worry about your problems and bring about their solution."

Besides receiving that official report from the American authorities in Berlin and the other letters that reached me later, through the assistance of my friend, the most precious and sweetest letter was the one written by my little daughter Ruth. It read as follows:

> My beloved Papa,
>
> I am very glad that I have a sign of life from you. We have received your letter through the American Consul in Berlin. Karin and I are now at Aunt Elly and Aunt Gerda's home in Jerichow. We are well taken care of. Aunt Ella Staehler brought Karin to us. After Karin had been brought to Grandma's home she soon was stricken with typhoid. On the 10th of January she was released from the hospital and then Aunt Elly went over to fetch her. I also had typhoid before I left Danzig. In that sickness I lost all of my hair. Now it is growing nicely again but I still look like a boy. Since I am with Aunt Elly I have gained much in weight because it is better here. When I was with my grandma I didn't have much to eat. I am now going to school and am in the 6th grade. Aunt Elly wants to send me to the high school after Easter. Grandma is at present very weak and has but very little to eat. She has only dry bread and some watery potato soup. While I was with my grandma I weighed only 51 pounds, now I weigh 67. How are you, my dear Papa? I hope that you are in good health. I would be very glad and rejoice if I could visit you.

In that strain the child went on to write in her childish way, rejoicing that she could write a few lines to her Papa.

56. Anxious Waiting

The greatest anxiety was over. I knew that my girls were safe; that they were in comparatively good health. I now had the satisfying feeling that they were under the supervision of the American authorities. God had answered prayer. The only problem left was how to get them over to Sweden, away from Germany. That proved to be very difficult. Many, many formalities were necessary to go through in order to pave the way for my children finally to be brought to me, but my Jesus was fully equal to finish what he had begun, all glory be to his matchless name forever!

The first letter which I received giving me information about my children was the one from Mrs. Staehler who had taken Karin away from Danzig. That letter was enclosed in a communication from Brother Greenstreet, a friend of mine in London. He wrote as follows:

> The enclosed letter from Mrs. Staehler has been received here through my correspondent in Germany and we hasten to send it on to you as requested. We have only delayed just long enough to extract any information likely to prove helpful in further developments that may arise. I am told that the letter was received by a Mr. Moller, the German brother who wrote to Suhl to obtain information as mentioned in my last letter to you. We rejoice for any news which we can obtain to help you and your dear girls. If anything further comes to hand we will not delay to advise you. Should you have any news, kindly let me know as soon as possible.
>
> It appears that the UNRA are on the lookout for your dear ones, as well, so I trust something will soon take place which will restore them to you before you sail for America.

On April 6, I received a letter from the Legation of the United States of America in Stockholm, which read:

> Dear Mr. Schmidt,

There is enclosed for your information a copy of a letter, with its enclosures concerning your two daughters, addressed to this Legation by the Office of the United States Political Adviser for Germany in Berlin. It is suggested that your reply to the letter mentioned above, be sent to this office for transmission to the United States Political Adviser's Office.

F. C. SIGMOND
American Vice-Consul

The letter indicated here is the lengthy report from Berlin, already brought to the attention of the reader in the previous chapter. Again I had to wait two weeks until I received further news regarding my daughters. On April 15, a letter reached me from the American Red Cross office in Stockholm, dated April 13, which contained the following message:

Dear Mr. Schmidt,

We have just received a cable from Paris in answer to our telegram of April 9, advising of the interest of the United States Political Adviser, Berlin, and suggesting your guarantee of payment for plane passage for the children to Stockholm. They tell us that the American Red Cross Area Executive, Berlin, advises that arrangements have been made for release of the children from the Russian Zone. They understand that the R.A.F. Transport Command will take them to Stockholm. They will advise us further when there is additional information available.

ALICE G. GILLEN
Assistant to the Director

The thrills that surged through me as I held that letter from the Red Cross in my hands, cannot easily be described. There was a similar moment when there in the dark cell in Danzig, after not having seen any sunshine for four months, the first sun-ray burst into my cell and lingered on the wall of my dark and dismal room. This

294

letter from the Red Cross had a peculiarly pleasant effect on me. It seemed as if I had been walking along my weary way through a cold and dismal tunnel and suddenly emerged from its dark and gloomy confines into the golden sunshine of God's out-of-doors. As in a daze, I boarded the bus in front of our house in Möklinta and made my way to the station, twelve (English) miles away—then rushed to Stockholm by train.

First, I went to the American Red Cross office and there found that it was not so easy to make arrangements for payment of the fares for my girls and to get permission for them to be transported from Berlin by plane. After several futile efforts I was advised to appeal to Mrs. Soderberg, head of the International Department of the Swedish Red Cross at Stockholm. She knew the details about the desperate case of my lost children and showed a real heart interest. It was through her efforts that final arrangements for the payment of my children's fare by plane were made, as she picked up the telephone and contacted the Minister of Foreign Affairs of the Swedish government.

After some minutes the difficulties were removed as the Foreign Department assumed the responsibility for payment of transportation. I was required to deposit the equivalent sum of money in the Treasury of the Red Cross. Then I gave my written statement about transporting my daughters by air which message was telegraphed to Berlin. I was told that it would take several days for that telegram to reach Berlin, as it had to pass through Paris and then via American Occupation Headquarters at Frankfurt, and from there, relayed to Berlin. Then I was also informed that after the message reached Berlin, the children could arrive in Stockholm anytime during the day or night without advance notice. So a time of waiting began. My vigil continued for the actual arrival of my girls. Day and night I was on the alert. I went to the Swedish airport and talked to an official who promised that should they receive any advance news, it would be transmitted to me immediately; otherwise, I would be informed as soon as the children arrived and they in turn would be held for me until I could reach the airport.

It was indeed anxious waiting, as hour by hour I had the little ones on my mind and heart. I pictured them as being up in the plane, I envisaged their arrival, but from day to day I waited, until a whole week passed—then another week crept by without any indication as to the date of their arrival.

Finally, Mrs. Söderberg, with other friends of mine, and I myself, despaired of waiting. "There is a possibility that your children have been taken to Lübeck and put aboard the Swedish steamer which plies between the German and a Swedish port," Mrs. Söderberg remarked.

As a steamer was due on Friday May 3, in the Port of Helsingborg at the very southern tip of Sweden, I was advised to proceed to that city. It was five hours by fast train from Stockholm, so I boarded the train and rushed over to that city at once. When I inquired about a steamer being due there from Lübeck, nobody seemed to know anything about it. I waited all day Friday, Saturday and Sunday. Then I was told that a ship might arrive on Monday or Tuesday. Finally, on Tuesday the steamer pulled in, but my children were not on board. Again I was at the end of my resources and did not know where to turn.

57. HAPPY REUNION

For hours I was near despair again, but then a telephone call reached me from Stockholm. It was from Mrs. Söderberg of the Swedish Red Cross. She had been very busy during those days following up my case. When she heard that the steamer did not arrive she moved to other authorities. Now her message was as follows:

Your children arrived in London by an American military plane. They will proceed from there to Sweden by plane, landing in Gothenburg. Go there immediately to await your daughters.

As in a trance I hung up the receiver and immediately, Brother Pfeifer, my friend in whose home I stayed, and I, made preparations for the trip to Gothenburg which was a three-hours train ride from Helsingborg. We went to the airport there when the London plane arrived, but my children were not on board. On Thursday noon, we again went to the airport—but in vain. On that afternoon I asked the airport office to telephone London and ask the officials there whether my children had arrived and what time they would proceed to Sweden. The information given was that two little girls were at the airport, but by another name, and would proceed to Sweden two days later, on Saturday.

Having received that news from the London Airport, we thought there was no use for us to go and meet the London plane, the airport being eight (English) miles distance, as my daughters would not be coming until Saturday anyway. Strange as it may seem, the London Airport official had mis-informed us. The truth was that my girls were already in a Swedish plane on their way to Gothenburg, Sweden, and arrived at the airport in the evening, while Brother Pfeifer and I were in the hotel. The children were put out of the plane and a search began for their father, who was to have come and claimed them, but I was not there; neither had I informed the officials at the airport about my place of lodging. The police began a search for me at the airport; they searched for me in the city—and I was ignorant of it all.

While all of this was going on, a thought seized me forcefully to call the Pastor of the Smyrna Church in

Gothenburg, with whom I was acquainted, to inform him that I had arrived and to give him my address. Likewise I phoned the pastor's home, but he was not there, so I gave his wife my number. It was only a quarter of an hour after I called, when there was a police call in the home of the pastor asking whether they knew where I was. The lost was found and I was informed that I should get in touch immediately with the police. When I contacted police headquarters, the officials were very much incensed against me, asking all kinds of questions, because as a refugee, I was not permitted to be in Gothenburg without permission of the Foreigner's Commission in Stockholm. When I explained sufficiently, they were satisfied and then they told me that my girls had arrived and as I was not there to receive them, they were returned to the plane and taken on to Stockholm. This was late in the evening. I had placed a telephone call to my friend, Pastor Weger, in Stockholm a few minutes before ten o'clock in the evening to ask whether he knew anything about my daughters.

"Have you heard anything about my girls?" I asked.

"Yes," was his reply. "In fifteen minutes I am going to meet your daughters at the bus, coming from the airport, and I am going to take them into my home where they will spend their first night."

That was one time in my life when I had a strong desire to jump through the telephone and reach Stockholm immediately, to be on hand and receive my girls upon their arrival. To my great sorrow, that was impossible. Strange things happen in the world. Here I was waiting and agonizing before the Lord for years for my daughters, then when the time of their arrival came, I raced across Sweden to receive them, and now they actually got ahead of me, just because the wrong information was given me in London regarding the time of their arrival. I had to catch up with them. Brother Pfeifer and I had barely enough time to settle the hotel bill and board the fast train for

Stockholm. All night we speeded along, arriving in Stockholm at seven o'clock in the morning. It was the tenth of May, 1946. As we did not care to arouse the family too early, we lingered in the station until eight o'clock that morning before we entered the home of my friend, Pastor Weger.

The dramatic moment had finally come. I trembled with excitement as we were ushered into the room. My girls had been awakened. They sat up in the bed when I entered the room. Ruth gazed at me. Then she wept, and our tears were flowing over each other, mingled tears of joy and thankfulness to God. Little Karin, too, stared at me as if I were an apparition. Her face showed pain. She tried to fight back her tears but they were coursing down her cheeks. The time had come to press my daughters to my heart. The thrill of that reunion created reactions which happen only rarely in one's life. God alone had made it possible, this wondrous happiness of a lifetime crowded into a few moments, this happy reunion. As I gazed at them I had a profound feeling of thankfulness to God for preserving their lives, a thankfulness also to the many thousands of faithful saints who had been praying and interceding for us. And now the arm of the Lord had moved on our behalf and here they were, my precious daughters, as if they had emerged from the grave. God had graciously and in mercy brought them back to me, all praise and glory and thanksgiving be unto his mighty and wonderful name forever and forever!

Although through the letters I learned that they had had very good care since they had gone to Miss Klatt's home—especially the last few weeks, they had improved greatly, still, they looked emaciated, very thin and frail, Karin, more so than Ruth. I was greatly surprised when I was introduced to a young girl in uniform, an American military nurse who had been sent along with my girls, and who was to deliver them to me in person. That was very noble of the American officials in Berlin.

After Brother Weger, my friend, had observed the welcoming scene, he said to me, pointing to the bed where my girls had slept, "Hundreds of times my wife and I have knelt at this bedside praying for your girls to return. Now the Lord has honored us and given us the joy of having them spend their first night with us after their arrival in Stockholm, and in this very bed." God be praised forever! Amen! Amen! It resounded within me, "God had done all things well."

As in a dream, Brother Pfeifer and I took the girls along with us. Together with the nurse and Pastor Weger, we took a tour through that lovely city of Stockholm where such wealth and beauty is displayed. To my children, who had never seen such splendor, it was all an unreal display of a fairyland. Both of my darling girls had seen only misery, tragedy, blood, death and ruins. There they were, walking peacefully and joyously along in the streets of Stockholm! We went to a restaurant for lunch. It was pitiful to watch them eat. Karin cleared a whole rich portion of meat and vegetables with bread, and looked for more, but of course, it would not have been wise to give her more. They ate and ate and ate. They stared at those wonderful shop windows, they gazed through and saw the pastry and chocolates; the children's playthings—all was new to them. They were utterly fascinated. It was hard for me to keep back tears as I observed my precious children in their amazement. They were now with me, never to part again, if God in his wisdom and mercy so willed and decreed.

On the following Sunday, Brother and Sister Weger, the children and I took a walk in the city. I had Ruth with me and little Karin walked with my friends. It happened that Ruth and I were separated from the others while crossing the street. I was with Ruth on the other side and walked on slowly without waiting for the others to follow. In the next moment I heard a heart-rending child's scream; it was Karin who was trembling, in greatest distress because to her it seemed that I was going away from her. I could hear that scream for weeks, within me. After that, my girls held on to my hands when we walked, for fear that Papa would go away from them again.

"Papa, you will never go away from us again, will you?" little Karin said to me pleadingly during those first weeks of glad reunion.

"No, Karin, by God's grace, we are going to stay together now and always," I answered solemnly. How wonderful it was to be able to say that. "God had done all things well." Oh, could I only praise him enough!

58. PREPARING FOR OUR DEPARTURE

In January 1946, when I had exhausted every avenue of approach to do something actual for my children's rescue, I had despaired of waiting any longer, as I had begun to believe it was useless and that Sweden was not the place to accomplish anything further for my children's welfare. Perhaps I would have more opportunity to do something from home—the United States, I thought. With a heavy heart I had decided to return alone, to America. When I arrived in Sweden I had told the consul that I would not leave Sweden and return to America without my family. Afterward, when my wife passed on to be with Jesus, and my two little girls were left destitute in Germany, I continued in anxious helplessness waiting for them. Now I had no more hope remaining to do anything for them from there. I went on my way to the steamship office one day to book passage, since it took a long time to get reservations.

On the way a strong impression made me decide to book passage not only for myself, but also for my daughters.

"Where are your daughters?" I was asked.

"Oh, they are still in Germany, but they will be brought to me in the near future," I said, without having any tangible reason for making such a statement, but somehow I said it with the voice of faith.

When later I received notice from the steamship office that the M.S. *Gripsholm* would sail on May 14, and that places were reserved for my girls and me, I had a strange feeling, because I did not yet know whether my children were alive. However, we were to sail on May 14. That eventful day, March 8, came when I made that supreme surrender to my Jesus, placing my girls completely into God's keeping. Afterward the first reports about my daughters reached me, and finally my children arrived in Stockholm, four days before the ship was to sail. As I had spent several weeks waiting for the arrival of my girls, I had no time to prepare for sailing so quickly. I also realized that my daughters were very feeble, so I decided to defer our departure one month. Places were arranged for the next sailing of the Gripsholm on June 18, which gave us time to leisurely prepare for our voyage to the homeland.

That delay also gave opportunity for my girls to stay in Möklinta in the home of the Sisters Enagrius, where I had had such a blessed and quiet shelter during the anxious and seemingly endless years of vigil for my daughters. The loving care and attention which they received in that home has entered the hearts of my girls that even today they brighten up in delight when Aunt Hildur is mentioned. It was God's own arrangement that he prepared such a wondrous haven of restful care and love right after they came out of their tragic ordeal in Germany. And they did and still do appreciate it, as in their prayers, the names Aunt Hildur and Aunt Ellen are still heard. It is touching how they mention in their daily prayers, the names of a number of friends who have aroused their imagination and gratitude.

The Lord has a plan for us and sees events that still lie in the future. That I have fully realized in my own life, when the Lord revealed certain future developments. That was also the case during the time I waited anxiously and with such dire forebodings for my daughters. The month of January 1946 was a crucial month. All my efforts had ebbed out into blind alleys and the future was indeed black with uncertainty and helplessness.

In the night of January 31, I heard a voice while sleeping, which said: "a great thing will happen on June 8." I made a note of that strange occurrence in my daybook under that date. In the rush of time and overwhelming events I had forgotten that dream. Plans for leaving our peaceful haven of refuge and rest had to be made long in advance of our departure. Urgent invitations from friends who desired to see my daughters, made it necessary to fit the date of our departure sufficiently early to allow the necessary time for these visits and our departure from Möklinta was fixed for June 8. When my itinerary was arranged in all detail, I made a record of it in my daybook, and there found the note that a great thing would happen on that date.

It was on the eighth of June when we finally left the lovely home in Möklinta and said goodbye to our noble friends in the place to which God had called me aside to fight the desperate battles in quietness and solitude; the home where I had passed through so many agonies and anxieties for my family. On that eighth day of June, we left to proceed to Stockholm, and from there to Helsingborg—then to Gothenburg to board the ship which was to carry us homeward to America!

"Leave your case in my hands," the Lord had said to me that afternoon of March 8. "I will take care of your case," the Lord assured me now. He did take care of the case in a loving, marvelous and masterly way. It was a great miracle of God that had preserved my life in that terrible and dismal cell in Danzig. It was God who had finally helped me to escape out of the hands of the Nazis to that haven of safety in Sweden. It was God, through numerous miracles who had preserved the life of my daughters and kept them through typhoid and through perilous dangers of various kinds. Yes, he had preserved them! Praises be to his holy name! It was God who caused me to send a cablegram to the President, through which he worked and arranged the uniting of my daughters. Hallelujah!

It was God who brought them safely to Sweden and now I had them with me. It was like a dream. It was almost unreal after the cruel years of anxiety and uncertainty— after being accustomed to just thinking of my girls in uncertain and helpless, impotent ways, lingering between hope and fearful forebodings. It was quite a task for me to switch over into the reality of victory and just to look at my girls and rejoice with thanksgivings before the Lord.

59. LEAVING EUROPE'S SHORES

Many saints in Sweden who had faithfully prayed time and again and had tried to encourage me and lighten my burdens and anxiety, now rejoiced with me, manifesting their delight in wonderful ways. Seeking to give vent to their joy, sisters from the Philadelphia Church "borrowed" my daughters one afternoon in Stockholm, went into the stores and clothed them with wonderful things from head to foot. How lovely my girls looked when they were literally wrapped into the love of God's people—a love that can only be shown in such a noble beauty by those who have the love of God dwelling in their hearts. My many personal friends, especially Brother Pfeifer, who had time and again shown their wonderful interest and concern for my daughters, were now rejoicing with me to the full, and how full of thrills was I when we, my daughters, Brother Pfeifer and I finally made our way to Göteborg, the port of embarkation where the M. S. *Gripsholm* was waiting to receive us.

On the last Sunday before sailing I spoke in the Smyrna Tabernacle at Gothenburg, a church of 3,000 members.[15] There I voiced my final testimony, giving tribute to my wonderful Savior who terminated my great sorrow and period of anguished waiting, by uniting me with my precious daughters who had gone through so much suffering in near-starvation and sickness, that humanly speaking, there was no possible hope left for them to survive. God had made the impossibilities possible, answering the fervent prayers of the saints. That congregation who had often surrounded the throne of grace in pleading for the recovery of my daughters, now saw my two little girls sitting beside me on the platform in that great auditorium. Two living witnesses to the power of prayer and the faithfulness of God were in their midst. Reverend Harold Gustafson also gave expression and tribute to the marvelous grace, love and power of God in this complicated case which was from the human stand-point, so full of impossibilities.

I shall never forget those marvelous last days in Gothenburg. We moved about in that city, full of glad anticipation of boarding the ship. All had turned into such a wonderful victory. The Lord "had done all things well." He had changed the storm clouds' distress into the sunshine of peace, tranquility and rejoicing. HE was the ONE who turned the hopeless battle into a wonderful triumph by

---

[15] This church still meets in Gothenburg under the name Smyrna International.

reuniting me with my precious daughters. Again, as on the day when I walked out of that dismal prison in Danzig; the 126th Psalm was ringing in my heart:

When the LORD turned again the captivity of Zion, we were like them that dream. Then was our mouth filled with laughter and our tongue with singing; then said they among the heathen, The LORD hath done great things for us; whereof we are glad. They that sow in tears shall reap in joy. He that goeth forth and weepeth, bearing precious seed, shall doubtless come again with rejoicing, bringing his sheaves with him.

Those days of seven years ago also flashed through my memory. It was seven years ago almost to the day when my wife and I landed in Hamburg, coming from America on the May 31, 1939. And exactly seven years ago on June 6, we arrived in Danzig. The period of my life began which proved to be so tragic for the whole world as well as for my family and me.

My beloved wife fell in the heat of the battle. She wears now the crown of victory in glory. God has decreed it differently with me. I am in life, and my precious Savior did not let the cup of bitterness become too hard to drink. He modified it by giving me my girls again. Now I walked hand in hand with them through the streets of that clean and noble city of Gothenburg as if I had just succeeded in shaking off a terrible nightmare. No wonder my heart was singing—giving unending praises to my precious Redeemer, praise his holy name forever!

Finally, the afternoon of Tuesday, June 18, had come. The concluding preparations had been made. Luggage was examined and checked. Together with my friends, the Brothers Pfeifer and Kinderman, and my daughters, we found a corner on the pier in Göteborg, where we united in a last prayer and thanksgiving. I could not help but open my eyes during prayer to make sure that my daughters were present. There they stood with me, their little hands folded, their eyes closed and the expression in their features rather sad, imprinted during years of deep privation and the ravages of disease. They followed the prayers, also conscious of the import of the hour. No, it is not a glorious dream which crumbles into nothing when awakened. I see reality of delight as numberless times before. I was compelled to pick up the threads of anxiety and worries after dreams in which I had been with my children, only to awaken with a still greater pain, which at times had almost crushed my heart utterly by its iron grip. This was glorious reality! I saw the bowed heads of my precious children, saw their slightly curling hair, their folded hands; saw the serious expressions in their faces as if they felt their deep gratitude toward God who had brought such a glorious end to their suffering and pain. Yes, tears gathered in my eyes, also a tribute in thankfulness to my wonderful Savior who so marvelously answered the insistent and faithful prayers of thousands of his saints.

The time came for a last handshake and farewell to the friends who stayed behind. Then an excited, "Auf Wiedersehn" resounded from the lips of my girls who could not yet speak English—only German. Now my daughters grasped my hands more tightly as we stepped up a few steps and then walked over the gangplank to the promenade deck of the stately ship, *Gripsholm*. While crossing, such thrills of exuberant joy flooded my whole being as I had experienced but a few times before in my life. Then we stood on deck gazing down to the pier where the two brethren were still standing. We waved our hands as is usual, towards those remaining behind. The gangplank was finally lifted away and the last tie with the mainland severed. The ship began to float away slightly from the pier; tugs were towing and shoving the great ship, ever widening the gap between the pier and us until it moved along under its own power. I stood on the deck of that noble ship, the *Gripsholm*, which during the dreadful war had been a messenger of mercy to so many stranded and despairing refugees, carrying them back to their loved ones who awaited them in different parts of the globe.

Now, this was another errand of mercy, carrying us out of tragedy and sorrow, anxieties and fears indescribable, and back to our dear ones in our homeland—the United States. Praise God! My thoughts once more went back to the events of those three and a half years of anxious waiting and prayerful vigil; first for my beloved wife, and then for my children. I was thinking of the loving kindness of Swedish Christian people. I especially recalled the time when I walked out from the custody of the authorities in Stockholm, led by Pastor Lewi Pethrus, and then how I was clothed and cared for by the brethren in the Philadelphia Church for several months until help reached me from the United States. Many of the saints from that peaceful and noble country, Sweden, have done their utmost to encourage me in my distress, praying and interceding for me throughout those crucial years. They were one in like precious faith with the saints in our United States, England and other countries. They had trusted and believed that our precious Lord and Savior in his own good time would return my darling children to me.

Thus we had been borne on wings of loving and faithful intercession and prayer by thousands of God's people in many different parts of the world until the arm of our great God moved, marvelously intervening and preserving the lives of my little daughters and myself. He finally led us back into the circle of our dear friends.

Now we stood on the deck of that noble ship. We had heard the anchors being raised and the contact with the pier being broken. It was the visible symbol of that sad period of seven years having been brought to a termination; the ending of that period which had been filled with so many trials and tragedies. Now, that period had terminated in these very moments.

All was so thrilling to my girls, so new. They had seen many things; they had been thrown about much in Europe —they flew from Berlin via London to Stockholm. Now they were speeding on westward toward our homeland. Whatever was in store for us will be a new chapter in our lives. When leaving Europe's shores, physical contact with friends there was ended, the only tie remaining being the tie of friendship and thankfulness to my precious prayer-warrior friends whom we had won in times of trials, and who had prayed for us and helped win the victory. May God bless and reward each one of them abundantly.

The ship docked in Liverpool. Six hundred additional passengers came on board. I watched while the luggage was taken aboard. The irresponsible way in which they handled baggage of all sizes and descriptions astonished the on-lookers. Suitcases, hat boxes, valises, gladstones, steamer and wardrobe trunks were all thrown—not placed—on the giant netting, falling on it every which way. The luggage was piled up high, then the four corner loops were taken together, the derrick hooks placed into these loops and up they were lifted and squeezed together by the tremendous weight. Any frail pieces of luggage were simply squashed. I could hear the cracking of the framework of the luggage. The hundreds of passengers' eyes looked on merrily. Expressions of delight or astonishment were heard, just because the crushed hatbox or suitcase happened to belong to someone else. Many passengers watched and looked on with piercing eyes for fear their own luggage might be among the lot.

Those hustling workmen who were handling the whole "show" were operating in utmost haste to get the work done and have everything quickly loaded on deck of the ship.

When all the heap of luggage composing one load was carted down on deck, one side of the netting was retained in the hook of the derrick, which thus pulled the netting out from under the luggage. Some of the pieces of luggage were lifted bodily into the air, being caught in the netting and finally fell back onto the deck with a crash. I wonder what happened to mi-lady's eau de cologne, her hair tonic, or to the nicely folded clothes to be used for the next social event during the voyage? This way of handling things may spare time, but in my estimation comprises civilization's paradox. Our generation has learned how to split atoms, but they also continue to split their suitcases, the gladstones, the brave but feeble European steamer-trunks and hat-boxes. Insurance is available and the luggage manufacturers have their hey-day working overtime.

On Monday, June 24, the weather was getting rough. Lilliputian man began feeling a bit unpleasant and a number were not in such good humor, so they had to pause in their acts of sin and vice. Even the poisonous alcohol did not taste as good as usual to them, because Almighty God had framed them in such a peculiar way that they can be incapacitated. Yes, a temporary halt is dedicated at times by God of the universe, whom they deny or whom they locked into the church or chapel, visiting him occasionally—if at all—and finally expect him to provide for them a nice heaven after their wicked life.

Excepting a few foggy and rough days, the voyage was excellent. Sunny days on the decks of a ship cannot be easily excelled by anything on land. My daughters in their unassuming exuberant joyfulness won many new friends on that ship. They spoke only German and did so without being conscious of any offence. The passengers looked at them, some astonished enough as if to ask, "How is this possible, that German children are on board this ship?" A number of passengers had painful memories of concentration camps, tortures to their blood relatives, and one could not blame them if they received a shock at hearing the German language so openly spoken. But I must say something especially regarding the numerous Jewish passengers who had been in concentration camps. They befriended my children and conversed in German, entertaining them for long periods during the whole voyage. That proved to me that reconciliation among mankind is possible if not interfered with by vicious propagandists of hate.

My daughters had not been honored by being born here in the United States. The call of God upon my life made it necessary for me to spend most of my years beyond the borders of my country. So it happened that both of my girls were born in the Free City of Danzig, but both were registered immediately after their birth in the American Consulate and received their American birth certificates. They had never seen their homeland and were now under the greatest tension as we neared that grand home-country of ours, America!

60. COMING HOME

Longingly we stood on deck of that stately ship, *Gripsholm*, while it felt its way carefully ahead through the dense fog that had settled down over American waters. Just when we were nearing Sandy Hook, heading for New York Bay, I tried to pierce the dense wall of mist and get a glimpse of land. Then the *Gripsholm* glided through the New York Bay until on Sunday at noon the faint outline of New York's skyscrapers appeared in the distance. The thrills which millions of immigrants have lived through in their first moments of viewing the symbols of the new world were again enacted here on the decks of this Atlantic liner.

My young daughters had their first glimpse of their homeland.

We had ample time on deck of the *Gripsholm* to look around in all directions. There was the highway along the shore from New York to Coney Island. Thousands of cars passed. They looked—in little Karin's words, like "little bugs" crawling along on the land. On the other side we saw Staten Island. All was new to my girls.

The ship did not dock on Sunday, so preparations were made for disembarking Monday, as we anchored in view of the Statue of Liberty. Customs declaration forms were handed out and I, too, busied myself filling them out. Landing cards were distributed, which had to be stamped by American officials. The last day of the voyage came, Monday morning. With my two children, I made my way to the desks of the American customs officers for the first time in seven years. There they sat behind their desks. I handed over our passports, a glance at their lists checking our names, the stamp was impressed on our landing cards, all a matter of hardly a minute. I could not help but reflect in my mind that here was that which makes America uniquely grand and different from Europe. Our officials know what they want and carry out their duties in all seriousness, without show of bureaucracy. One feels that they can have confidence in these officials. The same feeling I noted on the pier during customs formalities.

On Monday morning the steamer slowly made her way to the pier and I truly experienced the feeling of "homecoming." When finally I stepped off the ship with my girls and walked on the floor of that pier, it seemed like those officials and the customs officers were close relatives of mine. Customs formalities were rather slow because of the throng and excessively large amount of baggage to be handled, but the officials were kind and patient, willing to explain why something must be done that way, and not another way. Still, they inspire confidence as they show interest without deviating from their strict duty. They serve without showing in their behavior a demand of recognizing their importance. Perhaps it can be termed an air of comradeship that prevails. That is America! This has made it a country which makes people want to return again and share the blessings of liberty and personal rights. How glad I was to tread American soil again after so many heartbreaking experiences in the seven years abroad! It surely was significant that I reached my homeland again on July 1—the exact date appearing on my naturalization certificate—July 1, 1919—just 27 years ago.

The seven years of my trials, anxieties and tragedies have finally come to an end! The seemingly impossible situations beyond remedy, had, with God's help merged into victory. I am reunited with my daughters. On May 9 of the year of grace, 1946, the Lord brought them to me after they had been flown from Berlin to Croydon in an American plane, and from there in a Swedish plane to Stockholm. The condition of my girls from that moment on improved rapidly under the loving care of our Swedish friends, especially there in that quiet, blessed, hospitable and comfortable residence in Möklinta, which had been my peaceful and lovely home for two and a half years.

To show how wonderfully the Lord cared for us in every detail, I must relate another phase of development regarding my homecoming. While I was in Sweden, I did not give a thought to what would happen after my return to the States. As usual, on my return from the mission field I had no occasion to give it even a fleeting thought as to where I would live and the home I would occupy after my home-coming. As I have loving relatives in California with whom I am in closest fellowship, being very faithful believers and consecrated to the Lord, it was evident that my girls and I would return to California for recuperation.

It was known to the Lord, however, that there is a great scarcity of homes in America and thousands upon thousands are looking in vain for a place of abode. One day my friend, Brother Pfeifer, on one of his visits to Möklinta, Sweden, remarked, "I wish the renters of my home could be made to vacate, then I would ask you to make your abode in my home, while I am here in Sweden, and later I would join you in case I return to the States again. I just made a casual remark and we passed on to other subjects. In the spring of 1946, Brother Pfeifer wrote me that he had just received news from the lady who takes care of his property, that the renters of his home had bought their own house and would vacate on May 22, 1946. "Now the way is clear to you, Brother Schmidt, to move into my home," he wrote, inviting me very warmly to take charge of the home "as if it were your own."

After I arrived in New York and realized that it was next to impossible to find a suitable home on short notice, I saw again the wonderful and loving hand of God moving in our behalf and taking care of a very urgent problem, even though I had not foreseen that need. The time came, after spending two months in the East and the Midwest, that we arrived in California and could then move into a ready and prepared home which was comfortable for the girls and myself, with a great garden with beautiful trees and shrubbery surrounding the house, being at our disposal.

God has done all things well. How could I thank him enough for what he had done and for what he is doing for me? I *do* praise God for my noble friend, Brother Pfeifer, who was willing to be used by the Lord to do his errand and help a servant of God who had spent years of trials in the mission fields and had lost everything; my nice home and furnishings, personal belongings, bedding, linens, clothing —everything had been lost during the war in the heat of the battles. I returned with my girls to America with a few suitcases and two medium-sized trunks. I had lost my expensive library, and in addition, also all of my writings and manuscripts. But the Lord had provided again. We moved into Brother Pfeifer's home at Redondo Beach, at the shore of Santa Monica Bay near Los Angeles, a quiet little town. The house overlooks the ocean, although it is five blocks away from the shore—and has a wonderful view. God has done all things well! To him we shall give praises in glory forever!

As my daughters did not speak English, having only been among German-speaking friends while they were lost in Germany, I was greatly concerned about the school problem. They might have become very conspicuous among the other children in the public school and be looked upon as German aliens. This became a heavy burden to me while we made our way westward to our new home in Redondo Beach. After our arrival in September, 1946, not being acquainted with the situation here, I sought for an opportunity to find a religious school in which to place my girls, but I seemed to find no solution to the problem.

One day while driving home to Redondo Beach from Alhambra, and passing through Maywood, I remembered dear Brother and Sister Erickson, who always treated me with special kindness in past years and I had a strong desire to say hello to them. Upon entering their home the same old warmth and love in Christ was extended to me immediately. The news thrilled me, as in glad surprise, I learned that Brother and Sister Erickson were conducting a Christian grade school, so that I did not only receive advice from them, but they were willing to do more than that.

"We really should take the girls into our school," Brother Erickson remarked questioningly to his wife.

"Yes, sure, that would be wonderful. We can make room for those little darlings," she replied with deep interest.

My heart was full of praise to my wonderful Jesus, as that was the beginning of God's hand visibly moving on our behalf. Not only were Brother and Sister Erickson willing to receive the girls in their school, but they also found a place for them to stay from Monday until Friday, and for the entire winter following, the school board defrayed the expenses for their lodgings as well as tuition fees. Very special attention was given to my girls by their teachers. Having begun in the fall when they could hardly speak a word of English, I was astonished that they soon were able to follow the lessons with the other American children. That could not have happened with competent teaching alone, but the instructors, who are faithful and experienced children of God, also carried them upon the arms of prayer.

It was then my privilege to attend the graduation day exercises presided over by Sister Erickson. My heart was filled with thankfulness and praise to God for his wonderful help in answering the prayers of his saints. My girls were especially honored and commended for their diligence during the school term by giving them gifts. Ruth received a lovely portfolio, and Karin was presented with the most precious gift of all—a New Testament. How proud she was when she found her name printed in gold on the cover! As I sat there in that celebration, my thoughts went to all the precious friends who had so faithfully prayed throughout the years of our trials. How I wish all of them could have seen my daughters that evening, they would have exclaimed before the Lord as I did: "The Lord hath done all things well; he has answered our prayers above and beyond all we can ask or think."

61. VIEWING THE FUTURE

I sincerely covet the earnest prayers of the saints regarding the future that lies before us. I have lost my helpmate, and my children their precious mother. It will remain an irreparable loss and my children are in special need of prayer. They do not yet fully realize the loss they have suffered, but I know. I tremble when I contemplate the future, looming up so dark and uncertain, by reason of Satan arraying his forces against us. Youth of today are exposed to the merciless spirit of this wicked world.

After having passed the storms of the past years and survived, I desire to serve him in spite of the physical strain occasioned by the sufferings during my imprisonment, and the long years of tension with anxieties and uncertainties that followed for my wife and daughters, the Lord has restored and very graciously and gloriously made his promises come true in my life. How forcefully real to me appear the words of the Psalmist when he says, "Who passing through the Valley of Baca [weeping], . . . they go from strength to strength" (Psalms 84:6–7) and the Apostle Paul, when writing to the Romans says: "In all these things we are more than conquerors through Christ" (Rom. 8:37). My Jesus led me to write down my testimony experienced during my imprisonment and Reverend Florentium Hallzon, owner of the Evangeliipress Publishing House in Örebro, Sweden, very nobly accepted the manuscript dealing with my imprisonment, *Songs in the Night*, as well as others of my writings for publication. God made the divine promises literally come true in my life. Many thousands of children of God have already read my books, especially *Songs in the Night*. Thousands expressed verbally or by letter their thankfulness to me for the testimony contained in these volumes which demonstrates the faithfulness, love and power of God in our life. Yes, we are always on the safe side when trusting him, though the way may become rough at times and many seemingly unsurmountable obstacles confront us and hinder along our pathway. Jesus never fails nor forsakes us and he always finds a way of escape, leading us to final victory and triumph. Hallelujah!

Tragic times and trouble undoubtedly lie ahead of us. We shall be called upon to prove the great promises of our

God in a special way, even in the future. We look around us and see the sure signs of his coming soon. Let us lift up our heads, gaze heavenward and rejoice, for "our redemption draws nigh" (Luke 21:18). May we not be deceived by the enemy in hoping for better conditions on this tired and decaying old earth. We know that better times will not come to us here below, but will only be realized in Jesus at his second coming. May we prepare in all earnestness for that Day when the trumpet of God shall sound and the dead in Christ rise and we with them, to meet the Lord in the air and be forever with him in the glory (1 Thess. 4:13–18).

The testings in my body were severe at times even after I arrived in California. Somehow the Lord did not see fit to enable me to carry on an extensive lecturing service in meetings. Mixing among people made me very tired and nervous, still, I was fully active for the Lord. In a most wonderful way he enabled me to do service of another nature. Four radio stations daily broadcasted my lectures on the religious, political and prophetic aspects in Europe. These lectures were inspired not only by my actual, personal knowledge of existing conditions, but also by the intense sufferings of God's people in Europe. Those of us who know the conditions over there and know the saints personally, especially the Christian leaders, realize that it is beyond endurance. For the sake of making the need of Europe's suffering saints known, the burden which the Lord had put upon me and the compassion for the destitute saints that filled my mind and heart, compelled me to undertake this radio work. The Lord of the Harvest sanctioned my desire by making it possible for me to give forty-eight talks under the caption, *Europe's Gospel Call*, a whole category of information enabling honest Christians to grasp the situation and act upon the strong appeals which were made for the temporal and spiritual relief of the saints in Europe. As a result, Brother Pfeifer and I have sent many scores of packages to Europe during this year. For the present time the radio work has been discontinued, but we hope it is only an interruption.

Europe's Gospel Call is upon my heart. *Europe's Gospel Call* is burning in the hearts of many of God's people causing them to respond to the appeal. Although the radio messages have stopped, *Europe's Gospel Call* is still being answered and help is still going forth. We will do so as long as the burden for the sufferings of the saints in Europe will cause God's people to respond to the desperate gospel call of Europe's saints. We will faithfully carry on for him who says: "inasmuch as you have done it to one of the least of these, my brethren, ye have done it unto me" (Matt. 25:40). If everyone does his duty before the Lord, obeying his promptings, many tears will be dried and many of his dear ones in Europe will be kept from actual starvation and death. My longing and plan for the future is to send many hundreds of "CARE" packages to Europe. These parcels contain twenty-one pounds of good food and cost $10.00 each. Besides food, many more clothing packages must be sent to these destitute people of God on that bleeding and weeping continent of Europe, if whole households are to be saved from sickness and death.

On the horizon of our time I see the dark clouds gathering for a new and final outburst of rape, murder and bloodshed which undoubtedly will carry us into the great tribulation. Many saints have more means than is required for happiness and comfortable living. The Holy Spirit desires to pry loose that excessive money and make it useful for God *now,* and thus prevent such capital from falling into the hands of the Anti-Christ. Every really consecrated saint, waiting and looking for the return of our blessed Lord and Christ, should pray and intercede for all wealthy but often lukewarm followers of our dear Lord and Master.

To all our noble and loving friends, I desire to express my own and my daughters' appreciation for the deep and heart-felt interest shown toward us by the pastors of the Maywood Assembly, the School Board and the teachers, then to all those saints who prayed during the years when testings and trials well nigh overwhelmed me. Now that the *Journey Home* is completed and we are safely placed among our precious friends, my heart is filled with rejoicings because of the overwhelming kindness and love so lavishly extended to my girls and myself. The Lord will not forget or fail to reward you all. God bless every one of you richly and abundantly. It is my heart's desire to keep alive our fellowship in the Lord and I shall endeavor to keep you informed as to the future guidings of the Lord and hope that you will continue to pray for us.

We had a very happy and glorious *journey home* to our *homeland*. We moved into that humble but cozy little home in Redondo Beach. But we are still on the way of the great *journey homeward*—the last one—*that* homecoming is still awaiting us. Let us live for our blessed Master and work for him in order that the "homecoming" to our eternal abode in the realm of eternity shall be all the more glorious. Out of the Valley of "Baca," out of the field of the world with its tears and trials and testings where we have been sowing and toiling for our blessed Master, we shall come to appear before him, our Savior and Judge (2 Cor. 5:10). When we shall hear his "well done," it will be our reaping time, our time of harvest in joy (Psalms 126:5).

O Lord, give us grace on our final *Journey Home* that our homecoming into your eternal realm may be glorious for thy precious name's sake.

While I am in my exultant joy over the reunion with my children and *The Journey Home*, untold thousands mourn because of separation from their loved ones whom they shall never see again on this earth. I also remember with tears the thousands of children who are looking for their parents whom they have hopelessly lost and have nobody to love or care for, or comfort them—no mother's love—no father's care.

"O merciful God, dry the tears of the many, many broken-hearted parents who wait for their darling children. Help them as you helped me, as you wiped away my tears of longing by bringing my precious daughters to me again, for Jesus' sake and in his holy and wonderful name, to whom be glory and majesty, dominion and power forever and forever. Amen!"

AFTERWORD

HERBERT SCHMIDT was the first Assemblies of God missionary to eastern Europe, who founded the region's first Pentecostal Bible school. When he returned from furlough in 1939, little did he know that a Nazi prison cell awaited him. In the midst of tragedy and war, God preserved his life, filling his heart with songs of praise in prison.

God's story and mission in the heart of Europe continues today. The area of Poland where Herbert was imprisoned is fertile ground for church planting again after a time when Christianity floundered. Following World War II, Poland was subject to a communist regime while the Church continued to suffer much persecution.

After the fall of the Iron Curtain, the Polish Pentecostal Fellowship, *Kościół Zielonoświątkowy* (the Polish Assemblies of God) emerged from the United Evangelical Church of Poland, comprising five Protestant denominations fused together first under the Nazis and continued under communism. The P.P.F. runs three Bible schools with extension programs training approximately 150 students and facilitating several ministries. Assemblies of God workers labor alongside the national church and its 500-plus ministers, serving approximately 22,000 members and adherents in 250 churches and outstations.

The church has faced many adversities yet continues to grow and even lead the charge in responding to the Ukraine crisis where the entire movement was mobilized to help. Despite the tragedy, hundreds have been saved and dozens of new churches were planted.

Poland is a country that is perceived as a Christian nation. However, the vast majority of people do not know Jesus Christ personally. Of the 38 million people who live in Poland, missiologists expect that only a fraction—0.03%—are born again. Of its 940 metropolitan areas, 700 Polish cities do not have a single gospel-preaching church. These Poles have limited access to the gospel.

The Polish Pentecostal church is a church-planting movement with a vision called "700 Miast." 'Miast' is the Polish word for "cities." Consequently, the "700 Cities" church-planting movement represents a heartfelt response to this situation. The vision is to see a Bible-preaching, Pentecostal church planted in all 700 towns in the country where one currently does not exist.

Of course, achieving such a long-term goal requires that national church planters and leaders be equipped, trained, and mentored. Assemblies of God World Missions (AGWM) has formed a strategic partnership with the Polish Pentecostal church, supporting these church-planting efforts.

If you would like to help write the next chapter of what God is doing in Poland and in the heart of Europe today, please connect with us here:

May God richly bless and encourage you as you read this book about his faithfulness in the past. May the Lord lead you to consider how you can be a part of what he is doing today.

KIRK PRIEST
Area Director, Central Europe
Assemblies of God World Missions

324

REFERENCES

Edward Czajko. [In Polish.] "Historia Kościoła." *Kościół Zielonoświątkowy w PL.* https://kz.pl/historia-kosciola/

Wojciech Gajewski. [In Polish.] "Gdański Instytut Biblijny." *Gedanopedia.* Fundacja Gdańska, Muzeum Gdańska. https://gdansk.gedanopedia.pl/gdansk/?title=GDAŃSKI_INSTYTUT_BIBLIJNY

Roman Soloviy. "Pentecostalism in Western Ukraine: Historical Development and Current Theological Challenges," Occasional Papers on Religion in Eastern Europe, vol. 40 (2020), no. 7.

Wayne Warner. "An American Missionary in Nazi Hands: The Story of G. Herbert Schmidt." A/G Heritage, vol. 11, no. 4. Winter 1991–1992.

—. "Daylight Pushes Back the Night." A/G Heritage, vol. 12, no. 2. Summer 1992.

Articles in *The Pentecostal Evangel*:

"Prayer Request." August 18, 1945.

"News From Europe." September 15, 1945.

"Heavenly Songs in a Nazi Prison Cell: A Review of Gustav Herbert Schmidt's New Book, *Songs in the Night.*" January 12, 1946.

"German Branch Conference and Camp Meeting." September 14, 1946.

G. Herbert Schmidt. "Where Are We in Prophecy?" October 26, 1946.

"G. H. Schmidt Dies in Germany." July 13, 1958.

BOOKS BY HERBERT SCHMIDT

1. Songs in the Night
Swedish: Sånger i natten, 1943
Norwegian: Sanger i natten, 1945
English: Songs in the Night, 1946

2. God in My Life
Swedish: Gud i mitt liv, 1945

3. God Finds Ways
Swedish: Gud finner utvägar, 1946

4. The Journey Home
Swedish: Resan hem, 1947
English: The Journey Home, 1948

5. Faithful unto Death
Swedish: Trogen intill döden, 1962
Norwegian: Tro inntil døden, n.d.
Finnish: Uskollinen kuolemaan asti, n.d.

Made in the USA
Monee, IL
17 September 2023

42785133R00194